Change and Adaptation in Soviet and East European Politics

edited by
Jane P. Shapiro
Peter J. Potichnyj

The seventh of eight volumes of papers from the first international conference sponsored by the American Association for the Advancement of Slavic Studies, British National Association for Soviet and East European Studies, British Universities Association of Slavists, and Canadian Association of Slavists
General Editor: Roger E. Kanet

The Praeger Special Studies program—utilizing the most modern and efficient book production techniques and a selective worldwide distribution network—makes available to the academic, government, and business communities significant, timely research in U.S. and international economic, social, and political development.

Change and Adaptation in Soviet and East European Politics

PRAEGER SPECIAL STUDIES IN INTERNATIONAL POLITICS AND GOVERNMENT

Praeger Publishers   New York   Washington   London

Library of Congress Cataloging in Publication Data
Main entry under title:

Change and adaptation in Soviet and East European politics.

 (Praeger special studies in international politics and government)
 "Papers from the first international conference sponsored by the American Association for the Advancement of Slavic Studies ... [and other bodies]."
 Includes bibliographical references and indexes.
 1. Europe, Eastern—Politics and government—Congresses. I. Shapiro, Jane P. II. Potichnyj, Peter J. III. American Association for the Advancement of Slavic Studies.
DJK50.C48 320.9'47 76-8415
ISBN 0-275-56190-9

PRAEGER PUBLISHERS
111 Fourth Avenue, New York, N.Y. 10003, U.S.A.

Published in the United States of America in 1976
by Praeger Publishers, Inc.

All rights reserved

© 1976 by Praeger Publishers, Inc.

Printed in the United States of America

GENERAL EDITOR'S FOREWORD
Roger E. Kanet

The studies published in this volume were selected from those presented at the First International Slavic Conference, held in Banff, Alberta, Canada, September 4-7, 1974. The conference, which was attended by approximately 1,500 persons, was sponsored by the American Association for the Advancement of Slavic Studies, the British Universities Association of Slavists, the British National Association for Soviet and East European Studies, and the Canadian Association of Slavists. Although the sponsorship of the conference was limited to the four major English-speaking Slavic associations, attendance and participation were much broader and included numerous scholars from continental Western Europe, Asia, Africa, Latin America, and Oceania. In addition, a substantial number of scholars from the Soviet Union and Eastern Europe participated in the deliberations of the conference.

Among the more than 250 papers presented, a relatively large number have been selected for publication in two series of conference volumes. Papers in the social sciences are included in the series of volumes being published by Praeger Publishers of New York; those in the humanities are appearing in the series of books being published by Slavica Publishers of Cambridge, Massachusetts.

As general editor of both the Praeger and Slavica series of Banff publications, I wish to express my sincere appreciation to all the individuals and institutions that made the conference possible, including the numerous government and private organizations that provided financial assistance, the members of the International Planning Committee who prepared the conference, and the participants themselves. Finally, I wish to thank the editors of the individual volumes in the two series and the authors of the essays for their major contributions.

CONTENTS

	Page
GENERAL EDITOR'S FOREWORD By Roger E. Kanet	v
LIST OF TABLES	viii
INTRODUCTION	x

Chapter

PART I: POLITICAL CULTURE

1 POLITICAL CULTURE AND THE SOCIALIST PURPOSE 3
   By David W. Paul

2 DIVERSITY AND ADAPTATION IN SOVIET POLITICAL
   CULTURE: THE ATTITUDES OF THE SOVIET
   POLITICAL ELITE 18
   By Philip D. Stewart

3 STRUCTURAL CHANGE UNDER STATE SOCIALISM:
   THE POLISH CASE 40
   By Alexander Matejko

4 THE PROCESS OF REFORM IN POST-1970 POLAND:
   THE CASE OF THE PEOPLE'S COUNCILS SYSTEM 58
   By Ray Taras

5 INNOVATIONS IN THE MODEL OF SOCIALISM:
   POLITICAL REFORMS IN CZECHOSLOVAKIA, 1968 77
   By Galia Golan

6 CONTINUITY AND CHANGE IN HUNGARY IN HIS-
   TORICAL PERSPECTIVE: THE MODERN PERIOD 95
   By Joseph Held

7 DICTATORSHIP OF THE PROLETARIAT: A SLAVIC
   MODEL FOR THE NON-SLAVIC WORLD 110
   By Lubos G. Hejl

Chapter		Page

PART II: CENSORSHIP

8 SOVIET PUBLIC COMMUNICATIONS IN THE
   POST-STALIN PERIOD   133
   By Gayle Durham Hannah

9 LITERARY POLICY UNDER STALIN IN
   RETROSPECT: A CASE STUDY, 1952-53   161
   By Edith Rogovin Frankel

10 INTELLECTUALS AND THE PARTY IN BULGARIA   179
   By Peter Raina

PART III: NATIONALITIES

11 SOVIET HISTORIOGRAPHY AND THE NEW
   NATIONALITIES' POLICY, A CASE STUDY:
   BELORUSSIA AND UKRAINE   201
   By Stephan M. Horak

12 MODERNIZATION, POPULATION CHANGE AND
   NATIONALITY IN SOVIET CENTRAL ASIA AND
   KAZAKHSTAN   217
   By Robert A. Lewis, Richard H. Rowland,
   and Ralph S. Clem

NAME INDEX   234

SUBJECT INDEX   235

ABOUT THE EDITORS AND CONTRIBUTORS   237

LIST OF TABLES

Table		Page
1	Schematic Representation of Attitude Antecedents, Attitudes, and Behavioral Expectations for Three Images of Soviet Political Change	20
2	Attitudes of Regional Party Secretaries	23
3	Impact of Background and Experience on Ideological and Leadership Style Attitudes	29
4	Impact of Background and Experience on Consumer Welfare and Production and Manpower Attitudes	30
5	Equipment of Various Households: Appliances Per 100 Households	43
6	Educational Level of Councilors in 1949-69	61
7	People's Councils' Share of the Total State Budget, 1951-73	70
8	Aspirations of Local Activists on the Question of Autonomy	70
9	Total Population by Russians and Other Eastern Slavs in Kazakhstan and Central Asia, 1897-1970	221
10	Level of Urbanization by Russians and Major Nationalities of Central Asia and Kazakhstan, 1970	225
11	Russians As a Percent of Urban Population in Central Asia and Kazakhstan, 1970	226
12	Level of Urbanization by Russians and Turkic-Muslims, 1897-1970	227
13	Educational Levels by Russians and Major Nationalities of Central Asia and Kazakhstan, 1959 and 1970	228

Table		Page
14	Students in Higher Education Per 1,000 Population Aged 16-24 by Russians and Major Nationalities of Central Asia and Kazakhstan, 1959 and 1970	229
15	Specialists with Higher and Secondary Education Per 1,000 Population Aged 16-59 by Russians and Major Nationalities of Central Asia and Kazakhstan, 1959 and 1970	229

INTRODUCTION

CHANGE AND ADAPTATION IN SOVIET AND EAST EUROPEAN POLITICS

The First International Slavic Conference, Banff '74, produced several hundred studies on a variety of Soviet and East European themes. More than 20 of these studies, originally presented on various panels, were submitted for inclusion in this volume. They differ greatly in scope, subject matter, discipline, and methodological approach. In some fashion, however, each confronts the issues of tradition, change, and adaptation in societies experiencing modernization under communist rule. The editors were charged with the difficult task of determining some degree of coherence and scholarly competence for the essays to comprise the volume. Despite the comprehensiveness of the volume's theme, some studies could not be included because of relevance or space considerations. Others were omitted because their authors had arranged for publication prior to the conference. Several others were submitted for journal publication at the same time that they were sent to us, which accounts for their dual publication.

The essays in this volume raise a variety of questions related to rapid societal change, industrialization and modernization, and the capabilities of political leaderships to manage or restrict these changes. Why have the communist regimes of the Soviet Union and Eastern Europe sought to create modern, industrial, egalitarian societies from the multinational, largely rural, semiliterate, highly stratified societies they inherited? How did they seek to introduce rapid change? What elements existed within each society that served to resist change? What factors compelled the political leadership to modify and adapt its policies to existing realities? To what extent has each communist regime been limited by the particular culture and tradition of the society it rules? In seeking to answer these and related questions, an examination of the historical, sociological, and philosophical bases of a society is necessary. This is what the author of each essay in this volume has set out to do, with varying degrees of success.

The essays fall roughly into three sections: political culture, censorship, and nationalities problems. In the first section, David W. Paul analyzes the concept of political culture and suggests how it can be utilized in the study of communist societies despite the particular difficulties encountered in pursuing research on these societies. Philip D. Stewart asks how the Soviet political culture has shaped its political elite and how capable that elite has been in adapting to the challenges presented by the society's domestic and international environments. Alexander Matejko examines some aspects of Polish political culture that have resisted change and assesses the regime's response to such resistance, while Ray Taras analyzes the process of reform on the local government level in Poland after 1970. Galia Golan discusses one aspect of the Czechoslovak reform effort of the 1960s, namely the creation of pluralist rather than monolithic Communist Party rule within a socialist structure of society, guided in some fashion by Marxist-Leninist ideology. Joseph Held inquires into the nature of modernization in Hungarian society by analyzing its impact on the peasantry, blue- and white-collar industrial workers, and the bourgeoisie. Lubos G. Hejl probes the nature and meaning of the Marxian slogan "dictatorship of the proletariat" and its application to already industrialized societies, namely Czechoslovakia in 1945-48 and Chile in 1970-73.

Essays in the section on censorship are concerned primarily with the extent to which communist regimes are successful in controlling the information to which citizens have access. Gayle Durham Hannah suggests that, in seeking to become a major world power, the Soviet Union necessarily has had to permit contacts between Soviet citizens and the outside world. This has resulted in increased pressures, largely from the intelligentsia, for more accurate and more complete information, which the political leadership has found increasingly difficult to restrain. Edith Rogovin Frankel reviews official Soviet literary policy in the last year of Stalin's rule and suggests that there was not the high degree of uniformity and monolithism in censorship that typically has been assumed. Peter Raina outlines the nature of published debates during the late 1960s among Bulgarian writers and philosophers on a variety of issues and concludes that there are clearly discernible differences of opinion that the Party has been unable or unwilling to forge into a monolithic mold.

The final section is concerned with the manner in which the Soviet Communist Party has confronted and attempted to resolve the conflicts inherent in a multinational state. Stephan M. Horak examines the problem in light of Soviet historiography and focuses on the complex relationships among the main Slavic peoples within the USSR: Russians, Ukrainians, and Belorussians. Robert A. Lewis, Richard H. Rowland, and Ralph S. Clem investigate the impact of Soviet rule on the Central Asian nationalities and conclude that the latter have been largely excluded from the modernized sectors of society created in their traditional homelands.

The editors wish to thank McMaster University, the Russian Institute of Columbia University, and Manhattanville College for their generous assistance in the preparation of this volume.

PART I

POLITICAL CULTURE

CHAPTER 1

**POLITICAL CULTURE AND
THE SOCIALIST PURPOSE**
David W. Paul

The title of this volume focuses on the theme of change and adaptation in the socialist countries of Europe, and the various chapters speak to one or another of the obvious questions underlying the central theme. Most critical in understanding the nature of change is to determine the factors within society that promote, resist, and condition change. That there will always be change of some sort hardly needs to be emphasized here; similarly, that adaptations have to be made in some way should go without saying. Our general subject concerns not the presence or absence of change but the forms it adopts, which can be observed and described as objective facts. They can be explained as products of the people promoting the changes and analyzed in terms of their putative effects on society. Objective reasons for the specific nature of change and adaptation can be inferred from the nature of problems inherited from the recent past and the character of the people most influential in present-day policy making. However, one cannot reach a total understanding of change and adaptation in terms of these empirical facts alone. One needs, rather, to look more deeply within the fabric of each specific society to ascertain the nature of the forces for and against change in general, or for one change as opposed to another. Ultimately, one must consider the patterns of culture running through the social context in order to understand the factors predisposing human beings toward specific forms of behavior and self-perception. In short, to understand political change one must understand the political culture.

A number of scholars have examined the political culture of communist-ruled countries, either as the central focus of monographs or as an integral part of more general works.[1] Despite the relatively wide use of the concept, both in communist studies and elsewhere, the precise meaning of political culture is a matter of theoretical controversy. There are at least two schools of thought concerning the focus that should be adopted by the analyst of political culture, several ideas about the proper methodology of studying it, and no apparent consensus on what constitutes culture or what aspect of culture is in fact political.[2] Before examining the utility of the concept for studies of political change and adaptation in the socialist countries, therefore, it seems only fitting to reconsider these critical questions of purpose, content, and methodology.

THE CONCEPT

This study takes as its starting point a synthetic definition. Political culture as used herein refers to an observable configuration of values, symbols, orientations and behavior patterns related to the politics of a given society.[3] The assumptions underlying the concept as thus presented derive from a number of well-articulated fields within the social sciences, notably social psychology, cultural anthropology, national character analysis, and political development. (The author is aware that this position, as well as much of the ensuing argument, leaves him open to charges of eclecticism. Such is often the lot of the theorist who involves himself in cross-disciplinary scholarship.) Those who have previously written on the topic of political culture have often overlooked one or more of these important perspectives, resulting in analytical problems far deeper than just the definitional issue.[4] In any event, the matter of definition is the first order of business.

According to one school of thought, the central problem of political culture as a field of study is basically one of the linkage between micropolitical and macropolitical phenomena within a society, that is, between the causes and effects of individual motivation and the broader historical and sociocultural context.[5] This is the more conventional interpretation of the concept, associated very closely with the work of Gabriel A. Almond, Lucian W. Pye, and Sidney Verba.[6] A second approach, less well known but held with an equal degree of conviction, seeks to emphasize the broader problem of accounting for elements of historical change and continuity. The latter approach corresponds to the position of Robert C. Tucker.[7] Far from being mutually exclusive, however, the two approaches should properly be seen as complementary; both are essential to a full understanding of a political culture.[8]

Before proceeding further, it must be mentioned that, in speaking of the political culture, we are referring to the specific manifestation of a society's culture in the political realm of life. What is true of culture in relation to behavior, generally speaking, is true of political culture in relation to political behavior. Within their proper frames of reference, culture and political culture have the same attributes and play the same role. Therefore, on the level of micropolitics, where we must begin our analysis, the political culture relates to the individual exactly as the general culture does.[9]

Culture enters into micropolitics as an intervening variable influencing individual behavior between the time of a stimulus (S) and the response (R) to that stimulus. Thus the culture (that is, the political culture) can be said to play some role in the paradigmatic black box of the conventional S → M → R social behavior model, where M represents various unseen mediatory forces conditioning the action taken by an individual once he has been affected by an external stimulus (see diagram). (There are circumstances in which action takes place directly in response to the stimulus without the mediatory process, but these are limited to circumstances of reflexive behavior or behavior produced under conditions of extreme physiological stress.) Before the response takes place, the individual will perceive the stimulus in a specific way (cognition), attach some degree of significance to the situation (cathexis), and apply some set of value judgments (evaluation) before choosing a course of action.[10]

Stimulus → | cognition
cathexis
evaluation | → Response

Paramount to the mediatory process, and particularly to the role therein of the political culture, is apperception. Previous experiences and the knowledge of historical precedent will obviously color one's perception of contemporary reality. What one knows and experiences are part of one's culture, and by means of the apperceptive process an individual translates the knowledge and impulses he derives from his culture into an orientation toward contemporary reality. Similar impulses derived from his culture will condition his cathectic and evaluative processes. Thus it is because of his culture that an individual perceives a stimulus as significant or insignificant, and it is at least partly because of his culture that he then chooses (or is driven) to respond in a given way.[11]

This suggests that culture is not must an intervening variable but indeed a supervenient one, something at least partly extraneous to the individual's apperceptive process but yet connected to it as a source of influence. The psychological processes mediating between stimulus and response are conditioned by the individual's cultural environment. A second diagram may help to illustrate:

$$S \to M \to R$$
(culture) above, (culture) below

The mediatory forces at work inside the black box of M function under the impact of the cultural context. The latter envelops the entire situation; culture thus conditions not only the cognitive processes of M but also can condition the nature of the stimulus. In turn, the response (R) may make some contribution to the development of the culture itself.

It is here that the element of behavior in my definition becomes important, for behavior not only reflects culture but is itself a component of culture. It is at once the end product of the social action paradigm (S → M → R) and an element in the further development of culture. This is as true with regard to political culture as it is to culture more generally speaking; patterns of behavior are a component of culture, and patterns of political behavior are a component of the political culture.[12] This relationship between culture and behavior, while reciprocal, is by no means symmetrical. The impact of behavior on the development of culture is much more remote than that of culture on behavior. Specific behavioral actions may be decisively conditioned by their cultural context, but the culture itself will be influenced by behavior only in the aggregate (behavioral patterns), over relatively long periods of time, and selectively—that is, only some patterns will have an impact on the culture.

A further theoretical question concerns the specifically political character of the political culture: What in a culture is political and what is not? This is problematic, for the boundary between the political and the nonpolitical in any culture is imprecise, often shifting, and sometimes arbitrary. Something considered political by one person may not be by another. In modern totalitarian societies, almost anything may take on political significance, whereas to the nineteenth-century American pioneer, politics was usually remote and impinged upon one's life only exceptionally. Depending on the political salience attached by society to a given phenomenon, it may or may not be relevant.

As examples, consider religious beliefs, public gatherings, and literary forms. In a laissez-faire society, religious beliefs are assumed not to interfere with politics (separation of church and state), public gatherings are not inherently political, and most literature will be considered politically neutral. In a totalitarian society, on the other hand, these phenomena will generally tend to be construed (at least by rulers, if not always by the public) as politically salient. Religious beliefs will either support or threaten the official ideology; any public gathering will be suspected of having a political purpose; literary forms have an explicit propaganda value and therefore must conform to approved norms. Moreover, the same comparison can be made of certain value-related personality traits (avarice, skepticism) and cultural symbols (the color red).

Most societies are neither totalitarian nor laissez-faire, but those of the communist world approach the point at which all reality is imbued with political significance. The subjective, psychological processes referred to above are nonetheless important here. Citizens' perceptions of and affective orientations toward political realities play a critical role in the translation of the political culture into political behavior, assigning specific political meanings to events and evaluating one's course of action in terms of what one has learned to be permissible or advantageous.

This brings us to the methodological question: How does one get to the bottom of this complicated set of subjective and objective phenomena? Ever since The Civic Culture was published, the conventional wisdom has centered around survey research of the kind exemplified in the Almond and Verba book, aimed at eliciting from a scientifically chosen sampling of citizens their responses indicative of cognitive and normative patterns that, it was inferred, derived from their political culture. Because such data are scarce or unavailable in many societies, and because it is impossible to conduct one's own surveys in countries whose governments frown upon such research, the applicability of political culture as an approach to comparative politics seemed to be restricted to open societies whose governments allowed attitudinal research. For the most part, this would exclude communist-ruled societies, for, with some ephemeral exceptions, it has not been possible to do systematic survey research in those countries.[13]

Political culture, however, can be studied by means other than attitude surveys.[14] In fact, as our conception of political culture has expanded from its original formulation as applied in the studies of The Civic Culture, the utility of survey research itself has become somewhat dubious. In the first place, the results of any sample survey, regardless of how rigorously scientific the procedures involved, are at best definitive only for the specific moment at which they are taken and with regard to the specific questions asked. It seems disingenuous to draw wider interpretations about source and duration of public attitudes from a random polling at a given moment, for public attitudes can sometimes shift unpredictably.[15] Second, the difficulties inherent in polling citizens of closed societies— problems of access to the public as well as reliability of information obtained from people conditioned by past experience to guard their true feelings—are so serious as to render this method of analysis of limited use outside relatively open societies.

This is not meant to deny the utility of attitudinal data, where available, but to suggest that this type of evidence, if it is to be of value, must be supplemented by other kinds of information. Indeed, culture is much more than attitudes, and to study culture one must look at a wide variety of sources. Among these are interpretations of the society's nature and values by the broadest possible representation of spokesmen—philosophers, government leaders, opposition leaders, novelists and poets, counterculture spokesmen, social scientists, film producers, and so on. The more diverse the forms of evidence one uses, the richer and fuller will be one's understanding of a political culture.

One of the most illustrative single forms of evidence is behavior itself, specifically behavioral patterns. When observed diachronically, patterns of political behavior can shed more light on a society's political culture than can the best attitudinal data. The ways in which citizens tend to respond to such political circumstances as election campaigns, military invasions, taxation, physical coercion, and economic policy decisions can be enormously enlightening. They can aid in describing social values, delineating the options open to political leaders, and even predicting future trends in the general relationship between rulers and ruled.

Reliability and equivalence of data are problems faced by all social scientists, and they raise particular difficulties in the study of political culture.[16] Delicate judgments must often be made, challenging the scholar to reach deeply into his overall knowledge of the society under examination. Indeed, it would even seem appropriate to suggest that a study of the political culture of any society must proceed from a broadly based familiarity with the history, politics, sociology, economics, and intellectual patterns of that society—just as anthropological studies of specific cultures must proceed from a similar familiarity. Thus conceived, the political culture approach is not merely a tool of analysis to be taken into the study of this or that element in this or that society. It presents, rather, a framework for the examination of relatively specific questions that can be answered only from the basis of a broad empirical perspective. These questions, dealing with culturally derived predispositions to political behavior, have a theoretical impact on the study of politics universally; what one learns about one specific society should stimulate analogous studies of other societies, thus generating a body of information truly comparative in nature. As an approach to comparative politics, therefore, the study of political culture should combine elements of induction and deduction in an integrated and comprehensive way.

For many years the study of communist societies was not closely linked to the general concerns of comparative politics. This has

POLITICAL CULTURE AND SOCIALIST PURPOSE 9

changed in the past decade, however, as more and more attempts have been made to ask of these societies and their polities questions that concern the study of politics more generally.[17] By focusing on the political culture, therefore, we are contributing to the further integration of communist studies into the discipline of political science while exploring urgent questions related to change and adaptation in a specifically socialist context.

CONTINUITY, CHANGE, AND REVOLUTION

As we know from earlier treatises on the subject, a political culture is generally acquired over many years or generations of a society's experience through a learning process, explicit or implicit, of one generation to another. It can nevertheless be substantially changed under the impact of new circumstances, such as the development of unprecedented problems or the ascendance of a previously subdominant pattern of values. The process through which a political culture is learned is the complex of experiences, instruction, indoctrination, and passively acquired assumptions known as political socialization.[18]

Each generation tends to fashion its politics from cultural patterns handed down by its parent generation—but not entirely so. Unforeseen issues can arise, or old issues can take on a new complexion. Attitudes sometimes change, and a new generation may adapt, reject, or ignore some of the values and orientations of the parent generation. This is not easily done, for cultures tend to resist large-scale changes and such changes are generally accompanied by strain and cultural tension. This is especially true of changes promulgated on the basis of sudden decisions by a ruling group. This is, of course, the nature of most political change in socialist Europe; the regime decrees the necessity of change and policy is immediately aimed at bringing about specified changes, usually in the face of one or another form of cultural resistance.

On the whole, political cultures tend to be rather durable and resilient. This is not to say that they are static, but inertial tendencies within them are very strong. A culture will generally absorb gradual changes without undoing the overall configuration of value and behavior patterns, but large-scale changes will tend to occur only under exceptional circumstances, usually of a revolutionary nature.

Revolutionary societies are, in fact, characterized by radical changes in the critical elements of the political culture (values, orientations, and behavior patterns). A revolution, in essence, is a violent rupture of traditional norms and practices, invariably accompanied by severe stress and generally in the face of strong resistance from one or another quarter. Revolutions in this sense occur only infrequently. A successful revolution must prevail over great obstacles, for the revolutionary process invariably involves an upheaval in value standards, institutions, and symbols that are usually very deeply rooted.

Communist revolutions, whatever their particular historical or national forms, have had in common the goal of fundamental change in the dominant values, orientations, and behavior patterns of citizens. Lenin certainly had this in mind when he wrote in 1918 of the necessity to rid Soviet society of what he called "all the habits and traditions of the bourgeoisie"—habits and traditions running the gamut from laziness to profiteering.[19] Stalin carried this to an extreme, assuming that the radical transformation of Soviet society by means of the "revolution from above" would necessarily lead to the creation of the "new Soviet man." This new creature would be an individual enthusiastically committed to the goals of communism and unwaveringly obedient to the authority of the Party.[20] The transformation of attitudes and behavior at the very base of society has been an explicit aim of the Chinese, Cuban, and East European revolutions as well, and each regime has fashioned its own image of the emerging "new man." To have a radically new society, one must have qualitatively different citizens. Communist revolutionary policies, from Lenin to Khrushchev and from Peking to Havana, have sought to construct the "new man" with an outlook and lifestyle consistent with the ends of the revolution.

Communist ruling groups, then, have by and large articulated the goals toward which they wish to lead their societies—goals first articulated by Marx and Engels, later refined somewhat by Lenin, Stalin, and Mao, and most recently by a number of lesser authorities. Setting goals and attaining them are, of course, two different things, and the student of political culture in socialist societies is inevitably faced with the question, how has the revolution fared? That is, to what extent have society and the individuals within it actually been transformed as a result of the socialist revolution? Given the goal of transforming the political culture, to what extent has the revolution wrought its intended effect?

When the means of attaining social goals necessarily include fundamental upheavals of traditional norms, the purposes of the ruling group present a challenge that is difficult indeed. Ruling communist parties have always been sensitive to the danger posed by bourgeois and other nonproletarian class forces, but they have underestimated and misinterpreted the resilience of traditional impulses even among the working class. The question at this point becomes the following: To what extent to revolutionary changes in the political and economic superstructure (macrostructure) correspond to, result from, or give rise to coordinate changes in the psychosocial (micropolitical) base of society? To what extent are the orientations and behavior patterns of individuals conditioned by long-standing historical and evolutionary trends, "glacial in character" as Stephen White has said,[21] and to what extent are they capable of being reformed or redirected?

THE SPECIAL NATURE OF SOCIALIST REVOLUTIONS

Revolution, by any definition, connotes change. Basic to a successful revolution is some semblance of a collective social outlook that countenances, if not demands, fundamental change in the existing order. Marx had assumed that socialist revolutions would come about as a result of changes already well developed in the collective mentality of the working class, the driving force of the future. The revolution would succeed only when the workers identified the source of their immediate misery and alienation as the capitalist order, with all its moral and institutional trappings, for only then would the downtrodden of the societal substructure be able to focus their discontent against the established powers of the capitalist system and clear away the imposing obstacles to freedom, harmony, and self-fulfillment. Thus, only when the workers more or less universally felt the need to destroy the existing system would the revolution succeed.

Marx's theory of revolution presupposed a society that was modern—industrialized and capitalist, with class lines clearly drawn between the bourgeoisie and the proletariat, the only two important survivors of postfeudal social development. When socialism came to Eastern Europe, however, the region as a whole was not prepared for it, according to Marx's criteria. With the exception of Bohemia, Moravia, and a few industrial enclaves in Poland and Hungary, the region was one of relative socioeconomic backwardness. A diversity of national and local cultural patterns confronted the communists after 1945, just as they had confronted and frequently baffled the rulers of pre-1945 days. The working class, by and large, formed a small and weak basis of support for the communist governments. In the regions where the working class was strong, such as in Bohemia and Moravia, its support for communism had traditionally been diminished by the appeal of social democracy. Large peasant populations complicated the social systems, and in some cases vestiges of the feudal nobility were still salient political forces.

As in the Soviet Union, building the "objective" conditions of socialism became a necessary aim of the state's policy after the seizure of power. Thus the revolution in Eastern Europe was a modernizing movement as well as a political one. Having seized power, the communists were faced with the task of fabricating socioeconomic systems with at least some of the characteristics that Marx had assumed to be fundamental to the new order. This meant that the basis for an industrial order had to be established, with the state acting in the entrepreneurial capacity. Farming had to be revolutionized in order to consolidate small landholdings, release laborers from the fields for industrial manpower, and produce geometrically greater amounts of food to feed a rapidly expanding industrial labor force. Many of these policies were begun during the brief interlude of national front governments, in which communists shared but did not monopolize power. The process was accelerated after the elimination of the communists' political rivals, and the modernizing policies of the immediate post-1945 period took on the form of the Stalinist development model: totally nationalized industry, collectivized agriculture, comprehensive centralized economic planning, and so on.

Again as in Stalinist Russia, the marriage of the two revolutions—a socialist one and a modernizing one—was accompanied by conditions of extreme social and cultural stress. The communists sought to accelerate not only the economic revolution but the cultural transformation characteristic of modernization as well. They sought to eliminate the influence of the churches, to break the hold of traditional customs, to undermine long-established authority patterns, to supplant the impulse toward private acquisitiveness with collectivist values, and everywhere to instill a deep-seated hope and optimism in the socialist future.

All this required radical changes in the outlook of the people who made up these societies. Because the socioeconomic systems had not developed to the level foreseen by Marx, the ideal proletarian citizen, class-conscious and revolutionary-minded, did not yet exist. He did not exist, so he had to be created through a combination of myth and psychological wishful thinking. The myth derived in large part from Lenin's image of the true Bolshevik, the wishful thinking from the so-called psychological revolution in the Soviet Union. Lenin's ideal Bolshevik was a person of unfailing loyalty to the Party, a person of dedication, self-discipline, and clearsightedness. Under Stalin, this image had come to represent a model of the socialist citizen, the new man whom the regime sought to create universally. The new man was expected to internalize the norms of socialism, as determined by the Party. He was portrayed as the embodiment of patriotism, partiinost', vigilance, and collective-mindedness.[22]

The communist governments of Eastern Europe have borrowed heavily from the Soviet new man model in formulating their own images of the ideal citizen. Despite significant developments in indigenous social theory and psychology in Eastern Europe during the past twenty years, the regimes have consistently maintained the basic assumptions of character development derived from the Soviet model. The ideal citizen fervently believes the myths of the Marxist-Leninist ideological system and accepts the Party as the interpreter of that gospel. He feely chooses socialism over capitalism and does not resent the inperfections of the transitional present, for he knows that the future will be worth today's hardships. To this end, he participates in the programs fostered by the regime and he does so with enthusiasm.

The new man is, of course, more symbolic than actual. No man or woman is perfect, and the communists would undoubtedly be pleased with partial success and a gradual momentum toward the ideal. Just as the Christian model of a sinless life is a symbol and a guideline for believers, the new man is an ideal type for Marxist-Leninist believers. Socialism, as Petrovic and others have argued, is a process of becoming rather than a condition of being, and the end product of the process—the perfectly harmonious society—is only a dim vision.[23]

Indeed, the task of political socialization is a long-term, continuous process for all societies. Changing the nature of productive relations does not automatically produce socialist citizens, and rapid modernization does not automatically produce "modern" mentalities on a universal scale. It may be a long time before the norms of all the people are identical or even thoroughly consistent with those of the communists.

Meanwhile, the regimes in power in socialist Europe are confronted with the challenge of establishing and maintaining momentum toward that ultimate communist ideal. Politics, construed as the authoritative allocation of values, means several difficult things in this context. It means making and administering policy aimed at furthering both revolutions, socialist and modernizing. It means overseeing the process of reshaping citizens' political orientations and mobilizing the population in support of society's purposes. It means fighting the influence of old traditions on all levels of social organization. We read of Polish villages desperately in need of new school facilities yet enthusiastically engaged in erecting new church buildings[24]; and of the difficulties in drumming up enthusiasm for the task of self-management in Yugoslav workers' councils.[25] Large numbers of Soviet Jews find their traditional identity as Jews so compelling that they choose to reject the promise of communism, belied by the systematic repression of the present, and apply for emigration to Israel. We read sympathetic accounts of village life in Hungary's past, when custom and ritual underlay a society that was primitive and harsh—but stable and meaningful.[26]

In conclusion, the success or failure of any revolution can be measured by the effectiveness of its leaders in winning widespread public acceptance of the revolution's purpose. Put another way, the values, symbols, orientations, and behavioral patterns common to society as a whole—or to the largest possible part of it—must conform, or be changed so as to conform, with those of the revolution. This basic socialization function is more complicated than those in non-revolutionary societies because of the inherent contradiction between the revolution and the traditions of the past. This contradiction has underlain the history of Eastern Europe since the communists came to power.

It is beyond the scope of this study to begin to answer the questions raised in the preceding pages. My purpose here has been to suggest that empirical studies of policies, reforms, institutional adaptation, group conflicts, mobilization, and so on do not go far enough in our attempt to understand the nature of social change. To go beyond conventional empirical approaches, we need to explore systematically and in detail the cultures of the various societies in the socialist world. To do so might require some quite unconventional approaches to the study of politics.

NOTES

1. Of the former, see Frederick C. Barghoorn, Politics in the USSR (Boston: Little, Brown, 1966, 1972); Richard R. Fagen, The Transformation of Political Culture in Cuba (Stanford, Calif.: Stanford University Press, 1969); and Richard H. Solomon, Mao's Revolution and the Chinese Political Culture (Berkeley and Los Angeles: University of California Press, 1971). A forthcoming volume edited by A. H. Brown, Political Culture and Political Change in Communist States (London: Macmillan), will add new dimensions to the literature already published. For additional usages of the political culture concept see John S. Reshetar, The Soviet Polity (New York: Dodd, Mead, 1971); A. H. Brown, "Political Change in Czechoslovakia," in Political Opposition in One-Party States, ed. Leonard Schapiro (New York: John Wiley and Sons, 1972), pp. 110-37; and, by the same author, Soviet Politics and Political Science (London: Macmillan, 1974), pp. 89-104.

2. An interesting unpublished discussion of this is a paper by Robert C. Tucker, "Culture, Political Culture, Communism," prepared for the Arden House Conference on Communist Studies and Political Culture, November 1971. See Dorothy Knapp, David W. Paul, and Gerson S. Sher, "Digest of the Proceedings of the Arden

House Conference," Newsletter on Comparative Studies of Communism 5, no. 3 (May 1972): 2-17.

3. Elements of this definition can be found in the definitions put forth by Almond, Verba, Pye, Black, and Rosenbaum, among others. See Gabriel A. Almond, "Comparative Political Systems," The Journal of Politics 18, no. 3 (August 1956): 396; Almond and Sidney Verba, eds., The Civic Culture (Princeton: Princeton University Press, 1963), passim.; Verba and Lucian W. Pye, eds., Political Culture and Political Development (Princeton: Princeton University Press, 1965), esp. p. 513; and Walter A. Rosenbaum, Political Culture (New York: Praeger Publishers, 1975), pp. 4 ff. Cyril E. Black's definition appeared in an unpublished paper, "Theories of Political Development and American Foreign Policy," presented to the Dartmouth Bicentennial Conference on International Affairs, April 1970, p. 13.

4. See, for example, anthropologist Clifford Geertz's criticism of Pye's book dealing to a large extent with the political culture of Burma: Geertz, "A Study of National Character," review of Pye, Politics, Personality, and Nation Building, in the journal Economic Development and Cultural Change 12, no. 2 (January 1964): 205-09.

5. Walter A. Rosenbaum, who assumes this overall focus, argues that within it there are two somewhat separate levels of approach concentrating on the individual and his orientation toward politics (the micro level) and the collective patterns of such orientations within the whole society (the macro level). Rosenbaum, Political Culture, p. 4.

6. See note 3.

7. See note 2.

8. In the words of A. H. Brown, political culture has "a psychological as well as an historical dimension." Brown, Soviet Politics and Political Science, p. 89.

9. Verba, in Political Culture and Political Development, p. 521; Tucker, "Culture," p. 13; also Edward W. Lehman, "On the Concept of Political Culture: A Theoretical Reassessment," Social Forces 50, no. 3 (March 1972): 364.

10. Almond, "Comparative Political Systems," p. 396; cf. Edward C. Tolman, "A Psychological Model," Part 3 of Toward a General Theory of Action, ed. Talcott Parsons and Edward A. Shils (Cambridge, Mass.: Harvard University Press, 1951).

11. See Clyde Kluckhohn, Culture and Behavior (New York: The Free Press of Glencoe, 1962), pp. 46 ff. Kluckhohn stresses that culture does not, strictly speaking, cause anything. It predisposes one to a certain course of action, frequently setting limits or boundaries to the way in which one will perceive, evaluate, and ultimately respond to a stimulus.

12. The author is hereby aligning himself with Tucker (see "Culture") and others who argue that behavior be considered an integral part of political culture rather than just a reflection of subjective orientations to politics; the latter is the position of Almond, Verba, Pye, and Rosenbaum (see note 3). Cf. Moshe M. Czudnowski, "A Salience Dimension of Politics for the Study of Political Culture," American Political Science Review 62, no. 3 (September 1968): 884, and Fagen, The Transformation of Political Culture in Cuba, p. 5.

13. For a discussion of some exceptions, see Stephen White, "An Empirical Note on Communist Political Culture," Newsletter on Comparative Studies of Communism 6, no. 2 (February 1973): 41-44; David W. Paul, "A Further Empirical Note on Communist Political Culture," Newsletter 6, no. 4 (August 1973): 6-11.

14. Rosenbaum admits the utility of other methodological tools in addition to survey research but insists that the latter is still the "basic tool of contemporary political culture study." See Rosenbaum, Political Culture, pp. 21-29; citation is from p. 22.

15. As Harry Eckstein has argued with regard to The Civic Culture, we do not empirically know whether or not the values described in that study would be borne out by surveys conducted today. (Knapp, Paul, and Sher, "Digest," p. 9).

16. Rosenbaum, Political Culture, pp. 29-34.

17. See, for example, Frederic J. Fleron, ed., Communist Studies and the Social Sciences (New York: Rand-McNally, 1969); Roger E. Kanet, ed., The Behavioral Revolution and Communist Studies (New York: The Free Press, 1971); Lenard J. Cohen and Jane P. Shapiro, eds., Communist Studies in Comparative Perspective (Garden City, N.Y.: Anchor/Doubleday, 1974); and Brown, Soviet Studies and Political Science.

18. Fagen has defined political socialization most succinctly as "the inculcation of political information, values, and practices, whether formally or informally, in planned or unplanned fashion." (Fagen, The Transformation of Political Culture in Cuba, p. 2). See also Herbert H. Hyman, Political Socialization (Glencoe, Ill.: The Free Press, 1959); the discussion of "Political Socialization" by Fred I. Greenstein in the International Encyclopedia of the Social Sciences, vol. 14 (New York, 1968), pp. 551-55.

19. "The Immediate Tasks of the Soviet Government," abridged in Lenin on Politics and Revolution (New York: Pegasus, 1968), pp. 248-74.

20. For a detailed study of the Stalinist "new man" model, see Raymond A. Bauer, The New Man in Soviet Psychology (Cambridge, Mass.: Harvard University Press, 1952).

21. "An Empirical Note," p. 43.

22. For a discussion of this, see Robert C. Tucker, "Stalin and the Uses of Psychology," in *The Soviet Political Mind*, rev. ed. (New York: W. W. Norton, 1971), pp. 143-72.

23. Gajo Petrovic, *Marx in the Mid-Twentieth Century* (Garden City, N.Y.: Anchor/Doubleday, 1967).

24. Joseph Fiszman, *Revolution and Tradition in People's Poland* (Princeton: Princeton University Press, 1972), p. 37.

25. Branko Harvat, *An Essay on Yugoslav Society* (White Plains, N.Y.: International Arts and Sciences Press, 1969), pp. 210-24.

26. Edit Fel and Tamas Hofer, *Proper Peasants: Traditional Life in a Hungarian Village* (Chicago: Aldine, 1969), passim.

CHAPTER

2

DIVERSITY AND ADAPTATION IN SOVIET POLITICAL CULTURE: THE ATTITUDES OF THE SOVIET POLITICAL ELITE
Philip D. Stewart

IMAGES OF ADAPTATION IN SOVIET POLITICAL CULTURE

Can the Soviet Union survive until 1984? This question, made famous as the title of the controversial essay by dissident Soviet historian Andrei Amalrik,[1] is but an extreme variation of a concern that has increasingly engaged the attention of Soviet specialists in the West in recent years. While Amalrik characterizes the Soviet polity as hopelessly stifled by an unresponsive bureaucratic Party and envisions the system ultimately succumbing under the impact of a Sino-Soviet war, most Western views are less apocalyptic. Serious academic interpretations of the nature and direction of change in

---

The author wishes to express appreciation to those who assisted in this research: to Peg Hermann and Tom Milburn for inspiration and encouragement; to Judy Ruth for assistance in coding the data; to Bill Messmer and Barbara J. Nelson for assistance in developing some of the ideas presented here; to Dick Hofstetter, Giacomo Sani, and Herb Asher for conceptual and methodological guidance; to Jim McGregor and Jim Ludwig for programming and computer assistance; and to numerous graduate students for helpful comments. I am also indebted to the following facilities at Ohio State University: the Instruction and Research Computer Center, for generously allocating the required computer time; the Polimetrics Laboratory, Department of Political Science and College of Social and Behavioral Sciences, C. Richard Hofstetter, Director. Of course, responsibility for existing shortcomings belongs to the author alone.

Soviet politics range from a position that portrays a dynamic Stalinist totalitarianism degenerating into a kind of "oligarchic petrifaction,"[2] to an image of an essentially static, unchanging totalitarianism,[3] to an interpretation stressing gradual movement toward "institutional pluralism."[4] Table 1 summarizes three of these images. Although associated primarily with the work of a single scholar, as elaborated here each image incorporates the ideas of a number of observers who share similar perspectives.

Unfortunately, there exists no really satisfactory, relatively objective knowledge upon which either scholars or interested publics can rely in choosing among competing images of Soviet political culture and its adaptive potential.

The dramatic and fundamental differences in images of the Soviet political culture, reflected in Table 1, appear to be explained in part by the fact that, as T. Harry Rigby has noted, it is not the basic political structures, about which we have much information, that have been altered in the post-Stalin years but rather political processes, about which we know relatively little.[5] Much of what we do know, however, suggests that political processes reflect primarily the beliefs, orientations, values, and attitudes of the elites who fill political roles. Such abstract factors as norms, institutions, ideology, industrialization, and modernization find their impact on the political process primarily as they influence the attitudes and condition the behavior of individual political elites. Zbigniew Brzezinski notes, for example, that "political change in the Soviet Union will necessarily be influenced by the emergence of a new social elite . . . but it will be even more affected by the changes in the internal character and outlook of the professional, ruling Party bureaucracy."[6]

Only a few efforts have ever been made to study systematically the orientations, values or attitudes of the Soviet elite.[7] None of these, unfortunately, provides adequate evidence about the range of orientations or attitudes expressed by the most powerful Soviet elite—the Party leadership.

This essay reports a portion of an exploratory effort to examine the potential for long-term adaptation of the Soviet Party elite to challenges arising from the domestic and international environments.[8] The core assumption of this analysis is that the capacity for successful adaptation over the next ten to twenty years is dependent to a large degree on the extent to which attitudes responsive to and to a significant extent accommodative of a broad range of "legitimate" interests in Soviet society exist today among the next generation of the Soviet political leadership.

An adequate understanding of the leadership's long-term adaptive capacity not only depends upon the identification of responsive orientations but requires as well explanation of the relative salience of these

TABLE 1

Schematic Representation of Attitude Antecedents, Attitudes, and Behavioral Expectations for Three Images of Soviet Political Change

Antecedents	Attitudes	Behavioral Tendencies
Broker politician Younger; Post-1938 political generation; Co-opted into Party work; Agricultural or industrial education; Extensive agricultural or industrial experience	Ideology as instrumental effects; Trust in the masses; Industrial manpower orientation; Aggressive activism to improve consumer welfare	Institutional pluralism; Adaptive, responsive accommodation to "legitimate" interests of social forces; Creative change toward pluralism
Administrative dictator Older and younger; Pre-1939 and post-1938 political generation; Recruited or co-opted into Party work; Extensive Party experience; Industrial education	Ideology as doctrine; Distrust of the masses; Aggressive Party activism in agriculture; Symbolic affirmation of consumer welfare	"More perfect totalitarianism"; Greater Party control, repression of dissent, creation of new Soviet man, and remolding of society; Adaptation only to improve control
Regime of clerks Older and younger; Pre-1939 and post-1938 political generation; Recruited into Party work; Industrial or technical education; Extensive Party experience	Ideology as symbolic affirmation; Distrust in the masses; Assertive dissatisfaction with agriculture; Assertive dissatisfaction with consumer welfare	"Bureaucratic stagnation"; Rigid unresponsiveness, little innovation due to "ideological petrifaction," bureaucratic stability the most sought after goal; Minimal adaptation to social demands

orientations. In short, accommodative attitudes must be located within the overall outlook of the Party leadership. To accomplish this, a comprehensive approach is adopted here to assist in identification of elite attitudes.

THE RESEARCH DESIGN

The major premise underlying this research design is that individual attitudes of Soviet political elites can be measured through analysis of their writings in the Soviet press and periodic literature.[9] For a variety of reasons, including the significance of the position as a recruiting ground for new central Party elites,[10] this study focuses upon the writings of regional Party secretaries. The sample includes 75 articles by 39 different regional secretaries during their tenure as first secretaries. The articles, selected at random from a list of 1,200, appeared over a twelve-year time period, 1955 through 1966. Comparison of backgrounds and characteristics of regions represented by this sample and by a much larger group of RSFSR regional secretaries suggests that the sample group is representative both of the population of regional secretaries and of the conditions under which they worked during this time period.

Content analysis is the general approach most suited to the identification of opinions in public documents.[11] The specific form utilized here we call thematic analysis or opinion analysis. Rather than coding every aspect of every sentence in a variety of ways, or devising a set of coding categories requiring substantial coder judgment, we coded only statements of issue orientation or opinion, ignoring all purely cognitive statements.

An issue orientation or opinion is differentiated from other statements in that it contains both an affective or evaluative element and a cognitive or knowledge component.[12] In the thematic form of content analysis employed here, all themes containing both of these elements are coded.

Seeking a comprehensive mapping of issue orientations, a list was prepared of all cognitive objects occurring with any kind of associated affect from a sample of 25 percent of all articles to be coded.[13] Since virtually all expressions of affect found in the sample could be included unambiguously within one of three classes of affect—praise, criticism, or demands—these were selected as our coding categories for affect. All associated cognitive objects were grouped into thirteen items falling into four classes: ideology, leadership, production and manpower, and consumer welfare.

The unit of enumeration is the theme. If an individual secretary praised industrial production five times in all his coded articles, then his final raw score on this item would be five. Our assumption is that the intensity of an opinion is best measured here by the frequency with which it is expressed, in an additive manner.[14] In order to make scores comparable for all individuals (to control for differences in the total number of issue orientations expressed), all scores are converted into proportions. Application of this design to the sample articles resulted in the identification of 1,323 issue orientations or opinions expressed by the sample as a whole. These data formed the basis for the analysis of elite attitudes reported below.

ATTITUDES OF REGIONAL PARTY ELITES

The results of a principal component factor analysis of the correlations among the issue orientations of the regional Party first secretaries are presented in Table 2. Each of the resulting factors is considered as indicating one attitude. The factors or attitudes are orthogonal, based on a varimax rotation of the principal components solution.[15] Table 2 contains all factors in the analysis with an eigenvalue greater than unity; Table 2 also reports the issue orientations with factor loadings of ± 0.5 or higher on each factor and the percentage of the total variance explained by each factor.

The reader is asked to compare the attitudes in Table 2 with the Soviet elite attitudes listed in Table 1, which are implied by the three images of Soviet political change noted above. For the sample as a whole, many of the attitudes posited by the three images of change are found among Soviet regional Party first secretaries. Moreover, as might be expected from the careful, thoughtful scholarship represented by these three images, our analysis provides partial support for each one. In brief, we find widely divergent conceptions of their role and their world among regional Party officials.

Ideological Attitudes

More than 29 percent of the variation in all issue orientations is explained by attitude dimensions whose defining characteristics are predominantly ideological concerns. Comparing this percentage with the modest proportion (11.9 percent) of all expressed opinions that were considered directly ideological, ideology appears far more significant as an underlying, organizing concern than analysis of opinions alone might suggest. Indeed, the finding that nearly a third of all issue orientations are given directionality and coherence by

TABLE 2

Attitudes of Regional Party Secretaries

	Factor Loading	Eigenvalue	Percent Variance Explained
Ideological attitudes			29.06
1. Ideology as instrumental effects		4.34	
Criticize ideological preparedness	.923		
Demand ideological preparedness	.869		
Criticize level of Party initiative	.798		
2. Ideology as symbolic affirmation		3.90	10.56
Praise level of Party initiative	.927		
Praise ideological preparedness	.914		
Praise content of ideological work	.869		
3. Ideology as doctrine		2.71	7.31
Criticize content of ideological work	.899		
Demand improved content of ideological work	.851		
Praise upper level attention	.532		
Criticize upper level attention	.544		
Trust and distrust: leadership style			18.50
4. Distrust in masses: need for discipline		3.02	8.16
Demand concern for internal Party life	-.966		
Criticize state of internal Party life	-.964		
Criticize state of social and labor discipline	-.829		
5. Group cooperation: harmony through discipline		2.23	6.02
Demand improved group cooperation	.888		
Praise level of group cooperation	.861		
Criticize level of group cooperation	.578		
Demand improved social and labor discipline	.549		
Trust in masses: possibility of accommodation		1.60	4.32
Praise state of social and labor discipline	.813		
Praise state of internal Party life	.816		
Praise level of Party support	.714		
Production and Manpower Attitudes			24.66
7. General industrial manpower orientation		4.69	12.69
Criticize level of group cooperation	.577		
Criticize industrial manpower	.898		
Demand improved industrial manpower	.782		
Praise industrial manpower	.665		
Criticize industrial production	.547		
8. Aggressive Party activism in agricultural sphere		2.50	6.76
Demand improved agricultural production	.790		
Demand upper level attention	.727		
Demand Party initiatives	.693		
9. Assertive dissatisfaction with agriculture		1.93	5.21
Criticize agricultural manpower	-.753		
Demand improved agricultural production	-.686		
Criticize agricultural production	.515		
Praise industrial production	.579		
Consumer welfare attitudes			9.18
10. Assertive dissatisfaction with state of consumer affairs		1.33	3.59
Criticize level of consumer welfare	.806		
11. Symbolic affirmation of consumer well-being		1.05	2.83
Praise level of consumer welfare	-.806		
Praise agricultural manpower	-.658		
Praise agricultural production	-.514		
12. Aggressive activism to improve consumer welfare		1.02	2.76
Demand improved consumer welfare	.847		
Total variation in observed issue orientations explained by 12 attitude dimensions			81.94

ideological attitudes provides fairly striking confirmation of the widely accepted proposition about the dominant role of ideology in organizing the outlook of Soviet political elites.

When we examine the specific kinds of ideological attitudes, however, it is clear that each of the images of Soviet political elites is partially adequate but also to some degree inadequate in identifying salient ideological attitudes. The finding that an attitude conceptualizing ideology primarily as an object of symbolic affirmation accounts for more than 10 percent of all issue orientations is relevant to Brzezinski's view of "ideological petrifaction" and, in turn, to the "regime of clerks" image. Although it is the least significant organizer of opinions, "ideology as doctrine" does not disconfirm Allen Kassof's conception of the salience of ideology as content. This attitude lends support to the "administrative dictator" image. Similarly, that an instrumental attitude toward ideology, "ideology as instrumental effects," accounts for more variation in elite opinions than any other ideological attitude tends to justify Jerry Hough's emphasis on the "pragmatism" of political elites and the "broker politician." What is equally obvious, at the same time, is that all three ideological attitudes occur with similar degrees of salience. In other words, among the Soviet elite conceptions of ideology there is a range from an instrumentalist concern with impact to an unquestioned and positive acceptance of ideology to involvement with ideology as doctrine.

Leadership Style Attitudes

We find the same pattern of partial support for the three images of Soviet political elites in Table 2 when the other types of attitudes are examined—in this case, leadership style. Both Brzezinski and Kassof hypothesize a leadership style emphasizing dictatorship and control, stressing a perceived need for continuous if not ever-increasing social and labor discipline among the masses as well as tighter discipline within the Party. Fundamentally, the political elites are seen as suspicious and distrusting of the masses, both within the Party and in society. Certainly, this attitude is not absent among the regional political elite; indeed, this attitude accounts for more variation in elite orientations than either of the other two leadership attitudes.

At the time, irrespective of its relatively minor role in organizing orientations for the group as a whole, we cannot ignore the finding that the psychological bases for a "broker politician" leadership style also appear to exist among at least some elites. That we find

an attitude of trust in the masses and Party at all is significant in
light of the former predominance in Western images of Soviet politics
as totalitarianism dependent upon coercive terror for survival.[16]
Moreover, finding this attitude lends some credence to Merle Fainsod's
warning that we should not underestimate the impact on the Soviet
system of its many economic, social, and political successes in the
last twenty to thirty years.[17]

Perhaps we should not be surprised that a major organizing
dimension among attitudes toward the leadership function is an
orientation that appears to correspond closely to the official image
of the ideal Party leader—the leader who conceives his role as
essentially that of an orchestra conductor.[18] Two ingredients are
important to this image as portrayed in Soviet writings: (1) leadership resulting from group cooperation in the performance of Party
tasks and (2) a high level of conscious discipline among the masses.
Issue orientations indicative of both these positions define the group
cooperation attitude dimension. Although the model of the administered society appears to imply that this official image is only a mask
for a distrusting, disciplinary approach to total control, our findings
indicate that these are two separate, independent kinds of attitudes
toward leadership.

The identification of trust and distrust in the masses among
regional Party elites may have far-reaching significance for an
examination of Soviet political change. Considerable research on
trust and distrust has shown that persons exhibiting trust are far
more flexible and capable of absorbing and adapting to new information and situations than are those displaying distrust. If we later
find that trust is stronger than distrust among the emerging leadership, there may be some psychological basis for inferring a capacity
for effective adaptation to social and political change among at least
a portion of the Soviet political elite.

Production and Manpower Attitudes

The model of the broker politician is based upon the view that
the major, if not primary, preoccupation of political leadership is
physical production—planning, technology, material-technical supply.
As our analysis of issue orientations (reported elsewhere) has shown,
these concerns were the occasion for a large proportion of all
opinions expressed.[19] But the high frequency of comment in this
area may reflect the result of unavoidable environmental demands
more than underlying attitudes. Hough has also suggested that what
probably distinguishes Party officials from their similarly trained

colleagues in the industrial ministries is the preponderance of a political, generalizing approach in the former as contrasted with an essentially technical orientation to problems among the latter.[20] Our findings lend support to this interpretation. Although 37 percent of all issue orientations concerned the physical elements of industrial and agricultural production, these expressions constitute the defining characteristic of only one of the twelve principal attitudes identified by our method. While physical production orientations are moderately involved (factor loadings near 0.5) in several dimensions, the predominant elements in attitudes toward production are what the Party defines as a major political role, that is, recruiting and placing cadres and mobilizing people.[21]

The one exception is the attitude labeled "aggressive Party activism in the agricultural sphere." Here, demands for a greater Party role in agriculture (Party initiatives) and demands for more upper-level attention combine with demands for improved agricultural production to form a single attitude dimension. While in general, then, a political, mobilizational approach appears to characterize two of the identified attitudes toward production problems, an attitude supportive of intensive institutional and political involvement in agricultural production also is revealed. This "aggressive activism" may represent the psychological basis of what some[22] have identified as a "campaign approach" to production problems.[23] In effect, this attitude may be an extreme form of a more general but less intense mobilizational orientation to production problems by the political elite.

The findings on production attitudes are not inconsistent with any of the images of Soviet political change that we have reviewed. However, there are differences in emphasis. While the broker politician is seen as production-oriented, emphasizing pragmatic, efficiency concerns, our findings exhibit a mobilization approach more appropriate to the administrative dictatorship. Yet even here mobilization concerns are not as dominant as that model might suggest.

Consumer Welfare Attitudes

Differences in attitudes toward consumer welfare are more evident in the three images than was the case with production problems. The broker politician is postulated as exhibiting a strong, assertive commitment to improved consumer welfare, not merely for its utilitarian value but as a basic right. In the administrative dictatorship, welfare is only "an incidental and instrumental" element in the pursuit of more perfect social control. Brzezinski's regime of clerks tends to downplay the economic achievements of the Soviet economy, but he does appear to perceive some mild concern if not commitment to consumer well-being.

Again, we find evidence that all three of these attitudes exist among the regional elite. Moderate concern over consumer needs is the strongest organizing attitude dimension, but two sharply divergent attitudes on welfare also are of some importance. "Symbolic affirmation of consumer well-being" reflects a basic satisfaction both with the existing levels of welfare and with its most unreliable component—agricultural production. In sharp contrast is an attitude dimension defined almost entirely by an aggressive activism to improve well-being: demands for improved welfare.

SOURCES OF SOVIET ELITE ATTITUDES: POTENTIAL FOR ADAPTIVE CHANGE

Our analysis of Soviet regional political elite attitudes has shown that rather than a monolithic unity of views there exists within the Party elite a broad spectrum of attitudes. This range of attitudinal diversity, while in no sense embracing those views thought of as consistent with democratic politics,[24] does extend from the instrumental, responsive, trusting attitudes of the broker politician to embrace the outlook of the administrative dictator and attitudes consistent with a regime of clerks. In attempting to understand the present and to assess the direction of political change, each of the images of Soviet political change incorporates inferences about the background traits and kinds of experience necessary for the development of attitudes central to the image. These hypothesized antecedent characteristics, the reader will recall, are found in Table 1. Observed alterations in such elite characteristics can be used as a principal means of hypothesizing the pace and direction of change in elite attitudes and behavior and, in turn, of system transformation, perfection, or degeneration. Sincw we have now, in a tentative way, shown that attitudes consistent with each major image are found among the Soviet regional elite, it may be useful to seek to identify and to assess the impact of these antecedent factors on elite attitudes. By establishing whether, for example, it is the younger and those with extensive industrial experience who tend to display most strongly the attitudes of the broker politician as opposed to the administrative dictator or the regime of clerks, we may begin to create a more adequate basis for inferences about the probable direction of system development.[25]

The antecedent variables examined here are those suggested in the literature (see Table 1) as most directly related to the attitudinal differences postulated by the three images of Soviet elites. The four background variables employed are age, mode of entry into the Party, political generation, and type of education. Four measures of career experience are utilized. These are rate of career development, length of industrial experience (both in economic and Party posts), length of Party experience including all Party experience prior to acquiring the post of regional Party first secretary for the first time, and agricultural experience (both directly in agriculture and in related Party positions). Consistent with the illustrative approach taken here as well as to maximize clarity and ease of interpretation, each of the antecedent variables was dichotomized. The dividing point selected for each was the mean score for the sample on that indicator. Selected marginals for these variables in their continuous and dichotomous forms are found in the first two columns of Table 3. Table 3 also contains mean factor scores on the ideological and leadership style attitude dimensions for each subgroup created by dichotomizing the background and career experience variables. Table 4 presents mean factor scores for these same subgroups on the production and manpower as well as the consumer welfare attitude dimensions.

Factor scores are used in this analysis for several reasons. First, our measures of attitudes themselves are factored dimensions. Second, since factor scores are reported as standard scores and indicate the precise degree of individual involvement in each attitude, they make possible a clear and direct interpretation of the findings and results that are comparable across all attitudes. Third, the use of standardized factor scores means that a zero score represents just average involvement with an attitude. As a result, all positive scores indicate that the background or career experience variable has a greater than average involvement with the attitude, which is precisely the objective of this analysis. Finally, the interval level of measurement provided by factor scores means that the distances between unit scores are equal and conceptually meaningful, and thus interpretation is facilitated.

Several caveats are important at this point before we present the results of this analysis. Space does not permit presentation of findings showing the involvement of each background variable controlling for the others. Such an analysis provides a more complete understanding of the relationship between antecedent experiences and attitudes. This type of analysis has been performed on these data and is available upon request from the author.

With respect to our ability to generalize from the findings reported here, the reader should recall the descriptive, exploratory

TABLE 3

Impact of Background and Experience on Ideological and Leadership Style Attitudes

Antecedent Variables	Mean	N	Ideology Instrument	Ideology Symbolic	Ideology Doctrine	Distrust Masses	Trust Masses	Group Cooperation
Background Variables								
Year of birth								
Born post-1912	1916	19	-.028	.184	-.099	-.214	.044	-.291
Born pre-1913	1909	18	.072	-.135	.125	.216	-.208	.291
Mode of entry to Party[a]								
Recruited	3.4	15	-.175	-.143	-.144	.241	.044	-.108
Co-opted	15.0	12	.110	.089	.090	-.151	-.028	.067
Political generation								
Joined Party pre-1939	1929	10	-.142	-.365	.265	.375	-.217	-.187
Joined Party post-1938	1941	28	.060	.157	-.086	-.148	-.056	-.070
Education[b]								
Agricultural	—	16	-.343	.284	.153	.127	-.026	.015
Industrial	—	14	.551	-.042	-.050	-.015	-.178	.219
Experience Variables								
Career development[c]								
Slower than average	24.5	14	-.259	.248	.272	.287	.193	-.235
Faster than average	17.8	23	.162	-.155	-.170	-.179	-.120	.147
Industrial experience (yrs.)								
Lower than average	0.2	25	-.223	.005	.099	.020	.054	.137
Higher than average	8.4	12	.398	-.009	-.176	-.037	-.096	-.245
Party experience[d]								
Lower than average	6.3	18	.103	.008	-.197	-.193	-.031	.117
Higher than average	15.8	19	-.108	-.009	.208	.203	.032	-.123
Agricultural experience (yrs.)								
Lower than average	0.5	27	.166	-.155	-.145	.017	-.035	-.213
Higher than average	13.5	10	-.374	.259	.372	-.159	.079	.480

[a] Defined as years between education and first full-time Party post.
[b] Several categories are not included here because of small N's—political with N of 1, university with N of 3.
[c] Defined as years between joining Party and becoming regional Party first secretary.
[d] Defined as years in full-time Party positions.

TABLE 4

Impact of Background and Experience on Consumer Welfare and Production and Manpower Attitudes

Antecedent Variables	Industrial Manpower	Agricultural Dissatisfaction	Agricultural Activism	Consumer Welfare Dissatisfaction	Consumer Welfare Affirmation	Consumer Welfare Activism
Background Variables						
Year of birth						
Born post-1912	.048	.301	.063	-.156	-.225	.184
Born pre-1913	-.308	-.261	-.047	.194	.283	-.196
Mode of entry to Party[a]						
Recruited	-.020	-.146	-.098	-.068	-.297	-.039
Co-opted	.013	.091	.610	.042	.185	.024
Political generation						
Joined Party pre-1939	-.316	-.178	-.144	-.112	.357	-.198
Joined Party post-1938	.111	.083	.044	.043	-.085	.091
Education[b]						
Agricultural	-.238	.152	.216	-.393	.473	.213
Industrial	-.139	-.030	-.157	.473	-.393	-.003
Experience Variables						
Career development[c]						
Slower than average	-.191	.286	.194	.474	.040	-.191
Faster than average	.120	-.179	-.121	-.297	-.025	.120
Industrial experience (yrs.)						
Lower than average	-.246	.103	.096	-.202	.170	.078
Higher than average	.439	-.184	-.171	.362	-.304	-.139
Party experience[d]						
Lower than average	.281	-.061	-.003	.003	-.182	-.046
Higher than average	-.295	.065	.003	-.003	.192	.049
Agricultural experience						
Lower than average	-.032	.027	.080	.156	-.004	-.204
Higher than average	.073	-.061	-.180	-.350	.010	.460

[a] Defined as years between education and first full-time Party post.
[b] Several categories are not included here because of small N's—political with N of 1, university with N of 3.
[c] Defined as years between joining Party and becoming regional Party first secretary.
[d] Defined as years in full-time Party positions.

spirit in which these results are presented. While we are persuaded that our sample is representative of the larger universe, as we examine more cases and a larger sample of writings, the relationships reported here may well be altered in significant ways.

Ideological Attitudes

The attitude, "ideology as instrumental effects," is found predominantly among those with an industrial education and those who possess considerable industrial experience. This finding is consistent with the rational-technical image of Soviet political development[26] (of which the model of institutional pluralism is a contemporary adaptation), which suggests that industrial experience will lead to an instrumental, pragmatic orientation as contrasted with a dogmatic, ideological view of the world. But in contrast to the usual hypothesis in the literature that these tendencies will result in a lessening of the importance of ideology in the cognitive structure of industrialists, we find that this most salient of the three identified ideological attitudes is especially important to industrialist-politicians—just those whose background and experience is presumed to make ideology among the least important elements of their world view.

One kind of explanation for this phenomenon suggests itself. Ideology may be reconceptualized in a manner consistent with the industrialists' overall perspectives. Rather than developing affect toward its content or reducing ideology to the level of symbolic affirmation, the psychologically significant element of ideology becomes an overriding concern with the impact of ideological work on people. Ideology is valued pragmatically as a mechanism for motivating workers.

The conception of ideology as symbolic affirmation is found most clearly among those regional Party officials who (1) are younger than average, (2) joined the Party after 1938, (3) completed an agricultural education, (4) rose slower than normally expected in the apparatus, and (5) acquired greater than average experience in agricultural work. Whereas industrialist-politicians tend to adopt an instrumental view of ideology, agricultural specialists approach ideology as a set of symbols to be lauded.

Why should agriculturalist-politicians display this orientation? One possible explanation is that as the revolution recedes further into the past, even politically oriented younger cadres may find it increasingly difficult to become really involved with the ideology. While those from an urban, probably middle-class background transform their ideological interests in an instrumental direction in the process of industrial training and experience, the very abstractness of much of the ideology as doctrine may simply be beyond the grasp of those from a rural, peasant background who spend most of their lives in agricultural work. As a result of their political interests, however, the ideology becomes learned by rote and internalized; their superiors talk and think in ideological terms and the younger agriculturalists respond similarly, conscious of the need to observe ideological form. This process is seen by some as reinforcing an ideological vocabulary and style.[27] Rather than resulting in ideological erosion, the behavioral consequence of this process in Brzezinski's view is an "intensified emphasis on revolutionary rhetoric and symbolism."[28] This emphasis leads, in turn, to rigidity and inflexibility in thought and to a stifling of intellectual innovation.

Concern for ideology as doctrine also is salient for regional Party first secretaries with higher than average agricultural experience. Yet the fact that a concern for doctrine occurs predominantly among those who are older and those who joined the Party prior to 1938 provides some evidence of generational differences among the agriculturalist-politicians. For the younger agriculturalist-politicians, ideology as symbolic affirmation is more salient. Thus, rather than doctrinal concerns becoming ever more central to the leadership as implied by the model of the administrative dictator, these differences are precisely in the direction suggested by Brzezinski with his regime of clerks. There is an evident trend among these regional Party officials away from doctrine and toward ideology as more rhetoric and style than substance.

Leadership Styles

Three distinct approaches to leadership, reflecting divergent attitudes toward the masses were identified above: (1) distrust in the masses, (2) trust in the people, and (3) cooperation based upon discipline. Information on the impact of background and experience on these attitudes is found in Table 3.

From this table we note that distrust is a predominant orientation among older officials who were recruited into the Party, among those who joined the Party before 1938, among those whose career development was slower than average, and among those with higher than average Party experience. In striking contrast, the data for the trust attitude is more suggestive of types of regional Party secretaries who show little interest in trust than for which types of secretaries this attitude is salient. The attitude stressing group cooperation based upon discipline is found mainly among regional Party secretaries who older than average, who received an industrial education, and who have had extensive agricultural experience.

Many Western observers, pointing to the restrictions on individual, political, and administrative initiative during the Stalin period and to the general atmosphere of tension that existed throughout most of this period, argue that a basic distrust of the masses and an emphasis on the need for vigilance and control will characterize all political officials who acquired much experience in this repressive environment. Our findings lend support to this hypothesis. Regional officials who acquired their early political experience during the late 1920s and early 1930s (joined the Party pre-1939) show a distrusting orientation toward the masses.

The predominance of cooperation through discipline among older officials and among those with much agricultural experience, but not among their younger counterparts, suggests that the conditions associated with agricultural work in the 1930s and perhaps 1940s may have reinforced a belief in the value of cooperation and of discipline. One reasonable interpretation is that in an area of the economy where the Party assumed major responsibility for directly supervising production, but where relative few concrete rewards or coercive tactics could be used to increase productive activity, an emphasis on group cooperation combined with conscious discipline may well have been seen as the only effective style of leadership.[29] Why is this approach not found among younger agriculturalist-politicians? Khrushchev's half-hearted and Brezhnev's more extensive efforts at providing material rewards for agricultural production suggest evidence for the view that an instrumental approach, stressing material incentives over moral rewards, may now be perceived by younger cadres as both essential to motivate a more advanced and skilled peasantry and as appropriate in a more developed socialist economy.

While the general implication of these attitudes for conceptions of change was discussed in the previous section, we can see a clear trend away from both distrusting and cooperative disciplinary attitudes toward the masses. The younger regional officials display little interest in either of these attitudes. In effect, regime of clerks and administrative dictator images, with their emphasis on distrust of the masses, may well be more descriptive of the behavioral tendencies of older elites—those who are fairly rapidly leaving the scene except at the highest levels—than of the younger elites. The younger professional politicians may be still experimenting with their leadership style, some adopting the trust attitude, others using styles not identified in this study.

Production and Manpower Attitudes

As noted in Table 4, the "general industrial manpower orientation" is most pronounced in regional officials who have extensive industrial experience, belong to the post-1938 generation of Party members, and rose to prominence at an above-average rate. Regional elites with a birthdate post-1912, with an agricultural education, and with a slower than average career development exhibited the "assertive dissatisfaction with agriculture" attitude. Party first secretaries with an "aggressive Party activism in agriculture sphere" were those who were co-opted into the Party, who had an agricultural education, and who were slower than average in their movement up the career ladder.

It is reflective of the dominant role of the Party in agriculture that the strongest expression of agriculture manpower orientations (agricultural activism) is found primarily among the co-opted Party professional and not the agriculturalist-politician. The driving, critical, and demanding approach to agricultural manpower problems of these later-entering, slow-rising Party professionals contrasts sharply with the "group cooperation" orientation of the older agriculturalist-politicians.

The two attitudes concerned with agricultural production and manpower appear to be held by different regional officials. The younger officials express dissatisfaction with agricultural production and manpower while the co-opted officials demand changes in the agricultural sphere. The desire for change may result, in part, from a slow promotion rate within the Party.

Attitudes Toward Consumer Welfare

According to Table 4, differences in attitudes toward consumer welfare appear to correspond to variations in education and to diversity of career experiences. An attitude of assertive dissatisfaction with consumer welfare but with an underlying emphasis upon the value of moral rewards is expressed most strongly by regional Party secretaries with an industrial education and extensive industrial experience. Affirmation of consumer well-being and activism on consumer welfare, on the other hand, are found in regional officials with an agricultural education. Regional Party secretaries actively seeking changes in consumer welfare policies have had extensive agricultural experience, while those affirming present consumer well-being have higher than average Party experience. Dissatisfaction with consumer welfare appears to be the attitude of the industrialist-politician, affirmation of consumer well-being the attitude of the Party professional, and activism on consumer welfare the attitude of the agriculturalist-politician. Future consumer welfare policies will be determined by which type of politician goes on to higher office. Interestingly, the data in Table 4 suggest that regional officials with a faster than average career development exhibit the activism attitude on consumer welfare.

The three consumer welfare attitudes also are espoused by different age groups. Dissatisfaction with consumer welfare and affirmation of consumer well-being are expressed by older officials, while activism on consumer welfare is the attitude of the younger regional officials. The strength of the consumer welfare activism attitude among both the young and agriculturally-oriented officials lends support to Hough's contention that Brezhnev's "war on poverty," especially its agricultural component, probably has considerable support within this segment of the Party elite.[30] The relative youth of this supportive group also is a potential source of confirmation of Hough's image of the direction of political change within the Soviet Union. That conflict over the consumer welfare issue, particularly over the question of the right of Soviet citizens to a higher standard of living, does exist within the political elite itself and probably will continue to do so in the future is indicated by the contrasting views of the young and old officials. Support for the position that no real improvements are needed at all, however, appears to be a thing of the past, at least among the regional Party elite.

CONCLUSIONS

While some of the substantive conclusions presented in this report have been dramatic and unexpected and may even help to create a firmer empirical basis for our continuing efforts to understand Soviet political change, a more important objective will have been achieved if this research has contributed to the following ends: (1) increasing our awareness of the complexity and diversity of the Soviet political elite, a group all too often perceived as homogeneous in outlook; (2) enhancing our awareness that our efforts at constructing more adequate images of the Soviet political system should be based on systematic study of the attitudes of the Soviet elites; and (3) that it is possible to do so by using Soviet public documents. Only the reader can judge whether we have been successful in achieving these ends.

Identification of the diversity of attitudes among regional Party first secretaries and preliminary examination of the factors influencing this diversity, however, constitutes only a first, very tentative step in the elaboration of more adequate images of the political culture of the Soviet Party elite and of its potential for political adaptation. Some of the most important substantive questions and methodological issues either have been entirely ignored or only briefly touched upon here. Some discussion of a few of these may suggest appropriate directions for future work on Soviet political elites.

Ultimately, the crucial factor in the successful adaptation of the Soviet polity will be whether the policy behavior of the Party elite result in outcomes that increase support for the Party. Policies of international detente and cooperation, actions aimed at substantially improving the working and living conditions of the Soviet people, and a broadening of meaningful political participation would appear to indicate behavior appropriate to this end. Our analysis indicates that attitudes appropriate to the continuation of these policies are found among a portion of the regional elite. Yet the crucial linkage between attitudes and behavior in the Soviet case remains undemonstrated.

Future efforts must explore to what extent differences in attitudes among the Party elite lead to differences in policy emphases and to differences in other forms of behavior. If such relationships are found, it may then become possible to identify, on the basis of similarity of attitudes or policy positions, policy coalitions among the Party elite. Even rough estimates of the extent of support for, say, the policy of detente versus alternative foreign policies, would enormously enhance our understanding of the probable endurance of such policies. This knowledge would, moreover, provide a more adequate basis for conceptions of the policy process and leadership succession.

One of the critical methodological issues that must be confronted in order to address the attitude-behavior linkage in the Soviet context is creation of distinct measures of the separate components of attitude—belief, affect, and behavioral intention. As recent research has indicated, behavior tends not to be related to the belief and affect components of attitude but to be fairly consistently related to behavioral intentions.[31] Our own preliminary coding efforts from published materials suggest that such distinctions probably can be made with this type of data source.

A second important substantive issue is the extent to which the attitudinal diversity among the regional elite observed in the present research finds its reflection among members of the central Party leadership. Leadership recruitment policies that systematically screen out from top Party positions those with, for example, attitudes of the broker politician while advancing administrative dictators would result in far different policies and implications for long-term adaptation than if a different screening process took place. As the research reported here is carried into its next phase, our intention is to extend our sample both vertically (to include Politburo and Secretariat officials, as well as officials from major city Party organizations) and horizontally (to bring in a considerable portion of the regional Party officials). Such an approach should make it possible to address more adequately the issue of the impact of recruitment processes on policy and system change heretofore examined primarily on the basis of biographic data alone.

The durability of elite attitudes is a third important concern for future research. By examining the writings of individual Party elites over an extended time frame, the following question can be addressed: To what extent do measured attitudes change with alterations in the environment, such as (1) a shift in central policy, (2) change in issue addressed, (3) a shift in top leadership, (4) transfer from one region to another, or (5) promotion from the region to the center?

Only by intensive examination of these issues can we develop confidence in the validity of attitude measures derived from content analysis. By separating out the impact of situational factors, those elements of elite beliefs having a long-term impact can be specified. The end result should be considerably more sophisticated images of elite political culture and the potential for effective long-term adaptation.

NOTES

1. Andrei Amalrik, Will The Soviet Union Survive Until 1984? (New York: Praeger Publishers, 1971).
2. Zbigniew Brzezinski, Between Two Ages: America's Role in the Technetronic Era (New York: Viking, 1970).
3. Allen Kassof, "The Administered Society: Totalitarianism Without Terror," World Politics 16 (1964): 558-75.
4. Jerry Hough, "The Soviet System: Petrifaction or Pluralism?", Problems of Communism (1972), pp. 25-45.
5. T. Harry Rigby, "The Soviet Politbureau: A Comparative Profile 1951-1971," Soviet Studies 24 (1972): 3-23.
6. Brzezinski, Between Two Ages, p. 155.
7. R. C. Angell, "Social Values of Soviet and American Elites: Content Analysis of Elite Media," Journal of Conflict Resolution 8 (1964): 330-85; J. D. Singer, "Soviet and American Foreign Policy

Attitudes: Content Analysis of Elite Articulations," Journal of Conflict Resolution 8 (1964): 424-85; Milton Lodge, Soviet Elite Attitudes Since Stalin (Columbus: Charles Merrill, 1969).

8. Due to limitations of space, only a portion of this study is reported here. The reader is urged to consult the fuller report, Philip D. Stewart, "The Attitudes of the Soviet Political Elite: The Potential for Adaptation," in Margaret Hermann and Thomas Milburn, eds., Personality and Politics: A Psychological Examination of Political Man (New York: Free Press, 1975).

9. For an elaboration of this premise and of the research design as a whole, see ibid.

10. Rigby, "The Soviet Politbureau," pp. 15-20.

11. O. Holsti et al., Content Analysis (Evanston, Ill.: Northwestern University Press, 1963).

12. W. J. McGuire, "The Nature of Attitudes and Attitude Change," in The Handbook of Social Psychology, ed. G. Lindzey and E. Aronson, 2nd ed. (1969), vol. 3, pp. 136-314.

13. The specific coding categories and the coding form are reported in Stewart, "The Attitudes of the Soviet Political Elite."

14. McGuire, "The Nature of Attitudes," p. 154.

15. Since the use of orthogonal dimensions as descriptions of attitude structure is most appropriate only when there is reason to believe that the underlying structure is close to orthogonal, we compared our solution with an oblique rotation. We found that the highest intercorrelation of factors in the oblique solution was 0.2, with most factors intercorrelated in the range 0.02 to 0.08. The structure of each dimension was almost identical in the two rotations. This result gives confidence in the appropriateness of the varimax solution.

16. C. J. Friedrich and Z. K. Brzezinski, Totalitarian Dictatorship and Autocracy (Cambridge, Mass.: Harvard University Press, 1956).

17. Merle Fainsod, "Roads to the Future," in Dilemmas of Change in Soviet Politics, ed. Z. K. Brzezinski (New York: Columbia University Press, 1969.

18. Pravda, March 8, 1963.

19. Stewart, "The Attitudes of the Soviet Political Elite."

20. Jerry Hough, The Soviet Prefects: The Local Party Organs in Industrial Decision-Making (Cambridge, Mass.: Harvard University Press, 1969), pp. 66-69.

21. See Bogdan Harasymiw, "Nomenklatura: The Soviet Communist Party's Leadership Recruitment System," Canadian Journal of Political Science 2 (1969): 493-512.

22. R. A. Bauer, A. Inkeles, and C. Kluckhohn, How the Soviet System Works (Cambridge, Mass.: Harvard University Press, 1956), pp. 52-60.

23. For an illustration of this approach to agriculture, see P. D. Stewart, Political Power in the Soviet Union (Indianapolis: Bobbs-Merrill, 1968), Chapter 6.

24. Gabriel Almond and Sidney Verba, The Civic Culture (Boston: Little, Brown, 1965).

25. Another approach to this problem is to examine temporal trends in the expression of attitudes. Because of the small sample size, however, this approach is not appropriate here; in a later study, with a far larger sample, such an approach will become possible.

26. Barrington Moore, Jr., Terror and Progress USSR (Cambridge, Mass.: Harvard University Press, 1954); and Walt W. Rostow, The Dynamics of Soviet Society (Boston: MIT Press, 1953).

27. Zbigniew Brzezinski and Samuel Huntington, Political Power: USA/USSR (New York: Viking, 1963), pp. 42.

28. Brzezinski, Between Two Ages, p. 153.

29. For interesting evidence supporting this interpretation, see Merle Fainsod, Smolensk Under Soviet Rule (Cambridge, Mass.: Harvard University Press, 1958).

30. Hough, "The Soviet System."

31. M. Fishbein and I. Ajzen, "Attitudes and Opinions," in Annual Review of Psychology, ed. P. Mussen and M. Rosenzweig (Palo Alto: Annual Reviews, 1972), p. 516.

CHAPTER 3

STRUCTURAL CHANGE UNDER STATE SOCIALISM: THE POLISH CASE

Alexander Matejko

DYNAMICS OF SOCIAL SYSTEMS IN STATE SOCIALISM

Social systems are not very durable, even those maintained within the rigid framework of state socialism. They are exposed to pressures exercised by the various groups and individuals who participate in them. The uncertainties of socialization, perennial scarcity of resources relative to individual aspirations, contrasting types of social orientation, and variety of principles underlying the social organization[1]—all create problems for which there are no overall continuous solutions. Institutionalization within systems leads to the establishment of collectivities with their own vested interests, as well as to shifts in the balance of power and the creation of antisystems[2] that either challenge the status quo or try to defend it as long as possible. Resources and activities become disembodied from their ascriptive frameworks; differentiation takes place within systems in the shape of various "ways through which the main social functions or the major institutional spheres of society become dissociated from one another, attached to specialized collectivities and roles, and organized in relatively specific and autonomous symbolic and organizational frameworks within the confines of the same institutionalized system."[3]

Under state socialism in Eastern Europe, antisystems appear only rarely and temporarily as overt opposition to the status quo. It is in the nature of the communist political system that developing systemic differentiation and related social change[4] have only a limited opportunity to appear within new "specific and autonomous symbolic and organizational frameworks." A very heavy conservative bias in the Eastern European systems deters them from accepting new institutionalization. The case of the Polish workers' councils, to be discussed later in this essay, may serve as one of many possible examples.

Contrary to what is claimed by official Eastern European circles, the development of social systems in Eastern Europe does not constitute a cumulative and unilinear process. According to the official Marxist doctrine, these systems should make constant progress from lower to higher stages of development. However, it seems more reasonable to argue, after K. W. Deutsch, that from time to time the old social, economic, and psychological commitments become eroded and broken; then mobilization for the commitments is possible.[5] These new patterns reflect current political convenience more than blind acceptance of the doctrine.

Segmental (differentiation) and functional (integration) system components are bound together by the principle of solidarity and pluralism. Constraints must operate together with an interaction of actors in achieving common goals (the ideal of system as a perfect machine). The parts must be adequately arranged vis-a-vis one another. People must be motivated and cooperation promoted. The changing environment must be coped with. Power and resource distributions must be peacefully executed. Structural demands must be adequately related to the social configurations of power and influence. Potential energy must be transferred into fulfillment of tasks. Proper technologies must be found and applied (for the same final state can be reached from different initial conditions and in different ways).

The rigid Soviet model of state socialism that is dominant in Eastern Europe shows several obvious loopholes in all these aspects.[6] Attempts to reform the system so far have not been very successful, with the exception of the abandonment after Stalin's death of widespread persecution by the secret police. The Soviet system shows only a limited ability to absorb innovation and to learn from its own failures. There is rather a tendency to reduce any innovation to the previous state of affairs, as happened, for example, in regard to the Czechoslovak reforms or the Polish workers' councils.

DILEMMAS OF POLISH SOCIETY

Polish society provides a perfect example of specific problems that are peculiar to state socialism in a country with a long tradition and an advanced economy. Present-day Poland is a society of considerable strength (34 million in 1975) and dynamics, but it faces several dilemmas that expose the inability of Soviet-style state socialism to deal effectively with major problems of socioeconomic growth at the higher levels of industrialization.

It is a society of young people; 35 percent of the population is 20 years old or younger, in comparison with 28 percent in West Germany; 89 percent of youth 14 to 17 years old and 76 percent of youth 15 to 18 years old are in school; the number of students in postsecondary education per 10,000 population has grown from 50 in 1950 to 119 in 1973. However, the system has not grown accordingly. For 1,000 new marriages, there were in 1973 in the rural areas only 371 new dwellings; much more has been constructed in the urban sector, but even there in 1973 there were 116 households for 100 dwellings; average floor space per capita in square meters was 14 in urban as well as rural sectors; water supply installation in 1970 existed only in 12 percent of rural dwellings; even in urban dwellings only 36 percent had central heating and 50 percent had bathrooms. The housing shortage is one of the main problems confronting young people.[7]

Widespread education and culture contribute to the growing sophistication of the Polish people. In 1973 almost half the population 15 years old and over had primary education, 13 percent had basic vocational education, 14.5 percent had secondary education, and a little over 3 percent had postsecondary education. Women did not differ from men in any substantial degree in educational attainment, except in basic vocational education. In the period 1960-70 the percentage of the population 15 years old and over that did not attain at least primary education diminished from 45 to 24.5 (even among people age 60 and over, it diminished from 70 to 55 percent). Among the economically active population in the period 1960-72, the percentage of people with primary education grew from 35 to 45; the percentage with basic vocational education grew from 4 to 15.

Cultural consumption also has been growing. Consumption in the publication market is limited by the shortage of paper, as well as by censorship, but not by lack of interest or illiteracy. TV sets cost almost three average monthly earnings, but the number of TV subscribers per 1,000 population grew in the period 1965-73 from 111 to 217 among the urban population, and from 21 to 114 among the rural population (movie attendance per 1,000 population has diminished by half in the rural areas but much less in urban areas).

General consumption also has become more sophisticated. Food constitutes about two-fifths of the total household budget, but there is a progressive change of diet from an emphasis on potatoes and cereals to one on meat, milk, and fruit. The demand for manufactured foods has been growing rapidly. People from various strata differ less than in the past regarding possession of household appliances (see Table 5). Differences are much more evident among various income groups than

TABLE 5

Equipment of Various Households: Appliances per 100 Households
(end of 1973)

	Employees	Workers-Peasants	Peasants	Pensioners
Radio sets	118	89	71	83
TV sets	88	66	45	51
Record players	39	30	20	8
Washing machines	88	85	69	65
Refrigerators	59	21	12	27
Cars	8	4	3	1

Source: Rocznik Statystyczny (Warsaw: Central Statistical Office, 1974), p. 160.

among various strata. Thus, for example, the number of private cars increases in all strata when income increases (the total number of private cars in the country jumped from 91,000 in 1960 to 750,000 in 1973).

Growing consumer demands are far from being met. The percentage of national income allocated to personal consumption diminished in 1960-73 from 72 to 55, while the percentage allocated to capital formation grew from 21 to 35. This means that there is not very much room for improvement in living standards.

Social stratification of Poles today is based on income differentials, even if they are not so far-reaching as in the West. In 1972, the upper fifth of the population employed in the nationalized nonagricultural economy, who earned net 3,300 zloty (zl.) per month and more, accounted for 34 percent of the total wage fund in comparison with 13 percent accounted for by the lowest fifth, who earned no more than net 1,715 zl. (the average was net 2,542 zl.).

There are some striking differences in earnings in various branches. There are also notable differences in earnings of men and women. In trade, public health, social welfare, and physical culture, about 80 percent of the employees (three-quarters of whom are women) earned below the national average in 1972. Double the average net earnings were enjoyed by almost 7 percent of the men, but only by 0.4 percent of the women; even in the field of education (73 percent women), the respective percentages were 7.3 and 0.5. Over one-fifth of women employed in the fields of health, welfare, and education earned less than half the average national income, but only one-twentieth of men employed in these fields had such low wages.

Industrialization is the major factor in Poland's social change. The percentage of population outside agriculture grew from 53 in 1950 to 73 in 1973, and the urban population grew during the same period from 37 to 54 percent. In 1970, some 62 percent of the population depended on gainful employment in the nationalized economy and 25 percent depended on private agriculture (10 percent maintained themselves from pensions, etc.). In urban households with some gainfully employed members, 44 percent have one such member, 45 percent have two and 11 percent have three or more. The comparable data for rural households are 23 percent, 44 percent, and 33 percent. In 1970 some 52 percent of the population was economically active, mostly concentrated in agriculture or forestry (39 percent) and in industry (28 percent); only 15 percent were in services as contrasted with 20 to 30 percent in Western Europe.

THE HISTORICAL BACKGROUND AND ITS SIGNIFICANCE

Poland is one of the few countries in Europe in which the gentry used to be very numerous (12 to 15 percent of the population) and at the same time particularly influential. Poland constituted for centuries a gentry commonwealth in which not only were kings elected but even the powerful aristocratic circles were dependent to a large extent on the support of the lower and the middle gentry. It is therefore quite understandable why Polish national ideology even now is strongly influenced by the values and social patterns originated by the gentry and later cultivated by the intelligentsia. There is a long tradition of deep sociocultural divisions between various strata, widespread elitism, devotion to popular national myths, selectivity of private contacts, a warm attitude toward friends and guests but a distance or even prejudice toward strangers, and a defensive attitude toward formal authorities.

Many elements of the gentry ethos still exist in the Polish national character:

> On the one hand, cautiousness; on the other hand, risk and gesture, well known from the Polish saying "zastaw sie, a postaw sie" which, translated, means something like this: "pawn yourself, but keep your status." On the one hand, industriousness, on the other, contempt of work for profit, especially physical work; on the one hand desire for fame, on the other, desire for security.[8]

Although the Polish nobility ceased to exist in communist Poland, and therefore ceased to influence the national character, state socialism (as opposed to libertarian socialism) still tends toward elitist models in social and private life. Privileges are a principle of life. Look, for example, at the data on the availability of higher education for various social strata.

In 1960-73 white-collar workers (who constitute less than a quarter of the total population) improved their share among all day-course students from 48 to 52 percent, among first-year students from 49 to 55 percent, and among graduates from 41 to 49 percent. The share of blue-collar workers (who constitute half the total population) remained in all cases approximately 30 percent. The share of peasants (who constitute almost a third of the population) dropped from 20 to 14 percent of all students. Children of peasants have a much better share, around one-third, only in the extension courses. Blue-collar workers total three-fifths of the evening course students and half of those in extension courses. Of those who completed post-secondary education in 1945-73, 34 percent were of blue-collar origin, 22.5 percent of peasant origin, and 43.5 percent of other origin (mostly white-collar).[9]

Poland never really experienced capitalism, and therefore never had occasion to consolidate bourgeois morality in society. The national character, formed mainly by the feudal system, was transformed into one of Soviet-style state socialism. Both systems are similar in several important aspects. In both, the great majority of people have no privileges of importance and the most they can ever hope to achieve is to acquire some privileges illegally. In both systems, a man's value is measured primarily by loyalty and availability to the ruling elite. An ordinary citizen, by the simple fact of existence, is indebted to the establishment until the day he dies; this debt is expected to be paid continually by personal sacrifice for the good of the system. Whatever the official doctrine, it is always interpreted so as to enhance the cult of power, curb individual thinking and creativity, and rely on ritual rather than on intellectual and moral ferment.

The Protestant revolution hardly touched Poland[10] and, beginning with the eighteenth century, the question of keeping national identity alive eclipsed all other aspects of social awareness of the ruling classes. Soviet-style communism was forced on Poland when it already had become ideologically sterile. Thus, communism played the role of a bureaucracy that had the imperialistic tendencies of the Soviet state but at the same time a chauvinistic attitude toward everything non-Soviet. In addition, the version of communism forced on Poland absorbed without great difficulty many elements of traditional Polish ethos that could be treated as harmless ornaments: stress on military glory, pretense, cult of ritual and trinkets (medals, distinctions), treatment of "sacred values" with ostentatious pathos. Under present state socialism, the modern work ethic has had only a limited chance to establish itself. State socialism stresses the desirability of a high rate of industrial growth.[11] How is it possible to reach this goal without stimulating the basic moral virtues toward this end? Soviet-style bureaucracy in its very foundations requires blind obedience, if only in appearance. The endless argument between the experts and the apparatchiks must, in the end, be won by the latter if the model of state socialism and monopartyism is to remain in force.

The reconciliation of the individual good with the common welfare is an essential question in all social systems. Depending on the model adopted, one or the other is stressed. There is no room in a state socialist system for individual good, which is considered only a derivative of the common welfare, no room for a gentleman whose characteristics are "stateliness and security of an independent person," who is, at the same time, true, "trustful and inspiring trust."[12]

The Poles are becoming more and more charmed by the model of a perfect gentleman. This is due not only to a cult of all that comes from the West but probably also to the uncompromising loyalty required by bureaucratic institutions. These institutions usually function badly, disappoint citizens, and have no consideration for the public good. Bureaucratic organizations are used by preying cliques for their own particular goals and have been proven to be historically unstable.[13] Thus, it is necessary to rely only on oneself, rather than becoming involved in something that may disappear tomorrow. The younger generation appears to prefer the attitude of a gentleman who keeps his distance, rather than that of Party agitator or ardent revolutionary.

The clumsiness and conservatism characterizing Soviet-style state socialism are, in reality, the most important obstacles to the formation of a national ethos that would be convenient to the ruling communist elite in Poland. These characteristics have led to widespread criticism of the state socialist model. The country's rulers accuse the population from time to time of succumbing to Western influence and tastes. However, the real ethos of today's Poles reflects an escape to slightly updated traditional models, or to quite foreign models, such as that of the gentleman. But these models give, at least for the time being, a psychological shelter—to wait it all out.

In spite of the Catholic majority in Poland today, the influence of a truly Christian spirit should not be overestimated. As Maria Ossowska rightly underlines, the models of the knight, the gentleman, or even the courtier that are so attractive to the Poles are in many aspects contrary to the Christian spirit. "The ideal of a gentleman is not moral virtue but honour . . . anything that speaks highly in a social sense about the man is an asset for him. It is not, therefore, a set of Christian characteristics."[14]

The sense of honor among present-day Poles is probably no less significant than in previous generations; possibly it is even more important because of urbanization and the growing number of peasants in the ranks of the intelligentsia. However, over the years the meaning of honor has deviated considerably; now it very often means freedom from all outside criticism, or even even any critical allusion. Care is taken to prevent others from performing or saying anything offensive, which avoids a much more important question, that of what one is really like. Understood in this way, honor can very well exist side by side with dishonesty in public, or even in family matters, or in affairs between friends. This kind of manipulation is often used by bureaucrats who (as opposed to those who have to compete in a free market) obtain great gains from their monopoly. The dream of holding a monopoly or being indispensable and able to silence all others is, probably, not foreign to any of us.

Of course, these characteristics are not limited solely to Polish society. However, in Poland the gentry tradition and the postfeudal heritage seem particularly strong, especially in comparison with North American mass societies. Under communist rule, the massive social upgrading of people from the traditional lower classes has substantially contributed toward a model of mass society. However, the social attraction of the intelligentsia, which inherited directly from the gentry the "governance of souls," has yet to diminish. The dissemination of culture and mass education, as well as the numerical growth of white-collar workers from a sixth of the population before World War II to almost a quarter now, have both contributed to widespread acceptance in the society as a whole of the preferences and values typical of the intelligentsia.

Contrary to the situation before World War II, however, the intelligentsia no longer rules. In fact, it is subordinated to Party and state functionaries, and must obey them. On the other hand, it is practically impossible for functionaries to govern without all kinds of experts, who bring with them the traditional values and aspirations of the intelligentsia.[15]

THE CHANGING CONSTELLATION OF GROUPS

Poland's social structure has substantially changed since the interwar period. Manual workers and their families now constitute half the total population (they had been only one-third before). White-collar workers and their families have quadrupled, while the agricultural population has diminished from three-fifths to less than one-third and also has aged. Private farmers still constitute 27 percent of all working people, but even they depend very much on the state. Among medical doctors, only 16 percent practice privately (in Warsaw, 9 percent), and among dentists, 33 percent. The nonagricultural private sector of the Polish economy is of marginal importance, and its existence does not upset to any considerable degree the egalitarian structure of average incomes. Only 4 percent of the Polish people earn more than twice the average income, in comparison with 10 percent in the United States and 6 percent in Great Britain. White-collar workers, who earned twice as much as blue-collar workers before World War II, now have similar wages, at least insofar as manual workers and clerical staff are concerned. In comparison with blue-collar workers, technical staff people (engineers and technicians in industry) earn an average of 44 percent more.[16]

Under the impact of industrialization, Polish society has made obvious progress in several fields. During the 1960s alone, per capita production doubled in electric power, crude steel, and cement. It tripled in sulfuric acid and artificial fabrics. Consumption of meat, fat, and milk grew by 15 to 20 percent per capita. However, the population's aspirations have grown even faster, and people are by and large dissatisfied with their relatively low standard of living. One must take into consideration that food still represents the most important item in the family budget not only among farmers (50 percent of their budget) and blue-collar workers (45 percent) but also among white-collar workers (40 percent). There is a constantly growing demand for industrial goods. Purchases of shoes, sugar, and silk doubled per capita in the 1950s and 1960s.

In rural areas the situation is entirely different than before World War II. Not only is there no surplus of labor but agriculture even suffers from a labor shortage. Villages no longer increase in population because the natural population increase can only replace urban migration. There are proportionally fewer people of labor force age (18 to 64 for men, 18 to 59 for women) in villages than in towns.

The Soviet model of industrialization applied to Poland with some modifications (private agriculture, the autonomous cooperative sector until at least the early 1950s) is based, as everywhere, on the principle of low wages and relatively large fringe benefits. This principle should lead to egalitarianism, but the necessities of growth and the elitist bias of the political system constantly expose the obvious gap between the model and the social reality. There are several well-known and widely practiced semilegal or even illegal means of earning more and enjoying additional benefits. Moonlighting is widespread. Poles look to the West for a comparison of their standard of living with other societies. The Polish survey data show that, especially among the traditional lower classes, there is a widespread feeling of social inequality or even injustice.[17] Egalitarian demands are stronger among the blue-collar workers than among the relatively privileged strata of Party and state officials, managers, specialists, and intellectuals.

Each of the Polish social strata has its own legitimate reasons for dissatisfaction with the existing socioeconomic model, but each is also very limited in its ability to produce substantive change. First, the interests of each social stratum are not well articulated within the system. Bargaining within the system is of an individual nature; only in a few cases does it become a collective process. There is high risk involved when people join efforts to gain something substantial from the ruling circles, and so far only the blue-collar workers have succeeded: in 1956 and again in 1970. Private farmers bargain with the state indirectly by reacting more or less favorably to the trade conditions established unilaterally by the state. The same is true of various groups of white-collar specialists.[18]

This practice of indirect bargaining has obvious disadvantages. The authoritarian state is not obliged to keep promises, but on the other hand the people do not feel responsible for what happens around them. There are constant power demonstrations and cheating on both sides, and the common well-being suffers because of it. In this respect, the Polish institutional system evinces weaknesses quite typical of authoritarian regimes.

INTERNAL STRAINS

Several basic contradictions in Poland lead to internal social strains. First, there is the typical contradiction for communist countries between the very heavy rate of accumulation (between 23 and 30 percent of gross national income, services excluded) and the growing consumption demands. Second, there is a contradiction between the emphasis on growth and the rigidity of a bureaucratic structure and a doctrinaire ideology. Third, the egalitarian message of Marxism contradicts the strongly elitist biases of the authoritarian political system and local traditions (the gentry ideology and the "governance of minds" exercised by the intelligentsia). Fourth, the relatively well-educated and enlightened population needs leadership that could satisfy mass expectations, but this kind of leadership cannot develop under a system based on the perpetuation of bureaucratic authority.

Polish society is in constant flux, which makes its current problems even more complicated. Today, most Poles are uprooted.

Newcomers are very common in Polish towns (57 percent of the urban population) and villages (41 percent of the rural population). Among the urban population in 1970, less than half were born in the municipality where they were living; one-third were born in the rural areas, and one-tenth were born in a foreign country. In the rural areas, two-fifths of the population were born in the same village, one-third were born in another village, 5 percent were born in cities, and another 5 percent were born in a foreign country.

There is a high rate of vertical mobility. Even though students of white-collar background still dominate the day division of higher education, there is a considerable inflow of people from the traditionally lower classes to all important posts. These people already dominate the civil service, management, military, police, Party apparatus, elementary education, and several categories of graduate engineering. Many of these upgraded people owe their careers to the Party and are absolutely loyal to it. However, in the long run their aspirations must differ from the general Party line as long as the ideology of the intelligentsia dominates the Polish scene and the Party is doctrinaire in its commitment to Soviet-style state socialism.

The middle class has never had the chance to establish itself as an independent and influential sociopolitical factor. Now almost a quarter of all Poles belong to the white-collar stratum, and there are manual workers and peasant families that do everything they can to upgrade their children to that stratum; these groups provide a suitable base for some kind of semi-middle class.

PARTICIPATION AS A RESPONSE TO SYSTEMIC CHANGES

The development of social systems in general is based on the evolution from a multifunctional role structure to several more specialized structures. Literacy, urbanization, a money economy, political revolution, and the prior organizational density tend to increase the rate at which new organizational forms are developed. The new sets of roles established in the process of structural evolution are organized around basic rewards (generalized goals) built into each role: instrumental goal, security, response and recognition (Talcott Parsons). Without offering at least some of these rewards, it is not possible to establish authority as a legitimized power that brings about compliance to the will of those who occupy crucial positions.

The crisis of the highly centralized and rigid economic system in the middle 1950s made reform imperative. It was necessary to offer more material and social rewards to strengthen the legitimacy of the system. Workers' councils were formed in late 1956 as an expression of the growing dissatisfaction of industrial Party activists and managerial action groups with what was, in their opinion, overcentralization of the national economy. They suggested the formation of such councils as a means of bargaining with the upper levels of the industrial bureaucracy—which was particularly convenient because they themselves would not be directly involved. Participation of manual workers in management was from the beginning little more than a slogan. The summoning in 1958 of the Conference of Workers' Self-Government (KSR),[20] which coordinated the basic institutions of the factory (including the workers' council), was the logical outcome. The workers' councils grew into a popular myth of democratic industrial management not as a consequence of their actual role—they were dominated by technicians and economists, although supported by manual workers' votes—but of the large-scale expectations of a significant part of the population in the period after October 1956. The inadequacies of the centralist model of the economy (much of which is still unchanged) were then so obvious that council activists were able to suggest and often implement real improvements with relative ease—frequently with the tacit support of management, which was unable to speak out openly against the higher bureaucracy. In this sense, workers' councils and KSR became the instruments of indirect pressure by technocratic-political microelites in regional committees, the central committee of the Polish United Workers' Party (Communist Party), headquarters of industrial associations, and in the ministries.

However, as W. Morawski rightly pointed out,

> the situation of the workers' council became more difficult as the obvious reserves of productivity were exhausted; they entered a more stabilized phase, and the first wave of enthusiasm waned. Their activity became dominated by matters concerning further organizational streamlining.[21]

Since "the role of the workers' council depends on the general situation of the enterprise, on which the council has very limited influence,"[22] the council can in reality achieve little unless enterprises are allowed considerably more independence and unless the market is permitted to play a greater role in economic life. At KSR sessions and meetings of workers' councils, counterproposals to the industrial association are formulated with the purpose of facilitating the enterprise's attainment of planned targets.[23] As Morawski says, "These measures are as a rule either instigated by the administration, or strongly supported by it."[24] Whatever cannot easily be done by management (which is directly dependent on officials at a level above the enterprise) becomes the responsibility of the so-called self-government. Since leaders of the workers' councils participate in industrial association meetings, they are all the better able to play the roles expected of them by management: defenders against outside pressures and assistants to the administration within the enterprise.[25]

There seems to be little connection between this concept of the workers' council as "a grassroots warning signal of planning inadequacies and an instrument for the correction of plan indices"[26] and the wider concept of it as the nucleus of the collective initiative of all workers, or at least of the majority of them. A number of factors contribute to this situation: (1) the KSR and the presiding officers of the workers' council have no actual authority over management; (2) although both have the duty of encouraging the work force to increase output, they have no effective means of doing so; (3) the functioning of both has become ritualized—they are reduced to imitating the role of management but lack its power; (4) issues discussed at meetings of each are far removed from those relevant to the average worker[27] (Morawski states on the basis of survey data that 86 percent of workers did not know the subject matter of their workers' council session); (5) departmental workers' councils, which are in principle the lowest level in the workers' self-government system, in practice play a wholly marginal role; (6) there is an evident process of alienation whereby a small number of activists in the councils become separated from the rank and file who elect them. Collaboration with management and with the plant Party secretariat draws the activists into matters far removed from the actual interests of the workers and favors the development of an elitist orientation.

One must agree with Morawski that

> The organizational activity of the self-governing system has adapted itself to the limits dictated by the mechanisms of control of the economy. Since it was jointly responsible with management for the work of the enterprise, workers' self-government voted on plans and saw that they were executed in the enterprise. But the role of the enterprise (including workers' self-government) in establishing the plan was for many reasons very small, and the range of decision-making and initiative limited by the pressures of the plan indices. The self-governing body was therefore not so much a center for the activization of the work community, as a means for intervention, pressure, bargaining, etc. outside the enterprise. Instead of being the institution responsible for involving the workforce in the processes of social participation, it was used for carrying out formalized tasks.[28]

Neither workers' councils nor trade unions can be viewed as representative of working-class interests. It is true that "the setting up of the workers' councils was a way of exposing the reality of the industrial situation, the bureaucracy of administration, the inexpert management and the subservient trade unions."[29] In all these respects, however, the councils appeared to be more a response to the crisis of the totalitarian structure than a means of satisfying the interests of blue-collar workers, especially those in the lower ranks. Management, professional intelligentsia, and skilled workers had mutual interests in utilizing workers' councils as a tool for at least some degree of decentralization. "Workers' councils desired decentralization since they felt it a necessary prerequisite for democratization within the enterprise. Similarly, senior management argues for decentralization, considering it a necessary precondition to expert and rational management."[30]

However, the interests behind the whole idea of workers' councils were not sufficiently strong and consistent, and the top Party and state bureaucrats had enough power to slow down the spread of workers' councils. The electorate in the factories was internally split:

> Skilled workers had expectations concerning the role of the workers' councils which were considerably opposed or inconsistent with those of the unskilled manual workers. Young workers, educated and brought up under the conditions of socialism, displayed attitudes [toward] management, work relations and job content which were significantly different to those of their older colleagues. The questions of age difference, rural-urban origins and levels of skill influenced the representativeness of the workers' councils.[31]

In such a situation, it was possible for the political establishment to gradually maneuver the workers' councils into the position of minor bureaucratic units that would be subservient to the Party and would help implement production organization, efficiency, and productivity. Thus, the present role of workers' councils does not differ much from the traditional role of trade unions in the communist system. Whether or not the blue-collar workers comprise a majority within the executive boards of these bodies makes no great difference. They nevertheless have to obey blindly the commands that come from high echelons of the Party and state hierarchies. As a consequence, there is a breakdown in formal communication between the rank and file workers and the power centers.

The Conference of the Workers' Self-Government has continued to exist; in 1972, some 7,000 Polish enterprises in industry, construction, transport, and agriculture were affiliated with it. Members are those who participate in workers' councils, trade union councils, the Polish United Workers' Party committees, representatives of the

Socialist Youth Organization, and professional associations. Altogether, 240,000 people are members of the conference. In the workers' councils (a little over 6,000 of them in 1972), there were 86,000 representatives, among them 60,000 blue-collar workers, 19,000 technicians and engineers, 12,000 women, and 11,000 people below age 30.[32]

These numbers are quite impressive, but sociological research tells us a great deal more about the functioning of the councils and about workers' lack of support for them.[33] Research conducted during 1956-58 indicated that workers did not really feel themselves to be in collective charge of their places of work, and that the existence of workers' councils had achieved no fundamental improvement in this respect. Workers "do not clearly see the council's field of activity as a governing body. . . . They expect above all the solution of problems of living standards and social issues, while the council chiefly deals with questions of organization and production."[34] In a survey of manual workers in power plants and engineering plants, conducted by the Public Opinion Research Center in 1961, asking whose interests were represented by workers' self-government, 41 percent of those in power plants and 47 percent of those in engineering plants replied that management interests were represented. Only 8 percent and 5 percent respectively thought that workers' self-government represented the interests of manual workers.[35] Also, 35 percent of all workers (manual and white-collar) surveyed by the Public Opinion Research Center in 1960 thought that the blue-collar worker had no real influence on what happened at his work place; a further 32 percent thought that the situation varied considerably. Less than 50 percent of respondents thought that valid criticism of supervisors served any useful purpose, and only 23 percent reported they actively supported such criticism.[36]

Even though the councils are supposed to represent mainly manual workers, they show relatively less interest in them than the members of higher occupational strata. Research in 1958 indicated a connection between the extent of interest on the one hand and the level of qualifications on the other. Unskilled workers showed the least interest; the other categories (including engineers) on average showed a fairly large degree of interest. The main adverse criticism was that, in the respondents' opinion, the councils failed to act as representatives of the workers.[37] It is important to add here that later social research also indicated very limited worker interest in workers' councils. Only 5 percent of workers in the machinery and metal structures industry and only 19 percent of workers in the leather industry said that workers' councils really represented the interests of blue-collar workers (according to a survey by the Polish Center of Public Opinion Polls). In another study, 40 percent of blue-collar respondents had nothing to say about the activity of the workers' council in their own enterprise, and 86 percent knew nothing about the last session of that council.[38]

Self-management in the work place presents a problem whose importance increases with the rising qualifications and aspirations of the workers, particularly because there are tendencies among Polish experts to seek to improve the planned economy by giving the enterprises more freedom; moreover, there has been a notable stabilization of Polish management personnel. Some of the difficulties in making workers' participation effective may be related directly or indirectly to a number of factors. In factories that employ workers who have recently emigrated from the countryside (the first industrial generation), there is often only slight interest in self-government and a relatively low level of qualifications for participation in factory management. The knowledge and the practice necessary for self-government are especially low among uneducated workers.[39] Not surprisingly, the more educated strata of the work force (especially economists, engineers, and technicians) are also the most active participants in self-government.[40]

The level of organizational activity is high. In 1973 there were almost 15 million members of various types of cooperatives; 642,000 people took an active part on cooperative boards and committees, 135,000 people participated as councilors in the municipal councils, and 11,160,000 people were trade union members.

Polish nationalized enterprises have numerous committees and productivity meetings. Activists comprise only a small percentage of the total work force, but their role is essential because the attainment of production and other goals depends largely on them. They tend to come from the ranks of more highly skilled blue-collar workers who hold better positions.

As J. Kulpinska has noted, "The motives of activism frequently relate to the opportunities for contact with management during meetings and campaigns at a level of relative 'equality.' Linked to this motive is usually that of gaining promotion or other privileges. Activism is treated as the means of advancement in the organizational hierarchy."[41] People frequently engage in activism only for a limited period of time in order to achieve a specific goal—for instance, to gain enough credit to become eligible for staff housing. Some, however, treat their activism very seriously and jeopardize their futures by obstinately fighting for lost causes or annoying influential superiors.

This model of workers' activism has remained largely unchanged since Stalinist times. The fact that it was unsuited to the real situation was ignored for a number of years by the Party elite. Indeed, Gomulka once declared, "We have never had a situation in which the working class and the individual work forces of enterprises were completely deprived of opportunities to participate in the running of the national economy and of their workplaces, and in which they did not make use of these opportunities."[42] Obviously, Gomulka identified the working class with Party action groups and did not wish to acknowledge the totalitarian essence of Stalinist communism.

NOTES

1. See Wilbert E. Moore, Social Change (Englewood Cliffs, N.J.: Prentice-Hall, 1963).
2. S. N. Eisenstadt, "Social Change and Development," in Readings in Social Evolution and Development, ed. S. N. Eisenstadt (Oxford: Pergamon Press, 1970), p. 11.
3. Ibid., p. 15.
4. See Merwyn Matthews, Class and Society in Soviet Russia (New York: Walker Publishers, 1972); Alexander Matejko, Social Change and Stratification in East Europe: The Interpretive Analysis of Poland and Her Neighbours (New York: Praeger Publishers, 1974); Boris Meissner, ed., Social Change in the Soviet Union (Notre Dame: University of Notre Dame Press, 1972).
5. Karl W. Deutsch, "Social Mobilization and Political Development," American Political Science Review 65, no. 3 (September 1961): 493-514.
6. See Radoslav Selucky, Economic Reforms in Eastern Europe (New York: Praeger Publishers, 1972); Maria Hirszowicz, Komunistyczny Lewiatan (Paris: Instytut Literacki, 1973); Andrei Amalrik, "Will the USSR Survive until 1984?" Survey 73 (1969).
7. See Rocznik Statystyczny (Warsaw: Central Statistical Office, 1974); Concise Statistical Yearbook of Poland, 1974 (Warsaw: Central Statistical Office, 1974). Statistical data in the paper are from these two sources.
8. Maria Ossowska, Etyka rycerska [Ethics of knights] (Warsaw: Panstwowe Wydawnictwo Naukowe, 1973), p. 216.
9. Rocznik.
10. See Janusz Tazbir, A State Without States (New York: Kosciuszko Foundation, 1974).
11. Selucky, Economic Reforms.
12. Ossowska, Etyka, p. 170.
13. Matejko, Social Change.
14. Ossowska, Etyka, p. 171.
15. Matejko, Social Change, pp. 140-54.
16. Rocznik.
17. Matejko, Social Change, p. 151.

18. David Lane and George Kolankiewicz, eds., Social Groups in Polish Society (New York: Columbia University Press, 1973).
19. Janusz Zielinski, Economic Reforms in Polish Industry (London: Oxford University Press, 1973).
20. Lane and Kolankiewicz, Social Groups, pp. 137-38.
21. Witold Morawski, "Funkcje spoleczne samorzadu robotniczego w systemie zarzadzania przemyslem" [Social functions of workers' self-government in industrial management] in Przemysl i spoleczenstwo w Polsce Ludowej, ed. Jan Szczepanski (Wroclaw: Ossolineum, 1969), p. 249.
22. Ibid.
23. The industrial association represents the higher level of an administrative integration (something like a corporation in the West).
24. Morawski, "Funkcje Spoleczne."
25. Ibid., p. 252.
26. Ibid., p. 253.
27. Morawski states on the basis of surveys that 86 percent of workers did not know the subject matter of the most recent KSR session.
28. Morawski, "Funkcje spoleczne," p. 260.
29. George Kolankiewicz, "The Working Class," in Social Groups in Polish Society, ed. Lane and Kolankiewicz, pp. 137-51.
30. Ibid., p. 109.
31. Ibid., p. 113.
32. Rocznik, pp. 60-61.
33. On the origin of these councils, see Kolankiewicz, "The Working Class," pp. 137-51.
34. M. Jarosz et al., "Samorzad w opiniach zalog fabrycznych" in Studia nad rozwojem klasy robotniczej (Lodz-Warszawa, 1962), p. 146.
35. W. Wesolowski, "Rotobnicy o swojej pracy i swoich zakladach pracy," in Studia Socjologiczno-Polityczne 12 (1962).
36. A. Sicinski, "Postawy wobec pracy i wlasnosci oraz ich spoleczne uwarunkowanie," Studia Socjologiczne 2 (1961).
37. S. Szostkiewicz, "Two Researches in Industrial Society," The Polish Sociological Bulletin 1-2 (1962).
38. Morawski, "Funkcje Spoleczne," p. 259.
39. A. Meister, Socialisme et autosuggestion: L'experience Yugoslave (Paris, 1964). See also J. Kolaja, Workers' Councils: The Yugoslav Experiment (London: Tavistock, 1965).
40. L. Slejska, "Prace a rizeni," Sociologicky Casopis, no. 2 (1965).
41. Jan Szczepanski, ed., Przemysl i spoleczenstwo w Polsce Ludowej [Industry and society in People's Poland] (Wroclaw: Ossolineum, 1969), p. 275.
42. Nowe Drogi 6 (1957): 10.

CHAPTER

4

THE PROCESS OF REFORM IN POST-1970 POLAND: THE CASE OF THE PEOPLE'S COUNCILS SYSTEM

Ray Taras

The study of local government has been the focus of considerable social science research. Individual country studies together with comparative analyses have produced data indicating what local government structures have in common and in what respects they differ. The functioning of local government has been related to the political culture of a country, its rate of economic development, its process of making decisions, its local power structures, and the influence of bureaucratic elements. Relations between central and local governments also have been a primary concern. Here the question of local autonomy has been most important, and frequently a struggle is depicted between central and local tiers over the distribution of power. Local government is regarded as a fairly autonomous institution, to a large extent determining its own structures, processes, and goals, and occasionally having to resist encroachment by central authorities. Less frequently has the structure of local government been seen as the testing ground for the policies of national political leaders, as an institution reflecting the policy courses followed by these leaders.

In Poland it is possible to view the structures and functioning of local institutions as reflecting the policy of national leaders and the changes of policy that often occur. To change the structure or functioning of local government signifies for the central leadership its ability to implement policies throughout the nation. Inability to change local structures and processes implies weakness within the leadership. The major overhauls of local government in Poland have taken place during periods when the central leadership was strong: in 1950, following the full consolidation of the socialist system in Poland; in January 1958, when Gomulka was able to exploit popular support to carry out a series of reforms; and in 1972-73, when Gierek had established full control over the Party and state structures. When attempts to reform the local system have been unsuccessful—for example, in 1954 and in 1963-64, when legislative acts designed to delegate power to local councils failed—the leadership had become ossified: It had enough power to resist demands for change, but it did not have enough power to trigger change. The explanation, therefore, that in socialist states central control over all institutions is total does not tell us enough about the ability of central authorities to generate required change.

An examination of local institutions also may indicate the nature of the policies of central leadership. The system of people's councils in Poland, elected every four years by universal suffrage at provincial (wojewodztwo), county (powiat), and district (gminna) levels, is designed to ensure that local matters are decided by local representatives and that elected representatives control the work of the administration based at the local level. Polish theorists describe the councils as a form of local self-management, distinguishing them from the pure local government structures of capitalist states, which are considered to be basically the administrative agents for central government.[1] If the leadership is able to carry out policies that structurally affect the council system, it is possible to assess the value attached by the leadership to self-management at different times. An extension of authority to councils implies greater attachment to the principle of local self-management, and a resort to centralization means devaluing self-management.

Five years ago the Polish political system entered a period of change. There were demands for reform in all sectors of economic, social, and political life. The 6th Party Congress promised considerable reform, which ranged from the drawing up of a new constitution to the adoption of a system of one-man management in enterprises and state administration. Not all the resolutions passed by the congress have been executed, although a wide package of reform has been implemented since 1971. The system of people's councils is an area where reform has been most far-reaching, and the process may not yet be completed. This essay considers how the policies of the Gierek administration have affected the system of local representative government. In particular, four issues are analyzed: public participation, de-bureaucratization, local autonomy, and Party reform. The analysis considers the demands for change in each issue area, the degree to which the policies of the leadership coincided with the proposals for reform, and the general level of consensus or disagreement among key political institutions over reform measures. It may then be possible to suggest how power has been redistributed at the local level, emphasizing in particular the position of local Party committees and the degree of local self-management brought about under Gierek. Finally, there is an assessment of current proposals for further reorganization of the people's council system.

DEMANDS FOR REFORM

The 1970 seaport disturbances triggered a change in political leadership, in style of government, and in economic policy. By 1972 various groups in society, influenced by the new course the leadership was pursuing, began to articulate demands for concrete institutional change. By the end of 1973, the response to demands at the local level had been made: a general reorganization of local structures had been implemented. Similar processes were occurring in industry, the trade unions, the Party apparatus, and the central government structure. The demands, such as those for more autonomy, were often the same but the outcomes were different.

For the council system, the most pressing issue was to stem the stagnation that had begun nearly a decade earlier. Following a period of intense reform and decentralization in 1956-61, which made the concept of self-government a real possibility, a general malaise set in as reformist zeal ebbed. Centralization of decision making and strict control over local decision making were reintroduced by anxious ministries, jealous of any encroachment on their jurisdiction. The decentralization that had occurred in the early Gomulka years was of a quantitative rather than qualitative kind. The volume of central directives, recommendations, and reports had been reduced, but they were still numerous enough to permit strict limitations on local autonomy and initiative. A 1963 act added some powers to councils, and Jerzy Wiatr has argued that it made councils experienced and competent enough to assume further authority.[2] But this act turned out to be the last concession granted to local autonomy under Gomulka.

A second tendency in the 1960s was the gradual weakening of the position of elected representatives and a corresponding increase in the power of administrative elements. The council meeting was a large gathering that met infrequently, and it could not be expected to exercise supervision over the activity of administrative departments. Moreover, it was simply not qualified to assess administrative work. Whereas in 1965 some 54 percent of nonmanual department workers had completed secondary education,[3] the figure for councilors was only 28 percent (see Table 6). Councilors' educational qualifications had improved considerably since 1949, when over a third had not even completed elementary education. The first quinquennium under Gomulka showed marked improvement in educational attainment.

But by the mid-1960s the process had slowed down. As councils found they could not perform the functions ascribed to them because of central interference, many councilors resigned before finishing their terms of office. For example, one in seven councilors elected

TABLE 6

Educational Level of Councilors in 1949-69

Year	Percent of Councilors Without Elementary Education	Percent of Councilors With Secondary or Higher Education
1949	38.2	16.7
1955	43.9	15.9
1961	27.6	25.0
1965	19.1	28.2
1969	10.3	30.9

Source: Glowny Urzad Statystyczny, Radni rad narodowych (Warsaw, 1970), pp. 9-11.

in 1961 resigned within three and a half years, and their replacements were often losing candidates from the bottom of the previous electoral list who had been proposed because they had no chance of being elected.[4] Reasons for resigning included bad relations inside the council, a feeling of helplessness in relation to the administration, lack of help from Party authorities, and an inefficient style of work. Many councilors who did not resign began to neglect their work. On the Warsaw Praga-South council, 25 percent of councilors missed between one and three council meetings in 1961 (five were held); by 1963 this figure was 45 percent. This period of what was termed consolidation of councils' new powers was in fact the beginning of a serious process of stagnation in local political life.

To strengthen the position of representative institutions, the councils were empowered to set up commissions composed of councilors and co-opted specialists to supervise the performance of a specific function, for example, finance or housing. The relationship between commissions and administrative departments became the focal point of attempts to shift the balance of power between representatives and bureaucrats in favor of the former. For a start, commission membership reflected higher educational and professional expertise than did council membership (with a consequent drop in the proportion of manual workers and Party members).[5] A 1958 act gave commissions the right to issue "binding advice" to department heads on certain matters. In 1964, a Council of Ministers resolution consolidated this power by specifying the areas in which commission advice was binding. This alleged increase in the authority of a representative organ was supposed to form the cornerstone of the process of democratization of people's councils in the 1960s.

An examination of the facts points otherwise. The number of issues on which commissions were able to tender binding advice was low. In Krakow, Poznan, Wroclaw, Lublin, and Katowice provincial councils, for example, J. Chwistek found that only those areas cited as examplary ones in the 1964 resolution required binding commission advice.[6] Further illuminating evidence on the supposed increase in commissions' influence was provided by an attitudinal survey of department heads conducted in 1966.[7] Department heads might have been expected to take a critical attitude toward commissions because of the challenge they posed to the established position of departments. Instead, department heads made a number of demeaning assessments of commission work. Only 52 percent believed that commissions considered departmental matters with "animated activity," while 44 percent believed they considered such matters with barely any activity. Some 53 percent stated that commissions provided departments with very little or no assistance. In addition, 61 percent viewed the mechanism of binding advice as having had very limited or no influence in increasing contacts between commissions and departments. Only 3 percent of heads stated that there was relatively frequent controversy between the two organs, while 59 percent said there was never any controversy. Finally, nearly three-quarters of respondents asserted that the broadening of commission powers had no negative results whatever. Of 21 percent who attributed negative results, over a third said commissions had either slowed down or reduced the independence of departmental work. Clearly, the department heads' negative assessment of commission influence demonstrated that commissions had been unable to make full use of the powers given by the 1958 and 1964 legislation. It also showed that administrative organs had been able to resist reforms aimed at increasing the power of representatives.

A third tendency adversely affecting the council system in the 1960s was the uneven balance that had arisen between the performance of new functions and old methods of administration. According to S. Zawadzki, what was required was not new legislation but a modernization of administrative machinery.[8] Gierek himself was to describe the pitfalls of employing outdated modes of administration when he argued that a person who could not utilize modern methods often adopted a conservative posture and resisted change.[9] Traditional values among administrative personnel made it difficult to introduce novel methods of organization and management. Dziecolowska's study of the attitudes of 1,850 citizens toward local administrators revealed that more citizens found the bureaucracy sluggish than found it efficient.[10] Nearly 60 percent blamed the local authority for shortcomings in administration, and half of these respondents attributed such shortcomings to superciliousness or lack of interest on the part of officials. Clearly, the bureaucratization of councils had to be eliminated in order to restore dynamism to local councils.

Finally, a fourth tendency afflicting the council system was the dearth of information transmitted from lower to higher tiers. With local initiative thwarted, rigidity had spread throughout the government apparatus. If central institutions were to make decisions based on information from lower tiers, not only would local units increase their influence but a measure of decentralization would be injected into the political process. This particular defect, especially in the Party structure, was often given as a cause for the disturbances in 1970. Lack of communication from lower to higher tiers illustrated the extent of political stagnation that had set in during the 1960s.

RESOLUTIONS AND REFORMS

Some of the demands voiced when the ossified leadership was displaced in 1970 related to weaknesses in the political system described. Various groups and institutions articulated demands for change, and Party committees that had been dormant for some time suddenly became the aggregators of numerous interests seeking reform. The Party journal began to publish recommendations relating to improvements in local councils; the 6th Congress (December 1971) passed a number of resolutions spelling out concrete reform measures; by 1972 legislative acts were being drawn up, designed to bring about structural change; and the first national Party conference (October 1973) reviewed the reform measures and suggested others. The proposals for reform affecting the exercise of power at the local level can be grouped into four general categories: (1) wider public participation in local politics; (2) simultaneous de-bureaucratization of authority; (3) increased local autonomy; and (4) reform in the Party itself.

Public Participation

The proposal for integrating the public into the local political process appeared to be the solution put forward by the Party leadership to avoid a repetition of the 1970 events. As in France following the May 1968 riots, wider participation was viewed as a panacea for social and political ills, whether the public genuinely wanted it or not.* It is very difficult to determine the degree to which the public wishes to participate in any country's local government. Most studies of local political cultures depict a predominantly apathetic public, and investigators have been driven to the conclusion that "instead of asking why people are not interested in their local authority we should consider why we expect them to show interest."[11] In a socialist society it might be expected that the socialist man will be an ideal citizen, recognizing the truths of the Party's interpretation of Marxist-Leninist doctrine and playing an active part in the pursuit of its objectives. No systematic data have been provided by scholars in socialist systems to substantiate the claim that the ideal citizen is commonplace. Voter turnout is high, but it is thought that about 80 percent of people vote without striking names off the ballot.[12] Some indication of citizen involvement may be found by looking at the utilization of the opportunities for direct democracy that the public has. One of these is the frequency with which village meetings are held. A 1968 attitudinal survey of district council leaders in Krakow province showed that 43 percent of respondents thought village meetings were held at least six times a year; 42 percent believed two to four meetings were held each year. However, 68 percent stated that attendance at the meetings was poor or indifferent, and only 21 percent claimed that attendance was very good. Also, 39 percent said that at the meetings "the public showed initiative when discussing a problem," and 22 percent said "the public participated without showing initiative."[13] These data provide inconclusive evidence that the opportunities for direct participation are frequently exploited.

Data on citizens' exercise of the power to recall councilors also are difficult to interpret. In 1969-73, a total of 916 councilors were suspended (out of 165,725 elected).[14] Of these, 742 lost their positions because of inactivity on council and 95 because of court proceedings. Electors theoretically decide whether to recall councilors at specially convened electors' meetings, but in reality the National Unity Front (an organization encompassing members of the three political parties and other mass organizations) organizes such meetings.

Another possible index of citizen involvement in local political life is the extent of public participation in electoral campaigns. Research carried out in Lodz in 1969 revealed that 159 meetings were held with candidates for the council, in which over 61,000 citizens

---

*A French poster spoofed attempts by de Gaulle after May 1968 to increase public participation this way: "Je participe, tu participes, il participes, nous participons, vous participez, ils profitent." ("I participate, you participate, he participates, we participate, you participate, they profit.")

took part.[15] Of these, 2,400 people participated in the discussions and 1,022 suggestions were made about the Party platform, of which only 290 were dismissed. In the 1973 local election campaign, a total of 31,000 consultative meetings were held with the public and it was claimed that nearly three million citizens attended.[16] This evidence might suggest very high public involvement in local electoral campaigns. The qualification must be made, however, that most participants were probably members of political parties and other mass organizations, which attempt to mobilize their members during such campaigns.

Finally, one detailed study into Polish local political culture concluded that the public did not attach primary importance to participation in the political process.[17] Far more important a consideration was the extent of autonomy enjoyed by local councils (see discussion below). Factors that disinclined the public to value participation higher were the generally low level of conflict in the political process, the stable rotation of local leaders, and the fact that the leaders were usually drawn from outside the state apparatus (that is, the Party) in which participation would normally occur. These factors reduced the public's desire to become involved in local decision making.

The evidence that has been compiled has not shown the real level of citizen participation in local affairs in Poland, but it makes it possible to rule out the idea that there is mass public involvement. It is likely that participation is higher in nonstate institutions, such as the parties, to which 12 percent of the over-18 population belongs. In general, it can be said of Poland that "participant orientations have spread among only a part of the population"; thus, according to G. Almond and S. Verba, it is a subject participant culture.[18]

The 6th Congress passed a number of resolutions that sought to improve on this state of affairs. One exhorted citizens to become involved in factory decision making.[19] Another called for broader participation in the planning of social and economic policy. Gierek argued that government and Party functions had to become more distinct, and that this might inspire citizens to take a more active role in the political process. However, the actual measures taken to stimulate participation were modest. Under a 1972 act, village meetings were given the power to decide on issues delegated to them by district councils.[20] In 1973, residents' self-management was transformed from a form of voluntary organization to one existing in law with specific functions to carry out.[21] It was now to be consulted by councils on local matters; it was to participate in election campaigns and in consultations on the five-year plan; and it was to advise building enterprises and schools on various questions. The results of the 1973 elections doubled the number of councilors who were also activists in residents' self-management.[22] There was now a stronger possibility that involvement in this institution could lead to a political career on the local council.

The problem of increasing public participation in local government is difficult in any country, but especially in Poland after the lethargy with which councils operated in the late 1960s. Opportunities for citizens and groups to play a more influential part in local affairs have always been available, but in the past the local councils were not worth participating in. An examination of whether councils in the last few years have become less of a bureaucratic institution, and one with wider autonomy, can suggest whether participation would now be meaningful.

De-Bureaucratization

De-bureaucratization in the Polish context implied three important changes in the distribution of power that existed at the end of the 1960s. First, it meant the possibility of wider public involvement in the political process so as to be able to judge the decision makers. Since 1970, greater value has been attached to participation, as described. Second, it meant some decentralization of power to local units so that the near monopoly in major decision making enjoyed by ministries and other central institutions could be broken and could pass into the hands of local representatives and administrators. The distribution of power between officials and councilors would have to be clearly demarcated following such decentralization. Third, it meant not only that bureaucrats would have to share power with representatives but that their own exercise of power would have to become more expeditious, rational, and instrumental. The result of de-bureaucratization would be, therefore, that local representatives would wield greater influence and bureaucrats would employ more efficient managerial methods.

The established local bureaucracy, although interested in further devolution of authority, was naturally skeptical about new management techniques and opposed to transferring power to representative elements. Councilors and Party activists, in contrast, felt that one of the lessons of the 1970 disturbances was the need for a more responsive local political structure. The Party leadership believed that a sharper separation of functions between the state administration, the representative institutions, and the Party apparatus would bring about greater dedication to the proper execution of specific functions. In the 1960s, the Party could not make inroads on the entrenched position of the bureaucracy, either at ministerial or local level. But by 1970 Party objectives had gained the support of an emerging political entity that was striving to increase its influence—the economic and administrative managerial specialists.

The managerial elite had always had an influential role in postwar Poland, but until 1965 it owed this position not to meritocratic achievement nor to technical expertise but to the Party's system of nomenklatura. That is, the party nominated individuals to managerial positions on the basis of certain criteria. During the Stalinist period, the key factor was the class origin or Party allegiance of managerial cadres. After 1956, qualifications became the important criterion and the authority of managers and directors in enterprises was simultaneously increased. Under Gierek, professional qualifications assumed even greater importance: he demanded the right men for the right jobs (wlasciwi ludzie na wlasciwym miejscu). The old guard of political managers, who had been representatives of the state rather than the enterprise, finally gave way to the new managerial specialists, who stressed their professional competence by demanding control over criteria of appointment, promotion, and performance evaluation in their enterprises.[23] More and more managers had followed a managerial career path, that is, having always been employed as managers, independent of the nature of the enterprise. Highly qualified managerial cadres had permeated not only economic enterprises but also state administration, and Gierek's accession assured them of greater prominence in future decision making.

In the established local bureaucracy, a conflict had been raging for many years as to whether one-man management was preferable to collective management. The issue at stake was whether formal authority resided in administrative departments as a whole or in the department head alone.[24] Legislation had not been entirely clear, but the majority of administrative theorists concluded that the department head was in fact the source of legislative authority. This notion easily led to the principle of one-man management, adopted after 1970. Arguments against this system were that it would make the most powerful administrators even more remote from the public. Lower officials could take unfair advantage of the resulting anonymity. Department officials might feel that, not being vested with authority, they need not fulfill their responsibilities properly. There might be a lack of uniformity from one department to the next, due to the personal idiosyncracies of the heads. Or the possibility existed that department heads who were specialized in one area might be incompetent to reach decisions in other areas for which the department was responsible. Therefore, one-man management by department heads could lead to an administrative process insensitive to public needs.[25]

However, the new managers, who had supported the rationality of one-man management, won the day. The established local bureaucrats found that the new course and political style adopted by Gierek had no place for traditional, plodding, unclear methods of operation. Local representatives, who had been pressing for some of the bureaucrats' powers, also lost out to the new managers. Councilors were given more formal powers to supervise administrative activity, such as through issuing directives to the managerial overlords.[26] In practice, however, the managers now possessed more authority than bureaucrats enjoyed under the previous system. The long-standing conflict between elected representatives and the traditional bureaucrats had had a curious result. Neither gained influence from the reforms. Instead, the managerial specialists were granted the sweeping powers coveted by councilors and officials alike.

Who were the new managers in the local political system? The 1973 statute that implemented one-man administrative management termed them wojewoda in the seventeen provinces, presidents in the five principal cities, and executives at the county and district levels. They were appointed by the premier (at district level by the wojewoda) for an unspecified term of office. Their powers included final responsibility for all state administrative matters in their locality; residual power giving them jurisdiction over all unclarified functions; wide scope for patronage, such as appointment of department heads and directors of local enterprises; influence over centrally managed enterprises (such as suspension of their directors for dereliction of duty); and, in certain matters, the power to make decisions without being accountable to anyone. The first appointments were made in November 1973, and there are as yet no data on their background. But if the appointments were similar to recent ones in economic enterprises, then one would expect the managers to have followed managerial career paths and to be highly qualified technocrats.

The process of de-bureaucratization, therefore, has replaced traditional bureaucrats with specialists exercising new powers through the use of modern managerial techniques. For the elected representatives, the task of supervising the new administrative overlords will be even more difficult. The first detailed study of a council since the 1973 reform confirmed that the one-man executive was dominant over the representative institutions in terms of authority, prestige, and ability to have his policy applied.[27] The study found that the 1973 reform had considerably strengthened the hand of the state administration, and serious doubt was raised as to the value of having a council at all. However atypical a study of one district council may be, it reinforces the belief that the managerial specialists appointed under the reform may not regard themselves as answerable to representative elements. The role of the Party, considered below, becomes a crucial factor in assessing the extent of power held by the specialists.

Local Autonomy

Another reform that was demanded was an increase in autonomy for local councils. Here, too, the demand corresponded to the struggle by managerial specialists in economic enterprises for greater self-management and less central control. All three principal organizational structures—the representative institutions (councils), the Party (local committees), and the state administration (departments)—called for greater local autonomy. The first two in particular had lost power due to an overcentralization of decision making. The 6th Congress recommended, therefore, that central political institutions should formulate the general economic and social goals to be pursued, leaving lower tiers to decide on operational matters. The central authorities were to plan economic and social development, provide the necessary resources, and supervise implementation. Examinations of local operations were to be general, not like the detailed ones that had stultified local autonomy in the past.

The increase in the powers of local councils was one of the first structural reforms enacted under Gierek. In 1972, a legislative measure changed the lowest tier councils in two ways. First, their number was reduced from over 4,300 to 2,365 through a process of amalgamation and absorption. They were to become "economic microregions," that is, localities comprising town and countryside, harnessing both agrarian and industrial production, financially quite autonomous, and of a size to allow for local self-management. Second, the district councils were given new powers and sources of revenue. They could influence investment projects of local industry, they had more control in formulating local economic and social development plans, and they could undertake projects in conjunction with neighboring councils. They now had a higher turnover tax on local industry, and the central subsidies they received were for longer periods.

The economic emancipation of local authorities was reflected in their growing share of the total state budget (see Table 7). Trends during the 1950s and 1960s, described earlier, also are observable in the data. Local councils' share of the total state budget showed no increase in 1951-55 or in 1960-70. However, the first quinquennium of Gomulka's rule and the first three years under Gierek were marked by a sharp increase in councils' share of the state budget. These were periods when local autonomy was broadened considerably.

To increase local autonomy was a relatively straightforward matter, compared to the processes of democratization and de-bureaucratization. Ideologically more autonomous councils could be justified by referring to Lenin's concept of <u>soviets</u>. In practical terms, fewer but more powerful district councils were an integral part of the

TABLE 7

People's Councils' Share of the Total State Budget, 1951-73

Year	Local Budget (millions of zlotys)	Percent of Total State Budget
1951	7,859	15.2
1955	18,276	14.8
1960	52,703	26.3
1965	79,248	27.4
1970	100,300	26.4
1973	160,900	33.4

Source: Glowny Urzad Statystyczny, Maly Rocznik Statystyczny 1974 (Warsaw, 1974), p. 273.

TABLE 8

Aspirations of Local Activists on the Question of Autonomy

	Average Number of Issue Areas Cited As the Proper Responsibility of:*			
	Central Authority	Local Authority	Local Institutions	Public
India	3.32	2.44	0.57	0.62
Poland	1.47	4.83	0.50	0.18
United States	1.33	2.96	1.84	0.77
Yugoslavia	2.29	3.27	0.88	0.46

*Maximum number of issues was seven (housing, employment, schools, hospitals, arts, electrification, youth).

Source: J. Wiatr, Spoleczenstwo, Polityka, Nauka (Warsaw: KiW, 1973), pp. 130-36.

program of rationalization of the economic and political system. There also was less disagreement among various interests over the desirability of the objective. Although ministries might grumble about another intrusion into their domain, in reality neither they nor the provincial authorities were required to hand down any of their powers. Finally, the demand for an increase in local autonomy had popular support among a large proportion of citizens. An international study of political values found that Polish local activists were most decidedly in favor of greater delegation of authority to the local level (see Table 8). They were also the weakest proponents of public jurisdiction over local matters. The survey was conducted in 1966, at a time when local authorities were being resubjected to central control.[28]

These factors in favor of an increase in local autonomy did not mean that autonomy would be achieved once structural change was made. Local councils had to earn the right to exercise wider powers, their new role had to be legitimized through favorable public attitudes, they had to gain experience vital to the new tasks to be performed, and they might have to overcome quarters of resistance (especially at the county level, which did lose power and status). However, the balance of forces on the issue was weighted in favor of more local autonomy. Those opposed to the reform could find consolation in the fact that it is not difficult to deprive localities of their autonomy. The precedent exists in the decade that followed the last decentralization phase of 1956-61.

Party Reform

Perhaps the institution that required most serious revitalization after 1970, but the most difficult to carry out, was the Party. The communications gap between upper and lower Party echelons had been exposed by the seaport riots, and it is possible that a similar gap existed between lower Party levels and the public. A breakdown in legitimation had occurred between the public and the Party, although not between the public and the socialist state. Exhortations by the new leadership for a change in political style, followed by a reshuffling of leading cadres at all levels in the Party were the first steps taken by Gierek to remedy the problems. Political liberalization was not a crucial issue. Rather, it was the need to forge links within and outside the Party, in particular with a skeptical public, that became the main logistical difficulty.

The 6th Congress had argued the case for a clearer division of functions between the Party, the government, and the state bureaucracy. Gierek had to remind Party members of their role by stating the obvious: "The Party directs and the government governs." Reform was to be based on the premise that the Party had still to play a directing, programmatic role in the political process. Few seriously believed that this premise could be challenged. The first task was, therefore, to remove some of the pretense surrounding the 1952 constitution by giving the Party legislative recognition. Accordingly, in 1973 an electoral law was passed to recognize "the directing, ideological power of the Polish United Workers Party."[29] The National Unity Front was given sole responsibility for the submission of candidates' lists for elections. Requirements for the election of councilors remained unchanged: Turnout had to be 50 percent and an overall majority of votes was not necessary. This unadventurous reform demonstrated that the Party did not intend to surrender any of its powers.

At the local level the Party was to concentrate on issues of key political significance, leaving other matters to be resolved by councils. It was to become an ideological watchdog over the governmental apparatus, not an organizational substitute for it. But the Party was not to develop into an inactive and overcautious force. Studies had found that councilor clubs of the party seldom met[30] and that Party involvement in the resolution of an important dispute in Torun was minor.[31] The problem facing the local Party committees was, therefore, to find a median between unnecessary interference in certain spheres of activity and total inactivity in other spheres. The solution adopted was to have Party first secretaries become leaders of the councils. The first national Party conference concluded that representative institutions would be strengthened by injecting local Party notables at the top.[32] Following the local elections held in December 1973, all provincial, county, and most district Party first secretaries were duly elected as council leaders.

This overlap in leadership roles was perhaps designed to counterbalance the power of the wojewoda, presidents, and town executives. An axis of power could thereby be established between representative and Party elements on the one hand, and a group of managerial specialists on the other. A recent empirical study of a district council showed that the Party secretary and the executive were in constant touch each day and that the district was in effect governed by the two men.[33] How widespread this pattern is has not yet been determined, but Party secretaries are continually better qualified to take on the managerial specialists should such an axis arise. For example, by 1974 nearly all provincial and county secretaries had higher education. Significant developments in the drive to increase the quality of leadership cadres have been the establishment in 1973 of the Institute for the Training of Administrative Leadership Cadres under the auspices of the Council of Ministers, and in 1974 of the Institute of Marxism-Leninism under the auspices of the Central Committee to advise Party officials on various social, political, and economic problems. Both state and Party structures are anxious to produce experts in various fields, and are to a certain extent competing with each other to produce technocrats.

Two further problems confront the new Party style. The possibility remains that central control over local committees may not slacken. Organizational and policy directives may continue to flow from higher to lower tiers, thereby diminishing local initiative. Second, the electoral change made it easier rather than more difficult for the Party to control virtually all facets of the election procedure. This means lack of contestation for Party candidates, which might bring about a recurrence of unresponsiveness. No safeguards against these potential tendencies have been constructed. The danger is that the Party's good intentions may eventually wear thin, which would be unfortunate proof that the dynamism of the Party leader is a more important factor than the work of the mass Party.

THE EXERCISE OF POWER AND POLITICAL CHANGE

The description of the reform movement influencing post-1970 Polish political life has focused on the local arena, but the parallel with tendencies in economic enterprises also has been drawn. The four broad areas in which change occurred were: (1) wider public participation in the political process; (2) de-bureaucratization of state authority; (3) more local autonomy; and (4) a more streamlined Party profile in political life. The origin of demands for change varied from representative elements and Party rank and file to local bureaucracies and the managerial specialists. In other words, the reforms were debated by the most important political entities, which were sometimes in disagreement with each other as each sought to extend or at least maintain spheres of power.

The picture that emerges is one of considerable disparateness between the important political entities in a socialist system. The Party, the ministries, representative institutions, local bureaucracies, the managerial specialists, economic enterprises, workers' councils and possibly self-management organs have their own interests, values, and goals. Within each of these entities there usually exist differences of opinion between central and local structures. Control over these entities by the Party leadership varies in time and in degree, but it is rarely absolute.

Nevertheless, reform of the people's council system was primarily shaped by the general policy course adopted by the post-1970 leadership. Wider public participation, a more rational and efficient form of administration, and an expansion of local self-management were consistent with the ideology espoused by Gierek. But is the process of reform really completed? A new constitution has not been drafted because agreement cannot be reached among the political institutions on how power should be reallocated. One aspect of constitutional reform might be an even more drastic reform of the structure of the council system. A three-tier system of councils, with jurisdiction over many issues overlapping between tiers, appears to be inconsistent with the rational form of administration advocated by the leadership. (The three-tier system is more complex than it appears. There are five wojewodztwo city councils autonomous from the 17 provinces, 299 county councils, 15 amalgamated town and county councils, 441 town councils, 1,900 district councils, 375 amalgamated town and district councils, and 33 city district councils.)

One proposal is to dissolve the intermediary, county level, which lost most of its power through the 1972-73 reorganization.[34] This proposal is currently under discussion (although not in public), and it is significant that 10,000 jobs have been eliminated in the county administration since 1973.[35] The Party also has reduced its cadres at the county level and has strengthened them at the district level. The implications of eliminating counties are that the number of provinces would have to be increased from the traditional seventeen, so as to be able to supervise and coordinate the work of the 2,365 districts. A figure of about 75 to 80 provinces would be the optimum number and, additionally, several planning regions would be set up to consider long-term development proposals.

Arguments for and against such a drastic reorganization are many, but the most interesting aspect of the debate is whether the leadership is capable of implementing such wholesale change. The processes of widening public participation and ousting the entrenched bureaucrats from office were accomplished despite opposition from vested interests. The increase in local self-management and the reform of the local Party apparatus were also successfully carried out, based on a general consensus that these measures were necessary. These changes were made at a time when the leadership was completing the installation of new cadres holding progressive values at all levels of the political system. The reorganization of the three-tier system of councils, however, although justifiable in terms of efficiency, would cause havoc among the cadres who have been settling in during the last few years. The proposed reform would be strongly resisted by the affected state and Party cadres, in particular the seventeen powerful provincial Party secretaries.

Such reorganization of the council system may, like the question of a new constitution, have to be shelved, or it may be considered by the 7th Congress, scheduled to meet in late 1975. If the reform measure were adopted and carried out, it would be a considerable success for the Party leadership. To implement a reform of this magnitude after five years in power would demonstrate that the Gierek administration, and the policies it has, are still capable of bringing about sweeping change in as established an institution as people's councils.

NOTES

1. See J. Starosciak, Decentralizacja administracji (Warsaw, 1960), and the articles by Starosciak and M. Jaroszynski in Panstwo i Prawo, nos. 186-90 (1961).
2. J. Wiatr, "Demokracja—samorzadnosc—aktywnosc," Nowe Drogi, no. 10 (1971): 150-60.
3. Urzad Rady Ministrow, Struktura zatrudnienia w organach administracji prezydiow rad narodowych (Warsaw, 1966), p. 145.
4. T. Kolodziejczyk, "Zmeczeni kadencja," Polityka, no. 39 (September 21, 1964).
5. Kanceleria Rady Panstwa, Biuro Rad Narodowych, Struktura osobowa komisji stalych rad narodowych wedlug stanu w dniu 31.V.70 r. (Warsaw, 1970), pp. 2-9.
6. J. Chwistek, "Wplyw instytucji wiazacych zalecen i opinii na prawna i faktyczna pozycje komisji rad narodowych," Problemy Rad Narodowych, no. 12 (1968): 54.
7. W. Narojek and J. Swiatkiewicz, "Pozycja wydzialu w opinii kierownikow wydzialow presydiow WRN (Wyniki sondazu ankietowego)," Problemy Rad Narodowych, no. 11 (1968): 150-52.
8. S. Zawadzki, "Przeslanki i kierunki rozwoju systemu rad narodowych," Nowe Drogi, no. 8 (1971): 7.
9. Trybuna Ludu, no. 73 (1971). Quoted in Zawadzki, "Przeslanki," p. 13.
10. S. Dzieciolowska, "Rada narodowa w oczach mieszkancow (Wyniki ogolno-polskiego badania ankietowego)," Problemy Rad Narodowych, no. 13 (1969): 41-43.
11. W. Hampton, Democracy and Community (London: Oxford University Press, 1970).
12. Z. Jarosz, "Zmiana prawa wyborczego do rad narodowych," Panstwo i Prawo, no. 11 (1973): 29.
13. W. Zakrzewski, "Gromadzkie rady narodowe oczami swych przewodniczacych i sekretarzy," Problemy Rad Narodowych, no. 17 (1970): 94-95.
14. Jarosz, "Zmiana prawa," p. 30.

15. T. Szymczak, "Postulaty i wnioski wyborcow a decyzje miejskich rad narodowych," Problemy Rad Narodowych, no. 30 (1974): 146-47.

16. Rocznik polityczny i gospodarczy 1974 (Warsaw: PWE, 1975), p. 210.

17. International Studies of Values in Politics, Values and the Active Community (New York: Free Press, 1971), p. 282.

18. G. Almond and S. Verba, The Civic Culture (Boston: Little, Brown, 1965), p. 25.

19. VI Zjazd Polskiej Zjednoczonej Partii Robotniczej (Warsaw: KiW, 1972), pp. 261-68.

20. "Ustawa z dnia 29 listopada 1972 r. o utworzenia gmin i zmianie umstawy o radach narodowych," Dziennik Ustaw, no. 49 (December 1, 1972).

21. "Ustawa z dnia 22 listopada 1973 r. o zmianie ustawy o radach narodowych," Dziennik Ustaw, no. 47 (November 27, 1973).

22. S. Zawadzki, "Reforma wladz terenowych a rozwoj samorzadnosci w miastach," Nowe Drogi, no. 10 (1974): 40-49.

23. G. Kolankiewicz, "Class, State, Nation and Party." Unpublished paper presented to the British Sociological Association, 1973, p. 29.

24. For contrasting interpretations, see M. Jaroszynski, Zagadnienia rad narodowych (Warsaw, 1961), p. 206; Z. Leonski, Rady narodowe (Warsaw, 1969), pp. 146-47; T. Bochenski and S. Gebert, Nowa ustawa o radach narodowych (Warsaw, 1959), pp. 142ff.

25. See W. Sokolewicz, Przedstawicielstwo i administracja w systemie rad narodowych PRL (Wroclaw, 1968), pp. 275-77.

26. W. Sokolewicz, "Aktualne kierunki zmian w strukturze i dzialalnosci organow przedstawicielskich," Problemy Rad Narodowych, no. 25 (1973): 119.

27. J. Tarkowski, "Reforma wladz terenowych w gminie Zwierz," Problemy Rad Norodowych, no. 31 (1974): 76.

28. Values and the Active Community.

29. Jarosz, "Zmiana prawa," p. 24.

30. H. Rot, "Sesje rad narodowych w swietle badan empirycznych," Problemy Rad Narodowych, no. 26 (1973): 63-64.

31. A. Mrozek, "Udzial czynnika zawodowego i spolecznego w procesie podejmowania decyzji administracyjnych (studium jednego przypadku," Problemy Rad Narodowych, no. 28 (1974): 107.

32. "Deklaracja o roli i zadaniach rad narodowych w spoleczno-politycznym systemie Polskiej Rzeczypospolitej Ludowej," Nowe Drogi, no. 12 (1973): 6-7.

33. Tarkowski, "Reforma wladz," p. 75.

34. Rot, "Sesje rad," p. 158.

35. Rocznik polityczny i gospodarczy 1974, p. 134.

CHAPTER

5

INNOVATIONS IN THE MODEL OF SOCIALISM: POLITICAL REFORMS IN CZECHOSLOVAKIA, 1968

Galia Golan

The origins of the Czechoslovak reform movement, usually identified simply as the Prague Spring, may be traced back to 1956, developing and gaining momentum in 1963-67, and finally emerging as the ruling force in 1968. The various ideas for reform, in almost all spheres of Czechoslovak society, began to circulate and even appear publicly from 1963 to 1968, following a reluctant decision in 1962 on the part of the Stalinist leadership of Antonin Novotny to permit a very limited degree of de-Stalinization. This decision itself was due to a number of internal factors, such as a serious economic crisis, discontent among Slovak communists, and pressures from within the Czechoslovak Communist Party to repudiate the Stalinist methods of the past. The second wave of de-Stalinization, introduced in the USSR in 1961, further influenced the Czechoslovak leadership into attempting highly controlled change. Given the internal pressure— the weight of fourteen years of unabated Stalinism—it proved impossible, however, to control this process even at this early, tentative level within the Party. By 1967 it had in fact become uncontainable, the reformers—a disparate, often unlikely and unorganized collection of Party members—succeeded in January 1968 in overthrowing Novotny and installing a Party leader who accepted their own general viewpoint.

In the earlier period (1963-67), reform ideas and programs had appeared; some, such as the economic, education, and legal systems reforms, had even been accepted, although Novotny's basic opposition prevented full implementation. Although the proposals for reform tended to have a life of their own, proposed changes in one sphere demanding and generating reforms in other fields, the political sphere was, as the most dangerous one for the regime, the last to be openly discussed. Yet the pressures to go beyond limited parliamentary and even electoral reform were strong, and in 1966 the Party's Central Committee set up a committee to investigate political reform. Novotny himself may have hoped that this would funnel all such deliberations into an authorized channel, which itself might be occupied for years in devising long-term programs. The advent of the reformers to power in 1968, however, broke these bonds, converting this crucial sector into the very focal point of public as well as Party debate.

Broadly speaking, the Czechoslovak reformers sought an adjustment of the standard Soviet model of socialism to the realities of what they considered an advanced industrialized socialist country enjoying a tradition of democracy and humanitarianism. Lest they pose a threat in any way to the hegemony of the Soviet Union in the socialist community, most Czech and Slovak theoreticians emphasized the localized nature of the proposed reforms (the need for changes only in accord with Czechoslovak conditions); yet there were those, including Dubcek and other reform leaders, who occasionally let slip the clear implication that the new forms sought by Czechoslovakia could provide a model or an original contribution to socialism, particularly applicable in advanced Western societies.[1] Without going into the political consequences of such claims, it is clear that the Soviet Union was unwilling to tolerate even the implicit challenge of the type of revisions undertaken in Czechoslovakia.

These revisions did indeed tend toward a new model of socialism, intended to combine the pluralism, controls on power and freedoms generally associated with classical democracy with a socialist structure of society and economy guided in some way by the continued rule of communist ideology as defined by some type of communist political organization and/or institution.

Even this very general summary of the Czechoslovak model is subject to much dispute, for in fact there was no one model nor one blueprint that might be taken as the essence of the Czechoslovak experiment. Indeed, a vital characteristic of this experiment was perhaps the diversity of views that came to the fore, particularly in 1968, the lack (sometimes to the disadvantage of the reformers) of a unified program or movement, and the struggle between ideas—of liberalization versus democratization, change versus revolt, and in the case of certain segments of youth, organization versus anarchism. It is beyond the scope of this essay to go into all these proposals and ideas, even within the sphere of political, as distinct from economic or other reforms. Rather, an effort will be made to concentrate on the ideas that struck at perhaps the very heart of the Soviet political system and, because of the nature of this system, lay at the core of reforms designed for most other spheres of society: the role of the

Communist Party and the related topics of the National Front and the possibility of opposition.

One of the major theoretical foundations of the reform ideas was the argument that with the shift from people's democracy to socialist society (which had been formally declared in 1960), the dictatorship of the proletariat had achieved its task and was no longer applicable. With the elimination of classes (in the strict Marxist sense) and the emergence of legitimate (because no longer class-based) but conflicting interests, in what promised to be a relatively long period before the complete achievement of socialism, a new political structure was called for. What was necessary was a system in which these conflicting interests could be expressed and institutionally protected. Thus, the image of the Party's role, as it emerged in 1968, was that it act as a kind of programmatic arbitrator. The assumption was that the Party need no longer dictate (because it was no longer engaged in a struggle against opposing classes) nor seek (read impose) unity of views within society (for conflicting interests were now legitimate, being no longer expressions of class struggle). Thus the need for the Party (in the name of the proletariat) to control all organizations and institutions of society was surpassed in a socialist society, for its claim to be the sole representative of the proletariat's interest became meaningless when the society itself had been converted to a proletarian one.

As such, this was a relatively charitable view that upheld the role of the Party as it had been conceived even in the worst days of terror, justifying it as necessary for the struggle against hostile classes and private property interests.[2] The argument was, then, that this concept was simply no longer suitable, once socialism had been achieved. Only the more radical voices, such as that of philosopher Ivan Svitak (who had been expelled from the Party in 1964) expressed publicly what many probably held privately: The Leninist role of the Party had in fact been designed for Russia in which "the workers' class formed a negligible fraction of the illiterate masses under Czarist despotism" and was totally "unsuitable for democratic countries in which there are no illiterate people."[3]

On the whole, however, the validity of the Leninist concept was not openly challenged; rather, it was argued that a distortion had set in. Zdenek Mlynar, chairman of the Party's committee for political reform, claimed that "for many years the political system in this country was deliberately adjusted to conform to the demand that a <u>single interest</u>, embodied in the directives issued by the center, should be made to prevail without any resistance," so the Party not only interfered in and regulated all aspects of society but also regarded any interest or opinion beyond the appropriate directive as an obstacle to unity.[4] Slovak CP Central Committee member Ondrej Repka added that the Party had seen itself as infallible and therefore conceived its leading role as that of dictating—people's participation being limited to mere implementation of directives. This had led to a concentration of power and decision making by the few, the desired unity became no more than a "sterile and false" unity imposed from above, according to Repka.[5]

Both Repka and Mlynar argued that, if the existence of legitimate conflicts in socialist society (once classes in the Marxist sense were eliminated) were recognized, the Party would have to adjust to a "permanent class of views."[6] Its leading role, then, would have to be perceived as mediating between these conflicting views by permitting genuine and active participation, that is, by recognizing each of the components of society's political life as independent entities with their own contributions to make to the solution of problems and able, thereby, to provide also an element of control on concentrated power.

Indeed, reform leader Vaclav Slavik urged the Party to see itself as "merely one component, albeit the principal one, of the entire political and managerial system," a coparticipant together with other groups in society.[7] Thus, the Party would no longer dictate to or even through other organizations, be they the government, the mass organizations, the schools, the factories, or the cultural-artistic world. Psychology lecturer and Brno CP activist Jaroslav Sabata claimed that not only was the Party "not identical with organs and institutions which govern or should govern," it could not even pretend to represent all citizens, for the people were represented by their official elected bodies.[8] Thus, it was argued that the Party's leading role should not be achieved by the direction and control of the non-Party institutions and offices but by the influence of communists in these bodies. The point was that these communists should neither be imposed upon the non-Party groups (either by appointment or even by means of the cadre system), nor should they themselves dictate to these organizations or bodies.[9] The Party should play the role of an avant-garde or example for non-Party people, achieving its leading role by virtue of the success of this example.

This idea of achieving or earning its leading role underlay almost all of the different conceptions of the role the Party should play, be it that of mediator rather than dictator and/or independent coparticipant in rather than controller of the political scene. If the Party sought unity, through conflicts of views and discussion, it would be required constantly to invigorate its own arguments, adjusting and rejuvenating its own views to meet the challenges of others. Thus, instead of dogmatism, a living, suitable (to the conditions and demands of society) program would ensure the Party's leading role. In effect, the Party's authority as the leading force in the country, written into the Constitution, would no longer be a dictate but a constantly re-earned reality. Slavik went so far as to say, "These words of the Constitution are valid only if the Party fights and proves them by action."[10] (Against whom and how we shall see below.) Others, too, such as reform leader Josef Smrkovsky and Slovak CP Presidium member Miloslav Hruskovic, expressed reservations about the constitutional preference given the Communist Party, joining those who argued that the Party must continuously win anew its right to this leading role by seeking and fulfilling the public's trust.[11] This was the essence of Dubcek's position as well; he called for a broad programmatic rather than managerial role for the Party, which would provide room for the institutions of society to decide on their own plans and activities and room for a "confrontation and exchange of views."[12]

The stated opinions of most of the reformers concerning the new role of the Party could be summed up as follows: The Party should no longer maintain a monopoly of power and decision making; it should rather prove its goals through equal competition in offices, factories, and institutions by permitting a clash of ideas and interests; the abandonment of this monopoly would in effect mean a sharing of power and, implicit to all the above, permit criticism, opposition, and even control on the Party's own exercise of power. Wary of just these implications (which we shall examine below), and of the problem of getting such a view past the still numerous opponents of reform within the Party, the reformers were somewhat less forthcoming in the first official program, the Action Program, accepted by the Central Committee in early April 1968.[13] The Action Program maintained that the distortion that had entered the concept of the leading role of the Party was "the false thesis that the Party is the instrument of the dictatorship of the proletariat." It claimed that the state plus the economic and social institutions were the instruments of the proletariat while the Party's task was primarily to "encourage initiative, to point out the paths and realistic possibilities of Communist prospects and, by systematic persuasion and the personal example of Communists, to win over the working people to these prospects." This view, then, foresaw a "programmatic nature of Party activity" not unlike the role of any political party.

The Action Program also explicitly stated that the Party should not "rule over society" nor become a universal administration, "but limit itself to providing guidelines rather than concrete plans," continuously earning its leading role "by deeds." Still more specific, the program declared that the Party should not replace or dominate the social and political institutions, such as the National Front, for they, not the Party, represented the varied interests and groups in society. The Party, nonetheless, should play the role of arbitrator for the varying interests, seeking "a method of satisfying various interests

that will not threaten the long-term interests of society as a whole."
Nothing was said, however, about what body would determine the
definition or explanation of just which interests did or did not threaten
society. Moreover, the program also added:

> Through its members, organizations, and organs the Party
> must perform the practical organizational function of a
> political force in society. The political organizational
> activity of the Party coordinates the practical efforts of
> the people to ensure that the line and program of the Party
> are implemented in all sectors, that is, in the social,
> economic, and cultural life of society.

This statement would seem to negate all that had preceded it on non-
interference in social and cultural institutions, and so forth. The key
to this apparent paradox lay, perhaps, in the fact that the Action Program called for a change in the methods used by the Party in executing
its role. Instead of commanding, the Party was to exercise its authority informally, by means of persuasion and example, free of imposition
(that is, an end to the cadre system and the practice of controlling
the various institutions through communists placed in their leading
organs). To clarify this, the Action Program included almost word
for word a statement made by Dubcek in a speech one month earlier:

> Party policy must not lead to noncommunists[14] getting
> the impression that their rights and freedom are lim-
> ited by the role of the Party. On the contrary, they must
> see in the activity of the Party a guarantee of their rights,
> freedom, and interests.

The reformers' "Second Program," the policy outline prepared
for presentation to the 14th Party Congress[15] (and which may well
have undergone significant alteration at the Congress, given the
changes that had taken place within the Party itself between April and
September 1968[16]), faced the issue of the role of the Party in a more
general fashion in one sense, but altogether more concretely in another
sense. In referring to the role of the Party, this program said that
the Party must "cease to be an institution of power, dictating every
step taken by every member of society."[17] While continuing to be the
defender of "the working-man's essential interests," the Party should
function also as "the avant-garde of modern progress . . . an alliance
of all those creative forces in society which support the socialist and
Communist program and are able to contribute to its fulfillment."[18]
Going further than the Action Program in reflecting the views expressed by the reformers, the Second Program saw as the Party's

function an effort "unceasingly to maintain a position in our political system which will enable the exercise of power to be controlled by a system of partnership and balance, of competition between ideas and personalities, and which at the same time affords the best guarantee against any throwback to reactionary policies."[19] Moreover, the Party "is also a pioneer in furthering self-government by democratic institutions whose private activity must no longer be bound by Party regulations."[20] Behind these last two statements lay a wealth of discussion and debate over the exact meaning of this new role, that is, to what degree was the Party actually going to retire from the everyday direction of society and its members, to just what degree was it in fact going to permit genuine competition and share its power—would this be even to the point of endangering its own preeminent position by permitting a real opposition, and just what would such an opposition mean? To these crucial questions the Second Program sought to provide certain answers and solutions, but before turning to this more concrete side of the program it will be useful to examine some of the intervening debate.

It had been conceded before 1968, and confirmed by the Party's documents in 1968 if not by actual changes in the laws, that the government, the elected organs, the legal system, the social mass organizations (such as the trade unions or youth union), as well as the factories (within the framework of the economic reform), were to be given greater independence and possibility to participate in the decision-making process or conduct of society.[21] Specific reforms were worked out for each of these domains, designed both to provide the citizen with greater scope for genuine participation and to supply a means of control over power. While the basic principle involved in these reforms was the change in the role of the Party, one of the key instruments by which it was hoped to implement these reforms was a change in the political framework of the country as provided by the institution of the National Front. Whatever the concept of pluralism or democracy advocated by the reformers—be it self-rule through the social organizations or political groupings or workers councils, or parliamentary-type democracy, or some combination of these—the concept of the National Front was a central issue. For one could go only so far, so long as the National Front as conceived since 1948 continued to exist. It was the National Front that was to provide the overall conception for policy, that is, the platform for the government. It was the National Front that was to provide the framework for elections and the distribution of power within the government. Just how it was to do this was, therefore, considered crucial to the whole undertaking of political reform.

There were those who maintained that the reform of the National Front should focus on providing that body itself greater power to determine policy.[22] Thus, it should not be a subordinate organ (that is, subordinate to the Party) but, rather, independent, and indeed, the supreme political institution insofar as the platform and candidates (policy and elections) were concerned. This in itself was deemed sufficient for a pluralistic system, given the fact that the National Front consisted of all the authorized political and semipolitical (such as social organizations) groupings. For this to be effective, however, it was pointed out that the National Front would have to be changed internally as well. There should be a greater say within the National Front for all its component parts, equality within the National Front, and the possibility for each component to present its views (platform) and people (election list) within the National Front's deliberations.[23] In this way the National Front would no longer be just an instrument of the Party in its functions vis-a-vis the citizen, nor just a rubber stamp of the Party in its own internal functioning. Indeed, this principle was expressed in the Action Program and in the Party statutes drafted for the 14th Party Congress, both of which called for the separation of the National Front from the Party.[24]

This reform was not insignificant, for it would permit the competition of views within the National Front, with freedom to organize public opinion around a particular view in order to have it prevail within the National Front. Thus, at least at the stage of policy formulation, there would be a possibility for bargaining and convincing. It also would mean an end to the formal monopoly of the Party, at least as the constitutionally preferred group, in the policy-making sphere. Nonetheless, it would still mean the continuation of the post-1948 concept of the National Front insofar as there would still be only one list presented to the public at elections, one platform, and little chance for a genuine parliamentary system wherein relative strength within the government or at least the parliament would be determined by voting strength (based on separate lists and platforms).

There were also those, however, who opposed the whole post-1948 concept of the National Front for just these reasons, on the grounds that pluralism could not be achieved within the framework of a National Front.[25] Their concept of pluralism went beyond the idea of participation or expression of views within the social organizations and interest groups (and even "parties") within the National Front. The pluralism of a democratic society or what might be called political pluralism must include struggle and competition for power because, they argued, the essence of politics is competition for positions of power; that is, the struggle to have a particular platform and a particular list rule—and the possibility of losing this power to rule. In other words, the essence of politics in a democratic society is the possibility of presenting an alternative to those already in power. The exponents of this view did not say that this power need be monopolistic; indeed, they said that one of the flaws in the proposed reform of the National Front was that it, officially or theoretically, left little room for the other policy-making institutions of society, such as the government or in particular the parliament. The elected organs of government should have a say; the National Front could not be a substitute for representational government. It had to be remembered, some argued, that the National Front was not the result nor necessarily the reflection of the will of the people as expressed at elections—at least not if it continued to include the social organizations, in which membership was often overlapping. For example, trade union representation in the National Front might overlap in many cases with that of the women's organization, the youth organization, the veterans' association, a minorities' organization, the Party, and even others. Moreover, most of these organizations were based not on political views or platforms but on other interests.

This argument, then, asked the basic question: What is a political party if not a group struggling not only for power but for power for their interests, their candidates, and the platforms they present? It was posited that the new, genuine political parties might be based on functional interests, that is, that the social organizations and groupings might play the role of parties.[26] One could thus have a system without political parties at all, or conversely without a political role for the social organizations, but, with or without political parties, membership in the National Front was overlapping and, more important, the National Front prevented the real control function of pluralism by barring the way to a competition for power insofar as it presented one list, one platform. Here we have the essence of the debate over opposition, the right to political groupings outside the National Front, and the ultimate challenge to the leading role of the Party.

Dubcek and many of his reformer colleagues such as Smrkovsky, Spacek, Goldstucker, Colotka, and Mlynar continuously supported the idea of pluralism and encouraged a reform of the National Front whereby its component parts, including both political parties and the social organizations, would play an independent role as political representatives of their constituents. Yet they stopped short of the idea of an opposition or a genuine competition for power, be it inside or outside the National Front. Most thought it sufficient to democratize the Party itself to permit the conflict of views to be expressed—and fought out—there.[27] Some argued that sufficient controls on the Party's power could be achieved by the change of the Party's modus operandi from decree to persuasion, with the "function of power" (that is, everyday administration and decision making) shifted to the state, National Front, and elected organs.[28] Whether because of conservative pressures inside and outside Czechoslovakia or from a real concern that the Party could not survive the onslaught of an opposition party and a genuine competition for power, the more or less official position of the reform regime was expressed by Dubcek on a number of occasions in the spring of 1968. In a speech on April 20 he said that the question of "state, politics and power in conjunction with the development of socialism and communism" could be solved "not by forming opposition parties, but on the basis of the internal process of revival within the Party."[29] At the Central Committee plenum, which opened at the end of May in the midst of an acute struggle with the conservatives in the Party and under severe pressure from Moscow, Dubcek favored the participation of the people in the making of policy through these organizations in the National Front, but he stipulated that "it would be a distortion to maintain that the Party does not express the interests of society."[30] Thus, Dubcek was willing to grant these organizations the privilege of partnership with the Party but not the possibility of trying or even claiming to compete with it for the role of representative of the majority of the people's wishes. As he explained:

> The basic difference between bourgeois parliamentarianism and socialist democracy is the fact that relations between the political parties which preserve the foundations of the National Front must be relations of partnership and cooperation, not relationships of struggle for the repartition of power in the state—a struggle which is typical of the bourgeois political system.[31]

Moreover, he argued, the National Front should not be a coalition of political parties only but should provide an outlet for people of no party affiliation, by including the social organizations. According to Dubcek's formulation, however, there existed barely any difference between the parties and the social organizations. Not only was the element of competition for power to be completely absent but the right to an independent program within the National Front was neutralized by the fact that, according to Dubcek,

> The confrontation of views [within the National Front] must be based on the common socialist program. The leading role of the Czechoslovak Communist Party guarantees this program because there is no other realistic program for the building of socialism but the Marxist program, a program which leans on scientific knowledge and on the most progressive social interest.[32]

The most progressive social interest, according to Dubcek's earlier formulation, was expressed by the Communist Party.

Thus, wittingly or not, Dubcek reinstated the very concept of the infallibility of the Party that his program had sought to undo. He expressly closed the door to the possibility of any other valid program and thus barred the way to any hope for the genuine influence of non-communists upon policy making. He ruled out, emphatically, the creation of parties outside the National Front "because this is the road to a renewal of the power struggle." He warned that

> our Party will oppose such efforts by every possible means because under our present conditions—independently of the desire of the people who advocate such views—such efforts would finally result in an attempt first to undermine the position of the Czechoslovak Communist Party in the society, and finally, also to reverse socialist development.[33]

He argued that there would be enough room for mutual opposition within the National Front, but he had already said that the only program open for acceptance by the National Front was that of the Communist Party, so there seemed little hope that meaningful pluralism could emerge. Indeed, the draft law on the National Front as presented in June 1968 maintained that there was to be no competition for a redivision of political power in the state within the National Front,[34] no political groupings or program outside the Front, and no additional political parties even within the Front. (Moreover, the program of the National Front was declared to be that of the Czechoslovak Communist Party.[35])

The essence of Dubcek's reform conception, then, was not the possibility of pluralism in the accepted sense of the term but, rather, the obligation upon the Party to prove that its program was the only valid one for socialism and to win majority support for this nonetheless indisputable fact:

> In our country there is no other alternative to socialism than the Marxist program of socialist development which the Party upholds. Nor is there any other political force, loyal to revolutionary traditions, which would be a guarantee of the socialist process of democratization. That is why we are righteously defending the leading role of the Party in society. We know it is not given automatically. We want to contend for it.[36]

Yet by "contend" Dubcek did not mean against other contenders, nor that this role would be abandoned if not won, but merely that the Party would try to be worthy of it, through its deeds, rather than merely decree it. Differing views would no longer be suppressed; they could be heard and legally represented, but the only possibility they might have of becoming policy would depend on the ability of their proponents to convince the Party to accept them. While persuasion was indeed a step forward insofar as the Party's methods were concerned, it could hardly be a potent instrument in the hands of powerless non-Party groups, which lacked the possibility of presenting the electors with an alternative to the communists or of offering a real challenge to the communists' grip on power. Moreover, since the Party did not recognize the validity of any but its own program as genuinely socialist, it would make little difference if, in the confrontation of views so generously permitted, it gained or did not gain a majority. Aside from interests of good will or conscience, there was no need for the Party to heed the majority any more than it had in the past, and it stated, a priori, that it would not heed an opinion that might threaten its own right to rule. Thus, the system envisaged by Dubcek had no guarantees, particularly no guarantee that the Party would not once again misuse its power. What Dubcek offered, then, was not democracy but liberalization.

This enormous difference was indeed realized by many involved in the reform movement, and not only by the more extremist. Even within the Party, despite the line that emerged from Dubcek's pronouncements (and the draft law for the National Front), there was a struggle over the issue of opposition. The powerful Prague city Party organization, at its conference in July 1968, prepared a document that it intended to present at the 14th Party Congress in September.[37] This document urged a choice, at elections, between alternative programs and candidates, albeit "for the present" on the basis of the National Front, as well as the use of plebiscites and referendums on important political issues. If we are to believe the testimony of one person directly involved in the formulation of this position, the Prague delegates (representing some 150,000 members) under the leadership of Presidium member Bohumil Simon, intended to press the congress to reject the ban on political organizations and activity outside the National Front, thereby reversing the already drafted National Front law.[38]

This, then, is the background to the materials prepared for the 14th Congress—the programs referred to above and others—which remain the last blueprint left for judging just how the reform regime intended to cope with the crucial problem of the leading role of the Party versus pluralism. The program expressly recommended retention of what was called the "assured monopoly of the National Front" so as to prevent the "highly probable" conflict over the hegemony of the Communist Party.[39] This, however, was to be a temporary measure prior to the new constitution, which was to make the final decision on the openness of the political system, based on the experience of the intervening two years. Even in this two-year interim period, however, there was to be an effort to reduce the negative features of the one-list National Front system. Although no list outside of that of the National Front might be presented to the voters, the common list would list the candidates according to their organization or party (that is, their component of the National Front),[40] permitting the voter to select the organization or party he wanted with its list of candidates; places in the body to be elected would then be divided proportionally among the components of the National Front according to the votes received. Thus, the concept of the National Front as applied in the 1945-48 period was restored to some degree. In addition, however, a certain percentage of places (a suggested 25 percent) were to be put aside for candidates to be selected by the voter as individuals (regardless of organization or party), on the basis of a simple majority. Thus, the system would favor the party or organization that, although it might no do well as an organization, could achieve more seats through the direct election of individuals by the old one-list, absolute-majority system. A concomitant suggestion was to permit entirely independent candidates to appear on the list provided they had a certain minimum ("say, 2,000") of electors' signatures. The congress materials expressly acknowledged, however, that this combination of a proportional and absolute-majority voting system had been chosen so as to prevent the Communist Party from becoming a minority party.

The program also stipulated that the following two alternatives would be open for adoption in 1970 (for the next ten- to fifteen-year period):

(a) If the system of several political parties within a National Front were to "catch on" in such a way that the noncommunist parties formed a practical alternative to the communist hegemony, then the concept of the National Front outlined above [the "monopoly position" with no political organizations permitted outside] would have to continue in force.

(b) If on the other hand developments proceeded not in that direction but towards according a greater influence to the political interest-group organizations [which are also in the National Front] and to the self-management principle, then it would be possible to entertain an alternative constitutional solution. (This might be the inclusion in the Constitution of criteria for the existence of a party, and the creation and dissolution of parties could be decreed by a constitutional court.)[41]

These two alternatives could almost be seen as the juxtaposition between the Czech tradition of parliamentary democracy and something more akin to the Yugoslav system of self-rule. The second alternative was delineated in a way still closer to the Yugoslav system in the program's proposal that the parliament be multicameral on the basis of representation by social function (for example, an agricultural chamber elected by the agricultural units).[42] The implication was that this interest-group organization/self-management system would be less of a threat to the Communist Party than the parliamentary multiparty system, which would probably require the continuation of control through the National Front.

Theoretically the parliament, however organized, would be sufficiently free of Party control to be the locus of the creation of the state's political line.[43] Indeed even pre- and early 1968 reforms had offered greater independence and the right to initiate and/or reject government-proposed legislation, exercising even a control function over government.[44] Yet the materials presented for the 14th Congress evidenced a certain ambivalence as to the actual policy-making power of the parliament, speaking on the one hand of the "setting of the political line in the National Front" and on the other of functionally organized parliamentary chambers governed by a Yugoslav-type system of self-management.[45] The existence of a dilemma over this issue was in fact recognized, to be settled, it was recommended, together with and as a part of the overall electoral system/National Front/political pluralism/self-rule issue.[46]

The two tendencies—one toward a multiparty parliamentary system and one toward some sort of self-rule via the social organizations (trade unions, youth unions) plus workers' councils—were apparent not only in the Party's thinking but among the population at large. In the postinvasion period prior to the overthrow of Dubcek, in fact, the second tendency gained a certain ascendancy, for in the absence of any possibility to organize politically, the population sought to act through often spontaneously created self-managing bodies (unions, workers' councils). Yet in the preinvasion period the overall thrust seemed to be in the direction of a pluralistic political system based on parties and parliamentary democracy, with the self-management movement for the workers, for example, getting off only to a belated start. Indeed, the very workers' councils envisaged by a large part of the reform proposals were "enterprise councils" more broadly constituted than the strictly workers' councils of Yugoslavia. The Czechoslovak reforms admittedly called for decentralization and stronger local government, but in fact there was greater attention given to institutional controls on power and the classical means of representational participation. It was probably for this reason that the issue of the role of the Party could not be ignored or left for practice or even answered by a change in the character of Party work. It may well have been the Czech democratic tradition[47] with its institutional-legalistic penchant that made the reformers aware of the fact that even in a Yugoslav-type system of self-management, which does accord the citizen a great deal of direct participation and places the Party somewhat in the background, the monopoly on political power continues to be held by the communists, depriving the citizen both of any guarantee of the continuation or effectiveness of this participation and of controls on power (or misuses of power), making the whole system dependent upon the vicissitudes of arbitrary political life.

It must be borne in mind that much of the program discussed here, as well as the other documents and political ideas proposed in the Czechoslovak experiment, were conceived in an atmosphere of intense outside pressure, political struggle, and spontaneous activity. Foremost in the reformers' minds as they rushed to provide a coherent program for the scattered movement was the absolute imperative on the one hand to prove to Moscow that a socialist society would emerge intact and yet, on the other hand, to reflect the increasingly insistent demands (inside and outside the Party) for a humane and democratic system. The possible contradiction of these two imperatives tended to be driven home by the political atmosphere itself, undoubtedly affecting the content of the proposals ultimately worked out. Yet it is likely that any movement for genuine change of the Soviet political model in an East European country would result in the same pressures—both externally and internally. Genuine political reform cannot be undertaken without popular support (and indeed popular support tends to be sought by reformers in their struggle against conservatism), but once the public is involved, it is a natural development that their enthusiasm, while helpful, creates a new dynamism pushing the reformers for more thorough change than they had perhaps intended.

By the same token, it would be unrealistic to expect Moscow to remain indifferent to any such movement for change, the degree and rate of Soviet concern being determined additionally by the public involvement in and acceleration of the movement (or, in other terms, the degree of Party control over events). In this case, it would not necessarily be fruitful to enquire as to just what model might have emerged were it not for these two types of pressures, since such pressures were probably inevitable. The overall direction of the movement was clear and indeed consistent with the way in which the very issues and problems at hand were perceived. Basic to this lay the political traditions and spiritual heritage of the nation, which some even claimed had made the Prague Spring inevitable or, at the very least, determined the particular qualities of the model it produced.

NOTES

1. Dubcek speeches, Rude pravo, February 23, March 5, April 21, 1968. For others, see Josef Smrkovsky to Prague rally, Prague radio, March 20, 1968 or Peter Colotka in Zivot, April 17, 1968. For emphasis on specific conditions, see, for example, Smrkovsky in Rude pravo, February 9, 1968, or Josef Spacek, Rude pravo, April 11, 1968.
2. See, for example, Eduard Goldstucker in Prague rally, Prague radio, March 20, 1968.
3. Ivan Svitak, "A Conference Marked by the Sign of the Times," Filmovy a televizni noviny 11, no. 7 (1968): 7.
4. Rude pravo, January 13, 1968.
5. Rol'nicke noviny, January 20, 1968.
6. This point had been made by Mlynar as early as a 1965 article in The World Marxist Review, no. 12 (1965): 58-64 ("Problems of Political Leadership and the New Economic System").
7. Rude pravo, January 30, 1968.
8. Brno radio, February 7, 1968.
9. They did not go as far as the Yugoslav League of Communists, who theoretically at least permit Party members to act as individuals in their respective organizations, deciding themselves what line to take and thus not even having the added weight of "representing" the Party.
10. Prace, February 7, 1968.
11. Hruskovic on Czechoslovak television, February 29, 1968; Smrovsky, "Democracy Does Not Come Overnight," My 68 5, no. 4 (1968): 6.
12. Rude pravo, February 23, 1968 (February 22 speech, in the presence of visiting CP leaders, including Brezhnev). See also his speech of March 2, 1968 (Rude pravo, March 5, 1968).
13. Carried in full in Rude pravo, April 10, 1968.
14. "Of these there is a majority in our society," Dubcek said in the speech (Rude pravo, March 5, 1968).
15. "Analysis of the Party's Record and the Development of Society Since the Thirteenth Congress; The Party's Main Tasks for the Immediate Future," in Jiri Pelikan, The Secret Vysocany Congress (London: Allen Lane, 1971), pp. 187-253
16. The powerful Prague city Party committee planned to oppose certain parts of this program.
17. Pelikan, The Secret Vysocany Congress, p. 214.
18. Ibid., p. 215.
19. Ibid.
20. Ibid.

21. See Galia Golan, The Czechoslovak Reform Movement: Communism in Crisis 1962-1968 (Cambridge: Cambridge University Press, 1971), and Reform Rule in Czechoslovakia: The Dubcek Era 1968-1969 (Cambridge: Cambridge University Press, 1973).

22. Discussion on Prague radio, March 7, 1968; Alexandr Kliment in Literarni listy, July 4, 1968; Central Committee resolution, Rude pravo, April 6, 1968.

23. Mlynar argued this, for example, in Rude pravo, March 26 and April 5, 1968. See also economist Radoslav Selucky, Prace, April 11, 1968.

24. The draft statutes were published on August 10, 1968. In 1959 a Central Committee resolution had expressly placed the National Front under the Party's direction and it was customary to have the Party first secretary as chairman of the National Front.

25. For example, secretary of Mlynar's original committee, Petr Pithart, Literarni listy, May 1, 1968, or June 26, 1968. Vaclav Havel, Literarni listy, April 4, 1968; Jiri Hanak, Reporter, April 24, 1968; Pavol Stevcek, Kulturny zivot, April 12, 1968; Rudolf Battek, Literarni listy, March 21, 1968; Anton Hykisch, Kulturny zivot, May 31, 1968; Pavel Kohout, Literarni listy, May 16, 1968.

26. For example, Mlynar, Prague radio, May 17, 1968. The discussion on types of parties and the nature of political parties touched on many new and old ideas, from the functional basis to the idea of one mass, open Communist Party, or two competing CPs, or other such proposals.

27. The reforms envisaged for the Party itself were mapped out in the two drafts of the statutes to be presented at the 14th Congress. In addition to providing for the right to resign from the Party, limitations of the period of tenure and number of offices to be held simultaneously in the Party, greater authority for the elected organs of the Party, and greater information for and participation of the lower Party organizations, the statutes were to permit horizontal contact between Party units, the right to oppose a Party decision and to persist in this opposition even after the decision's acceptance—and to raise the issue again. In this way the door was opened to the "factions" forbidden by Lenin, but the second draft of the statutes, aware of this implication, was careful to add the caveat that dissent was acceptable if "not in fundamental conflict with the program and statutes of the Party." (Pelikan, The Secret Vysocany Congress, pp. 130-84, for both drafts.)

28. For example, Mlynar, Prague radio, March 6, 1968 or Rude pravo, March 26, May 16, June 6, 1968; Goldstucker, ASHAI (Tokyo), March 22, 1968, Volkstimme (Vienna), April 12, 1968; Spacek, Rude pravo, March 16, May 23, 1968.

29. Rude pravo, April 21, 1968.

30. Pravda (Bratislava), June 4, 1968.
31. Ibid.
32. Ibid.
33. Ibid.
34. Passed September 13, 1968 (No. 128/1968).
35. Rude pravo, June 16, 1968.
36. Rude pravo, July 1, 1968 (speech in Lisen); he repeated the same view in his speech to a Prague district meeting (Rude pravo, June 30, 1968).
37. "Stanovisko komunistu mimoradne mestke konference k obecnym politickym problemum," unpublished paper, Praha, 1968.
38. Josef Pokstefl in V. V. Kusin, ed., The Czechoslovak Reform Movement 1968 (Santa Barbara, Calif.: ABC-Clio, 1973).
39. "Analysis of the Party's Record . . ." in Pelikan, The Secret Vysocany Congress, p. 232.
40. The stipulated assumption was that the nominating procedure also would be reformed along democratic lines, as well as the technical side of the voting procedure.
41. Pelikan, The Secret Vysocany Congress, p. 232.
42. Ibid., pp. 233-34.
43. Ibid., p. 233.
44. Ibid.; Rude pravo, April 10, 1968 (Action Program); for reform of National Assembly and its role prior to 1968, see Golan, Czechoslovak Reform Movement, pp. 177-84.
45. Pelikan, The Secret Vysocany Congress, pp. 206, 224.
46. Ibid., pp. 233-35.
47. There were other elements of the Czech tradition at play, an analysis of which exceeds the scope of this essay; for example, one could find sources in the tradition for the concept of needing to "earn" the right to rule, the idea of a Czechoslovak "contribution" to the world, the emphasis on a program. See Galia Golan, "The Czech Democratic-Liberal Tradition and Czechoslovak Socialism" in Eisenstadt and Atzmon, eds., Tradition and Socialism (New York: The Free Press, 1974).

CHAPTER

6

CONTINUITY AND CHANGE IN HUNGARY IN HISTORICAL PERSPECTIVE: THE MODERN PERIOD

Joseph Held

Hungarian society has been undergoing a process of modernization for well over a century. By the 1970s, indicators to measure and compare the progress of "modernity" existed in abundance in Hungary.[1] These indicators include the level of industrialization and urbanization. Indeed, more than half of Hungary's population now earns a living in industrial enterprises, and two-thirds reside in urban or semiurban areas.[2] Another indicator is the growth of communications and the dissemination of knowledge. These diminish the most glaring differences between cities and villages, which in turn leads to a higher level of integration among the various strata of society. Additionally, in the Hungarian case, a leveling of individual incomes after 1945 contributed to the reduction, but not elimination, of long-standing class and sex inequalities.[3]

Modernization in Hungary, as elsewhere, has been an uneven process. On the one hand, it contributed to the disappearance of many historical traditions and the elimination of the landed aristocracy and the gentry,[4] and on the other, to the preservation of many attitudes and values dating back to premodern days. The consequent diversity of present-day social conditions makes generalization difficult indeed. Further compounding the problem is the continuing nature of the modernization process. An assertion that may seem valid at one moment could be outdated by the time it is committed to paper. In full awareness of this danger, the main assertion of this essay is that, despite the progress of modernization, Hungarian society in 1974 was not as drastically new as could be expected. Many material conditions of life have been fundamentally and rapidly changed. However, the rapidity of change in material conditions and social stratification has not always been accompanied by equally rapid change in traditional attitudes and values.

THE PEASANTRY IN THE 1970s

Out of a population of about 8 million, almost two-thirds were employed in agriculture during the interwar years. By 1974 this number had been halved—due to thoroughgoing land reform in 1945, followed by two separate collectivization drives after 1948, a flood of new jobs created by a very rapidly growing industry in the urban centers and various coercive "administrative" methods employed by the state.[5]

Young peasants were the first to flee their ancestral villages for new opportunities. The lure of better-paying jobs in the industrial centers, the opening of channels of secondary and higher education, and greater opportunities to meet other young people, attracted young peasants away from the villages. Many also shared a conviction that they had no future in agriculture. A collective farm chairman in the village of Bacsalmas in southern Hungary suggested an explanation based on past peasant experiences:

> The peasantry has always been held in contempt; when this attitude finally ceased to exist, the routes of escape were suddenly opened. It seems that the hopeless longing of generations of peasants to escape their fate has now come to bear fruit in the attitude of the upcoming young generation.[6]

Prior to the collectivization drives, most Hungarian peasants had one overriding ambition: to acquire a piece of land of their own. However, the peasants learned an important lesson by the 1970s: They realized that the land itself was not worth the price they were asked to pay because successive regimes in Hungary took advantage of their longings to extract the last ounce of their surpluses for state use. It did not matter whether this was done through the maintenance of price inequalities between industrial and agricultural goods—the infamous "agrarian scissor" of the interwar years—or through quotas for grain delivery at confiscatory prices as in the 1950s. What mattered was that the peasants of Hungary paid more for industrialization and economic modernization than any other group. No wonder the young peasants took the first opportunity to leave their villages.

However, in areas where intensive methods of agriculture have been traditionally practiced and where viable individual parcels of land were small enough to avoid the charge of being a kulak, many young peasants remained. In such regions, some peasant groups were able to turn the bitter lessons of the past to their advantage. This preserved ancient social stratification patterns in their villages.

In several other peasant communities close to urban centers, many families adopted a hybrid existence. The old families formed collective farms at the government's insistence. Such farms have thrived on the know-how of their members and often have continued many well-established practices of the past. The proximity of urban centers traditionally determined the crops: Vegetables and fruits continue to be the major produce, sold at considerable profit in the open markets of the urban centers. The government encourages the peasants to continue their traditional ways since their produce is important for the food supplies of the nearby cities. The income of these peasant families, therefore, is sufficient not only to satisfy their everyday needs but for the purchase of luxury articles as well.

Not all members of these families, however, joined the collectives; some commute to jobs in the nearby cities. In Vecses, a village of mixed population near Budapest, for example, some members of the old peasant families acquired a higher education. A few became lawyers and doctors, while others are white-collar workers in industry, commuting to the capital city. However, when work in the fields of the collective is pressing, the commuters take their vacations and help their relatives. In turn, they are assisted by their peasant families, made possible by the survival of an ancient peasant institution, the extended family.

The heads of extended families in Vecses control the common purse; they buy clothes, houses, and even automobiles for their "youngsters," many of whom are now in their forties. In turn, the latter take care of their parents in their old age; none of the old folks in the village has ever needed public assistance.[7] A similar situation exists in the village of Dunakeszi, located about eight miles north of Budapest, although here the influx of industry and the existence of the nearby stables of racing horses at Alag split the community more than in Vecses. But among the old peasant families a similar situation exists in Dunakeszi as in the other villages.[8] That these are not isolated cases is shown by the situation in villages away from urban centers, like the settlement in Soltvadkert.

Soltvadkert is located about 200 kilometers south of Budapest. The peasants in the area have, for generations, worked in viniculture. When they were forced into collective farms, each family "contracted" with the new institution to continue tending its own grapes. Since they continued working on their former private property, they labored very hard and prospered. From their considerable income they were able to maintain and even increase the harvest of their vineyards. They used large amounts of fertilizer and new strains of grape; their collective was able to buy the necessary machinery for mass production methods to maximize profits. The result was that many peasant families became wealthy, even by Western standards. In the 1970s they live in spacious brick homes in their village; they own television sets and some drive automobiles.[9]

However, the modernization of production and its concomitant, the acquisition of private wealth, left many peasant values and attitudes intact. For instance, birth control traditionally restricts each peasant family to one child, to preserve the family's wealth. Today, as for generations before, the peasant families arrange marriages for their children within the group. Today, such a marriage frequently draws 500 guests to the wedding. The collection at the bridal dance—another ancient peasant custom—seldom comes to less than 100,000 forints, the equivalent of about $5,000 at the current exchange rate.[10] On the other hand, marriage outside the circle of rich peasant families is discouraged and the offending young people are usually excluded.[11]

In both Vecses and Soltvadkert, and in other villages where similar conditions exist, social status continues to be determined by material possessions. This is no longer expressed by the size of the family's land holdings as in the past, but rather by the size of the home, the quality of the furnishings and gadgets. An important component of social status is the relation of rich families to the church. Although only about 30 percent of their children are enrolled in religious-education classes in the schools, their affiliation with the Catholic church is a measure of their social rank. Of course, the peasant way of life has undoubtedly changed. But the essence of the change is the adaptation of ancient institutions to new circumstances, not the abandonment of them. The process is even clearer in the case of the poor peasants in the countryside.

On the outskirts of the villages around Soltvadkert, shacks burrowed underground shelter the poorest families, often with half a dozen or more children each. They are despised even by the less rich peasants who work on the collectives but harvest crops other than grapes. The poorest peasants exist on the lowest rank of the social scale; their children do not mix with those of the rich peasants, and marriages between poor and rich children are practically nonexistent.[12] They have not been affected by modernization and live their life as in the past.

Another group of peasants live in isolated dwellings, far from other settlements. Their homes are without electricity or pumped water; they practice methods of agriculture that are centuries old.[13] Theirs is the famous world of the puszta, open lands of unlimited horizons, often of poor soil, with few opportunities for education or amusement. Traditionally the people of these dwellings, the tanyas, stood outside of any peasant community. Their lives were determined by their isolation. Today, they have the largest percentage of illiterates of all social strata, drinking is an important social problem, and they have not yet been touched by modernization.[14]

According to studies by the Institute of Social Research of the Hungarian Academy of Sciences, the old practice of religious sectarianism is on the rise once again among the people of the tanyas. This phenomenon was widely condemned in the 1930s, regarded as an expression of the hopelessness of the peasants who could not see anything promising in the future.[15] It seems that the people of these isolated dwellings are once again confronted by problems whose solution escapes them; therefore, they are turning to the sects for consolation.

In another area of Hungary, the Nyirseg, modernization has also proved uneven. According to the reports of Antal Vegh, a journalist who visited the region on several occasions (especially one village appropriately called Peneszlek, a name that includes the term for "mold"), poverty and ignorance continue to characterize the lives of many peasants. The soil is poor, natural resources are scarce, and opportunities for industrial work are limited. The collective farms are poorly organized and their leadership is often inefficient. Peasants who see little hope of escaping from their predicament turn to denatured alcohol—the cheapest drink available—which also was a scourge of the interwar years. Drinking is a great problem here; children whose apathetic parents send them to school without breakfast, clothed in filthy rags, often with lice in their hair, sometimes have a drink of denatured alcohol themselves before starting to school. Thus, at the ripe age of eight or ten they sleep through class in a drunken stupor.[16] There is little the state can do to help these people as long as they remain apathetic toward their fate.

In summing up the kaleidoscopic picture of peasant society in Hungary of the 1970s, one may say that life for the agricultural population has changed. Not only has the number of peasants diminished, but a greater number have been able to acquire a comfortable, secure existence. Some peasant families have even become wealthy in socialist Hungary.

At the same time, the process of modernization has not reached into every village. Hundreds of thousands of peasants continue to live as their ancestors lived, something that could be expected at this stage of modernization of Hungary. However, a puzzling phenomenon prevails: In some areas where modernization has penetrated into the villages, and where the peasants were able to turn the process to their advantage, they used the means so acquired for strengthening the traditional stratification of peasant society. Instead of abandoning the castes of the past, they want to retain their traditional social formations.

One final word should be said about peasant feelings toward the land, since this is the most important gauge of changing attitudes. As Hungarian authorities have observed, more than half of the agricultural workers' income in the 1970s is derived from private plots; these average about 1.25 acres (one hold, according to Hungarian measurements), an insignificantly small portion of the total arable land.[17] These plots also supply a considerable portion of the foodstuffs needed by Hungary's urban areas. Perhaps nothing illustrates better the lingering peasant love for private land than this. Not surprisingly, the current leaders of socialist Hungary regard the survival of castes in the countryside and the peasants' attitudes toward the land with alarm, for these certainly do not show a process of modernization in which social classes are "to wither away."

WHITE-COLLAR INDUSTRIAL WORKERS

There is no better indicator of the progress of modernization in Hungary than the increase in the number of people earning their living in industry. By 1970, this number stood at 3,160,593 wage earners out of a total labor force of 5,001,200 men and women, including both white- and blue-collar workers.[18] In the 1970s a total of 553,500 persons worked in white-collar jobs in three categories of industry: heavy industry, transportation-communication, and the building trades.[19]

White-collar industrial workers are not members of the Hungarian bourgeoisie. They are wage earners who sell their intellectual capacity and professional know-how to their employer—in most cases, the state. Their relationship to the mode of production—to use a favorite term of Marxist economists and politicians—does not determine their status in Hungarian society. Status is determined largely by the esteem that income-generating capacities inspire: The larger the income, the higher the status, regardless of the means by which income is acquired.

According to one report, professions based on the humanities have greater attraction for white-collar workers in the 1970s than the technical fields such as engineering, where mathematical knowledge is imperative.[20] The reason, according to the report, is not so much the reluctance of young people to enter occupations where responsibility for technical decisions is great, but a special stress on material compensation, which seems better in nontechnical managerial jobs. I suspect that historical traditions also play an important role, although this would be difficult to document. But Hungarian white-collar workers traditionally opted for a humanities-based education that could be used in such attractive fields as law and journalism. Practitioners of these professions were always highly regarded in Hungary in the past, for they commanded larger than average income and ample leisure time to enjoy it.

During the interwar years, jobs in industry on both the managerial and technical levels were scarce. Then the dream of white-collar workers was to acquire a steady, secure income—the legendary 200 pengos in fixed salary, in the 1930s the equivalent of about $40—and live a leisurely life. The acquisition of material goods as a primary aim in life was not a characteristic attitude for many white-collar workers at that time.

Rapid industrialization and modernization contributed to changing these attitudes after 1945. The socialist state's insistence upon increasing the volume of factory production, its stress upon material rewards for work exceeding the required norms, and, most important, the increasing number and variety of available consumer goods in the 1960s, started a race for acquisition by all segments of the population, especially white-collar workers. The race was encouraged by socialist theorists who insisted that the task of building socialism in Hungary necessitated as a first step the "catching up and overtaking" of production volume and living standards of the advanced industrialized countries of the West.[21]

The consequences included a steady increase in the standard of living of the white-collar wage earners (accompanied by increasing indebtedness of individuals and families). Many white-collar workers internalized the state's declared intention to overtake Western societies in the production and consumption of goods. But they turned around and substituted in their minds their fellow workers and neighbors for the "capitalists." Major status symbols in the 1970s, symbols of victory over less able competitors, were automobiles and weekend homes. As one observer remarked:

> Everybody is driving themselves hard . . . because without status symbols there is no respect. . . . And when one buys an automobile, one will try to exchange it for a more elegant one within a half a year, since [his neighbor] also bought a Western model. One must not fall behind, because it is not fashionable. Books? Theater? One should rather drive himself to exhaustion so that others would have no chance to feel superior.[22]

Not surprisingly, the best Hungarian white-collar workers want to live a life characteristic of the middle classes in the West before the present economic crisis. For them, this is the real meaning of modernization. At the same time, many realize that the race may lead to a way of life lacking in traditional values, that the fulfillment of material desires does not give full meaning to an individual's life. A woman white-collar worker explained:

[Among our social friends] those who have families play
the role of the petty bourgeois; for them, their child is
sacred; for him, they are willing to lick spittle, to exist
without a backbone, to elbow others out of the way. And
they are even proud of this! Books of poetry and novels
that they buy serve only as decoration on their shelves.
. . . Teachers, engineers, doctors, agro-technicians
must drive themselves hard. First of all, because they
want to catch up with the others. Secondly, because
they have to overtake them; with fur coats, cars, dogs,
the fashionable dresses of their children, and vacations.[23]

In the midst of a rushing life, in the feverish drive for the acquisition of material goods, some traditional attitudes did survive among the white-collar workers of Hungary. For instances, despite the high divorce rate, most white-collar families carried into the new age a Victorian attitude toward sex, an attitude reinforced by the ideological leaders of the Communist Party. Another attitude that has survived is nationalism. It is true that the virulent, chauvinistic nationalism of the interwar years (fostered by the aristocracy and the gentry) disappeared among white-collar workers in the 1970s. That current attitudes also include a strong feeling of nationalism is attested to by the decade-long arguments that periodically surface in journals and other publications.[24]

At the same time, the stress on work as the means of acquiring consumer goods has taken a great deal out of the creative nature of labor. Specialization and mechanization have also contributed to increasing alienation from work. Many white-collar workers choose their occupation not because they feel a calling but because it offers the highest possible material reward. Alienation from work has reinforced the tendency to compensate with acquisitiveness, creating a cycle in which competition for status and consumer goods has become a major characteristic of life.[25]

BLUE-COLLAR INDUSTRIAL WORKERS

Modernization has also increased the number of Hungary's blue-collar workers, recruited mainly from among peasants and women after 1945.[26] Many of these workers were considerably elated by the Red Army's liberation of the country; they had revolutionary expectations for a speedy transformation of society in which they would become an important force. These expectations were fueled by the nationalization of industry and banks in 1947-48, by the formation of workers' management councils in factories and the conquest of power by the communists, with Russian support, in 1948.[27] However, the blue-collar workers learned in the 1950s that the dictatorship of the proletariat in Hungary was a system led by foreigners, designed for the benefit of a privileged new class, and the modernization of economic and political life was to be achieved partly at their expense.

The steps in this process are well known and need little repetition here. The trade unions were transformed from workers' protective organizations to "transmission belts" for the flow of command from the top of the political hierarchy. Passbooks were introduced to tie workers to their jobs; the living standards of blue-collar workers steadily deteriorated as work norms were constantly increased and targets for the first five-year plan were revised.[28] Compounding these troubles was the lack of housing for the thousands of former peasants seeking jobs in industry as they were jammed into temporary housing in the urban centers. Purchase of government bonds, usually taking away 10 percent of the salaries of workers, was forced every year. No wonder the Hungarian blue-collar workers were the most stubborn, astute revolutionaries in 1956.[29]

By the 1970s, however, much of the antagonism and ill-feeling against the government that had been generated by these policies subsided. The economic reforms of 1968 laid stress on the profitability of enterprises, and bonuses for workers were introduced when profitability was achieved. The response of blue-collar workers was cautious and distrustful. A journalist reported that the attitude of young workers toward authority was characterized by a sense of separateness, as expressed in their use of the term "comrade":

> They do not consider the term "comrade" appropriate in addressing one another or their older fellow workers. . . . The opinion is common among them that this term is to be used only when talking to someone in higher authority.[30]

For decades the term was a bond between revolutionaries in Hungary; they recognized one another by using it. That many young workers no longer consider themselves "comrades," and that for them the term means people in higher authority, is the result of decades of strained relations between blue-collar workers and functionaries. Some blue-collar workers believe they are still being discriminated against for the benefit of other social strata. A Csepel iron works worker declared, for example, that the factory's managers favored white-collar workers over blue in the distribution of benefits, such as available apartments. A conversation between him and a reporter went this way:

> Reporter: . . . and the firm does not give you an apartment? After all, it is a large firm . . .
> Worker: It sure is, but it does not. I haven't yet seen a blue-collar worker who was given one . . .
> Reporter: And wouldn't they even encourage you? The trade union, or . . .
> Worker: They do encourage me but the apartments go to the technicians.[31]

A change in cultural and educational opportunities for workers in Hungary undoubtedly occurred in the 1960s. Many large firms now establish workers' clubs where entertainment, sports, and educational opportunities are available.[32] However, social mobility has slowed considerably. While a relatively large number of workers were promoted to positions of authority after 1948 (although seldom into positions of real political power), by the 1970s the requirements of modernization, which places a premium on higher education and technical training, tended to reduce the promotion opportunities for blue-collar workers. Furthermore, their children are now finding serious obstacles in the way of upward social mobility. According to the 1963 census, it was five times more difficult for children of blue-collar workers to acquire a university education than for the children of white-collar workers and intellectuals.[33] In all probability, this ratio has worsened in the 1970s because of the increasingly more complex, modernized social and economic processes.

Modernization in Hungary in the 1950s was paid for largely by the peasants and industrial workers. The loss of trust in government policies, the feeling of being once again left out of the process of sharing in the nation's wealth, disillusioned many blue-collar workers. Together with many peasants, blue-collar workers once again consider themselves the exploited masses, whose labors serve the interests of a new bourgeoisie.

THE BOURGEOISIE

If we define bourgeoisie by using Marx's classic view of a class that controls the means of production and, consequently, the political and economic processes, this definition would pertain to the Party apparatchiki, the privileged officers of the coercive arms of the state, the industrial managers, and a group of people standing apart from all of the above. The first group I would describe as the power bourgeoisie; the status of its members is determined by their relations to the higher bureaucratic institutions.

The members of the Hungarian power bourgeoisie pride themselves on being the guardians of political power, and they are unquestionably loyal to the ideals of the Communist Party. But some of their attitudes resemble those of the prewar gentry. Many are convinced that they possess an infallible guide to the future in Marxist theory and therefore are destined to lead the nation. They believe the rest of the population is not in a position to judge if they are right or wrong, which tends to breed contempt toward the common people.[34]

The number of the Hungarian power bourgeoisie is probably between 75,000 and 100,000 heads of households.[35] They have a vested interest in the status quo; they are, in the 1970s, a conservative class. Intolerant of political opposition, of "Western" music and abstract paintings, which they consider signs of decadence, they dislike avant-garde theater and long-haired youth. They are convinced that they are better Hungarians than the rest of the population and that they must guard the state against corruption by "outsiders," namely, all those outside their rank.[36] The characteristic attitudes of the Hungarian gentry in the interwar years would parallel many of the traits mentioned above, except Marxist ideology.[37]

The other segment of the Hungarian bourgeoisie I would label privateers, for they have little to do with political power. They exist—and prosper—because the socialist bureaucracy left a vacuum in certain areas of the national economy that must be filled if essential services are to be available. In most cases, these people are able to use existing laws for their benefit; their considerable wealth is, therefore, well protected unless the state decides that they are no longer needed. This is, however, unlikely to happen in the 1970s.

This segment of the Hungarian bourgeoisie numbers several tens of thousands of families. Their methods of acquiring wealth are often simple and would not raise an eyebrow in nonsocialist societies. For instance, an "organizer" with relatives abroad received several pieces of machinery for his own use over a period of time. (In all probability the machinery consisted of knitting machines that could be obtained cheaply in Western Europe and do not come under heavy duty in Hungary.) He then recruited factory workers, paying them better wages, and set them up in small shops. He arranged business deals, obtained raw materials, and collected payments. He was not officially the owner of the 25 to 30 shops that he organized; they operated as "craftsmen's collectives" so the "arranger" had no heavy taxes to pay the state. Consequently, his yearly income was about $100,000.

Others are not so squeamish about skirting the edges of laws. For instance, a pensioner bought apartments and inhabited houses for very low prices. Hungarian laws prohibit raising rents or expelling tenants. Such real estate, therefore, is practically valueless on the market and sells at low prices. However, the new house-owner usually informed tenants that their furnace was too old-fashioned and would have to be replaced. His workmen then dismantled the furnace; months went by and no new furnace was installed. By early winter the tenants were desperate and moved out at the first opportunity since they did not want to freeze to death. Now the house could be sold for a premium price and it was not difficult to find eager buyers who were willing to fix the furnace themselves. With such tricks the man collected hundreds of thousands of forints a year, without the authorities' intervention.[38]

Many in the Hungarian bourgeoisie are quite aware that (apart from those who openly defy the system) they are fulfilling a vital role in the national economy and that the state has a stake in their continued operations. Thus, they are not afraid of showing off their wealth. One reportedly bid top prices for paintings at an auction and counted money out of a briefcase; afterward he admitted that he wanted to show that he had plenty of money left. Others buy automobiles and other consumer goods and brag to their acquaintances. They also show a vulgarity in taste that recalls the nouveau riche in other societies.[39]

Private firms established by Hungarian bourgeoisie include small trucking concerns, stores that can be visited only by appointment (usually for foreigners only, featuring exquisite antiques), and small shops maintained by traveling salesmen. The salesmen also sell their wares at the regular fairs in the countryside, usually merchandise produced in "craftsmen's collectives" mentioned above. This segment of the Hungarian bourgeoisie, therefore, has established a comfortable existence and is not very different from similar classes in other modernizing societies.

SUMMARY

Hungarian society in the 1970s is more complex than it was during the interwar years. The major consequence of modernization is the enormous increase in the number of people earning their living in industry and the availability of consumer goods for all segments of the population. The social and occupational distribution of the population have been fundamentally altered; Hungarians in general live better than in the interwar years. But many values and attitudes from the past have been carried into the present. In some cases peasant groups used modernization to serve a rigid caste system that survived from another era; in others, old attitudes survived in new institutions—thus, attitudes that characterized the gentry of the interwar years reappeared among the power bourgeoisie.

It seems that social evolution in modernizing Hungary has its own dynamics. This often brings surprising results that are not always consistent with the desires and theories of social engineers.

NOTES

1. Cyril E. Black, Dynamics of Modernization: A Study in Comparative History (New York: Harper and Row, 1973), pp. 7, 21-22, discusses these indicators and includes among them urbanization, industrialization, and the diminishing differences between various social strata and the sexes.
2. See Miklos Gabor, ed., Hungary 73 (Budapest: Zrinyi, 1973), pp. 68-76. See also Ivan T. Berend and Gyorgy Ranki, Hungary: A Century of Economic Development (New York: Barnes and Noble, 1974), pp. 210-46.
3. For the problem of women's equality in modern Hungary, see Egon Szabady, "A nok helyzetenek hehany problemaja," Tarsadalmi Szemle 22, no. 4 (1967): 66-78; Magda Bronner, "A diplomas nok helyzete a gyogyszeripari kutatasban," Valosag 17, no. 2 (1974): 89-97; Katalin Sulyok, "Van-e a noknek szabad ideje?" Kortars 18, no. 4 (1974): 816-25.
4. For the collapse of the social structure of the 1930s and the subsequent changes in society, see Joseph Held, "Notes to the Collapse of Hungarian Society between the Two Wars," in Man, State and Society in East European History since the Renaissance, ed. Stephen Fischer-Galati (New York: Praeger Publishers, 1971), pp. 274-81.
5. See Mrs. Aladar Mod, ed., Tarsadalmi retegzodes Magyarorszagon (Budapest: Kozponti Statisztikai Hivatal, 1966), pp. 19-20.
6. Daniel Hatvani, "Egy eletforma szethullasa," Valosag 17, no. 11 (1974): 34-44.
7. See Gyorgy Berkovits, "Atmeneti telepules," Valosag 17, no. 11 (1974): 45-54.
8. Gyorgy Berkovits, "Nagykozseg gyarakkal, Dunakeszi," Valosag 17, no. 1 (1974): 73-84.
9. See Hatvani, "Egy eletforma," pp. 35-36.
10. Ibid., p. 35.
11. Ibid., p. 36.
12. Ibid., p. 43.
13. Ibid., p. 44.
14. According to the report of Jozsef Fekete and Gyula Pocs, more than 1.2 million peasants lived in isolated single-family dwellings in Hungary in the early 1970s, amounting to 34 percent of all wage earners in agriculture. Of these people, 6.7 percent were illiterates and

only 0.5 percent received a college education. See "Tanyavilag es ifjusag," Valosag 13, no. 7 (1970): 99-104.

15. The two most widely acclaimed works published in the 1930s were those by Gyula Illyes, Pusztak nepe (Budapest: Nyugat, 1936), and Imre Kovacs, Nema Forradalom (Budapest: Cserepfalvi, 1937); they discussed the life of the people of the isolated dwellings in often dramatic ways. See also Zoltan Szabo, A tardi helyzet (Budapest: Cserepfalvi, 1937); Peter Veres, Falusi Kronika (Budapest: Magyar Elet, 1941).

16. Antal Vegh, "Alloviz," Valosag 11, no. 4 (1968): 41-53.

17. Fekete-Pocs, "Tanyavilag," p. 101.

18. Gabor, Hungary 73, p. 13.

19. As compared to 41,224 in 1930. See Tibor Huszar, "Gondolatok az ertelmiseg szociologiai jellemzoirol es fogalmarol," Valosag 15, no. 2 (1972): 1-22. Huszar reports that of the half-million white-collar workers in industry, 32,165 are industrial engineers, 87,618 are technicians, and the rest work in lower and middle managerial positions and as clerks and semiskilled office helpers.

20. Sandor Somogyi-Toth, "Illusztraciok," Kortars 18, no. 8 (1974): 1325-26.

21. See, for instance, Arpad Thiery, "Portre-vazlatok egy kozseg ertelmisegerol," Tarsadalmi Szemle 22, no. 12 (1967): 77-86; Mihaly Sukosd, Ertelmiseg a kuszobon (Budapest: Gondolat, 1971).

22. Ferenc Baranyi, "Estek a verandan," Kortars 18, no. 7 (1974): 1143.

23. Laszlo Siklos, "Pazarlo ertelmiseg?" Kortars 18, no. 7 (1974): 1153.

24. The disputes over nationalism and the differences between this ideology and "socialist patriotism" opened in 1963 and have not yet ended. One of the best summaries of the disputes is Laszlo Peter, "Magyar nacionalizmus," in Eszmek Nyomaban (The Hague: Mikes Kelemen Kor, 1965), esp. pp. 218-24.

25. See Karoly Nagy, "The Impact of Communism in Hungary," East Europe 18, no. 3 (1969): 16-17.

26. Gabor, Hungary 73, p. 69.

27. See Zoltan Sztaray, "A magyar munkas utja a forradalomig," Szemle (Brussels) 3 (1961): 15-34.

28. See Ivan T. Berend, Gazdasagpolitika az elso oteves terv megindulasakor, 1948-1950 (Budapest: Kozgazdasagi es Jogi, 1964), pp. 97-126.

29. The literature about the role of Hungarian blue-collar workers in the events of 1956 is not very extensive, although each of the hundreds of volumes published on the revolution usually contains a section about the workers. Perhaps the best of these is a joint work: Tamas Aczel and Tibor Meray, The Revolt of the Mind (London: Big Ben,

1959). See also Gyula Borbandi and Jozsef Molnar, eds., Tanulmanyok a magyar forradalomrol (Munich: Aurora, 1966).

30. See Ferenc Bako, "Szakmunkastanulok erkolcsi fogalmai," Valosag 17, no. 5 (1974): 58. See also Mrs. Robert Kiss, "Munkasfiatalok kozott," Tarsadalmi Szemle 22, no. 6 (1967): 70-78.

31. Miklos Munkacsi, "Munkasok kozott," Kortars 18, no. 2 (1974): 308.

32. Istvan Agh and Istvan Balla, "Dunaujvarosi munkasok," Kortars 18, nos. 3,4 (1974): 475-84, 636-47.

33. See Mod, Tarsadalmi retegzodes, pp. 78-82.

34. See, for instance, George Heltai, "Some Thoughts on the Structural Changes in Hungarian Society since 1945," The Review (Brussels) 1, no. 4 (1960): 1-15.

35. The Hungarian statistical office, naturally, does not publish data about the number of secret police officers or officers in the armed forces, who would be included in this category. The total number, therefore, is necessarily speculatory.

36. See Aczel-Merey, The Revolt, pp. 102-04.

37. See Held, "Notes," pp. 304-05.

38. See Lajos Mesterhazi, "A gyerek es a furdoviz," Uj Iras 14, no. 1 (1974): 81.

39. Mesterhazi, "A gyerek," p. 80.

CHAPTER

7

DICTATORSHIP OF THE PROLETARIAT: A SLAVIC MODEL FOR THE NON-SLAVIC WORLD
Lubos J. Hejl

This essay seeks to dig out of Slavic experience some facts of real life that—when properly interpreted by means of theory—may be interesting even for the non-Slavic world. It deals with the Czechoslovak 1945-48 dictatorship of the proletariat (Marxist style), investigating mainly its power-status implications. The model of the dictatorship of the proletariat (DP), which I developed in 1969 on the basis of the Czechoslovak experience, was successfully tested by the Chilean events of 1970-73. The analogy of the Chilean narrative with the Czechoslovak experience of 1945-48 proved striking, despite the cultural differences between a mostly Slavic country and a nation south of the Andes.

Three periods of Czech postwar history fully support—each in its particular way—my thesis on the highly unstable character of the dictatorship of the proletariat:

1. The 1945-48 period, displaying "malignant growth" toward "dictatorship over the proletariat" (DOP).
2. The Czech Spring of 1968, featuring the "benign growth" of the DP, that is, development toward a pluralistic society.

This essay was written in late summer 1974. The contemporary developments in Portugal, especially after March 1975, may make the study even less academic. It represents a partial result of research made possible by a grant from The American Council of Learned Societies for summer 1973. The author expresses his thanks to Gary Francione, a student at the University of Rochester, for language and terminology editing.

3. The 1968-69 period, presenting a decelerated replica of the 1945-48 development, the second round of the "malignant growth," this time triggered by the Soviet invasion of August 1968.

This study deals only with the first case; reasons for this choice will be obvious immediately.

First, the Czechoslovak 1945-48 period will be described and analyzed. Then, after the period has been identified as the first DP organized in a politically and economically advanced country, the model of DP will be developed and causes of its built-in instability will be explained. Later, the process of malignant growth of DP into DOP, as observed in postwar Czechoslovakia, will be briefly described. Finally, the model will be tested against the Chilean developments of 1970-73.

THE CZECH REVOLUTION OF 1945: ESTABLISHMENT OF DP

The abrupt power change in Czechoslovakia in 1945 was, at the time, described as a "national-democratic revolution." This term, however, did not fully correspond to reality. The label originated in tactical political considerations and was excessively dependent on the forms this revolution assumed at the beginning. It started with the national resistance of Czechs and Slovaks against the rule of a foreign and totalitarian—that is, nonliberal and nondemocratic—regime. By its content, and over time this content grew steadily more apparent— this national-democratic revolution soon became a proletarian revolution and the power-political condition it created became a dictatorship of the proletariat.

The content of the dictatorship of the proletariat has undergone exhaustive changes during the past hundred years. It therefore needs clarification (the technical details are presented in the Appendix to this essay). Here it should suffice to say that the term is used in Marx and Engels' sense. According to them, a dictatorship of the proletariat, whether installed by force or through parliamentary democratic machinery, does not exclude broad suffrage even if this suffrage is limited to the "working class"; nor does it intend to abrogate freedom of speech for citizens possessing full rights, nor to preclude a representative government even if this rests on a narrow base limited by the revolution to "first-class citizens." However, this interpretation of the dictatorship of the proletariat has been almost forgotten.

The deviation from the original concept came about primarily by associating the term with the events that occurred in Russia soon after the October revolution of 1917. In March 1921 the dictatorship of the proletariat of the immediate post-October period was replaced by the authoritarian rule of the Central Committee of the Party. Its transformation into an oligarchic rule and later into an undisputed autocracy soon followed. These circumstances were responsible for the obvious change in connotations traditionally associated with DP.

Several facts confirming the interpretation of the Czechoslovak revolution of 1945 as a proletarian revolution come to mind. This list helps to clarify the concept of DP:

1. During the partisan and liberation struggle on the territory of Nazi-occupied Czechoslovakia, newly formed local bodies of administrative power—the so-called revolutionary national committees—took over the exercise of power from the fighting men while the old government machinery disintegrated. After 1938 this machinery had been usurped by the Nazis and partially compromised, as is well known.

2. The Kosice program of the new Czechoslovak coalition government, returning to Prague from Moscow and taking over the administration of the liberated territory from the Soviet Army or the Czechoslovak Army Corps, contained a large number of definite nationalization demands. These demands were tactically and skillfully associated with the call for punishment of treason and cooperation with the occupying power.

3. The coalition created in Moscow under the name of the "National Front of Czechs and Slovaks" included representatives of political forces acceptable only to each other. This coalition was an exclusive political club in spite of having broadly based support among the Czechoslovak people. Political parties allegedly or actually resisting the socialization program were not granted membership in the National Front. After the liberation, therefore, their activities were considered illegal by all the parties of the front.*

---

*So, for example, the Agrarian Party, for twenty years (1918-38) an influential political force in the Czechoslovak republic, was excluded from the coalition upon the suggestion of the communists. Other parties concurred, believing naively that each would gain a large share of the agricultural vote traditionally belonging to the Agrarian Party. Such political disqualification was made relatively easy by the alleged affiliation of this party with the Nazi power, especially at the beginning of the occupation, 1939-45.

4. Nationalization decrees (October 1945) of the president, which put into effect some of the demands of the Kosice program, expressed the will of the popular masses. They legally sanctioned the actual status quo: the control of large key industrial enterprises, transportation, banking, and mineral resources by the revolutionary workers' bodies.

5. The first stage of nationalization was effected by presidential decrees, that is, by executive power and not by an act of parliament. This is relevant although the decrees were signed by President Benes only under much pressure from the communist-led wing of the government and were actually the result of a complicated immediate postwar situation. Marx in his time extolled the merger of the executive and legislative powers when equating the Paris Commune with the dictatorship of the proletariat; the decrees signed by Benes expressed a similar fusion of power in Czechoslovakia of 1945. The club of political parties governing Czechoslovakia in 1945-48 assured this merger even in daily political life. It is interesting to note that communist and procommunist propaganda saw in this merger of executive and legislative powers (especially at the level of local government bodies, called "national committees") a significant new characteristic of the so-called people's democracy. This propaganda focused on the fact that in postwar Czechoslovakia the people's organizations not only formulated but also carried out the law. In this one saw its "people-oriented" character.

6. With the exception of the political exclusivity of the competing political parties, completely democratic elections were held on May 26, 1946, to elect deputies to the highest legislative body of Czechoslovakia, the National Assembly. From these first postwar elections the Czechoslovak Communist Party emerged as the strongest party, gaining 114 out of 298 seats (about 38.4 percent). Together with the Social Democratic Party and the National Socialist Party, it constituted more than a two-thirds majority.

All these facts confirm the overwhelmingly proletarian character of the revolutionary changes, that is, an orientation toward the redistribution of property, income, political influence, and social prestige for the benefit of wage earners in towns and the countryside.

Additional facts attest that the new Czechoslovak revolutionary government must be described as a dictatorship of the proletariat. Antisocialist or anti-Soviet propaganda was unthinkable, not only because of the pervasive political mood but also due to government control of newspapers and radio and to preferential allocations of newsprint.* The economy was under state control, partially reflecting the relics of the wartime economic management. The bourgeoisie was paralyzed by the harsh judicial revenge for cooperating with the Nazis (although that cooperation had often been imposed by Nazi terror), severely crushed by nationalization and workers' participation in the management of enterprises, and terrified by covert activity of the Czech and Slovak organs of the Soviet political police, which functioned at the time as a permanent warning rather than as a direct executor of arbitrary coercion. The warning was delivered mostly through acts against Soviet political emigres living in Czechoslovakia, perpetrated by the Soviet security forces immediately after liberation, that is, before the departure of the Red Army at the end of autumn 1945.

The proletarian character of the revolution, triggered by the fall of the German Reich and the proletarian character of the government created thereafter, is also demonstrated by the slogan "people's democracy," which appeared immediately after liberation.† I call it a slogan because the term "people's democracy" was not specifically defined until the end of 1948. In December of that year, the Bulgarian communist leader Georgi Dimitrov presented the following, later almost obligatory definition: "'People's Democracy' performs the function of the dictatorship of the proletariat."[1] In 1945 this slogan had a powerful appeal to the working population. They saw in it a new reality, fulfilling their prewar and wartime socialist hopes as well as the manifestation of their increased social prestige. The effort to differentiate the new regime from the so-called bourgeois democracy of the pre-Munich republic of 1918-38 was strong. Only tactical reasons dictated by the short-term program for the takeover of monopolistic power by the Communist Party prevented calling the situation by its true name: dictatorship of the proletariat. Later the Party could not easily justify the political and existential‡ destruction,

---

*Political periodicals could be published at that time, as after 1948, only by political parties and social organizations sanctioned by the National Front. Thus, political parties rather than the government controlled the media. Here we have not a monopolistic but an oligopolistic rule, including effective measures against the entry of other "producers."

†The fact that the official daily newspaper of the Czechoslovak Popular Party, which was close to the Roman Catholic Church, was started immediately after the liberation of Prague under the new heading People's Democracy belongs to the ironies of political life.

‡In Central Europe this term connotes the destruction of an individual's monetary possibilities through termination of employment and confiscation of all property. In addition, exclusion from housing often follows.

not to mention the physical liquidation of its socialist opponents, if dictatorship of the proletariat, fully in harmony with Marx's concept, should be identified with a political situation in which the Communist Party had to curry the favor of the working-class electorate. Such a political situation developed, however, in Czechoslovakia in 1945-47: the communists had to compete for the attention of the voters.

One more interesting circumstance must be noted. After February 1948 the Communist Party never admitted, not even during the self-criticism of 1968, that it seized power in 1948 by a putsch or any other unconstitutional means. It always insisted upon the continuity of the working-class rule already established in 1945. After 1948 the political apparatus of the Party and the state deprived the working class of Czechoslovakia, and in essence before 1951 even the rank and file membership of the Communist Party, of any control over the government. Yet this defense of an undemocratic seizure of monopolistic political power contains a grain of truth. During the period between 1945 and 1948 the working class, as well as small peasants and tradesmen, and the socialist-minded majority of the creative intelligentsia, were a decisive force and did rule Czechoslovakia. The remnants of the bourgeoisie were on the defensive. Nationalized property was safe from any effort to return it to private ownership. A thorough agrarian reform in a country with a long tradition of voluntary agricultural cooperatives created conditions for social reconstruction of the Czech village. A large majority of the population sincerely sought to develop a socialist economy.

Despite all the facts offered thus far, I do not yet consider fully proven the thesis that the revolution of 1945 installed in Czechoslovakia a dictatorship of the proletariat in Marx or Engels' sense. Only a return to the letter of the classical authors can confirm this. It is necessary to clarify in detail what Marx and Engels understood by dictatorship of the proletariat.

This is done in the Appendix. Its basic findings may be used here as follows: Marx's concept of dictatorship as a special power-political condition of society may be applied to the Czechoslovak political situation between 1945 and 1948 because Marx and Engels did not consider the dictatorship of the proletariat to be either a one-party political monopoly or a total concentration of economic power in one ruling organ.

Further, the political system in existence in Czechoslovakia in 1945-48 was the first dictatorship of the proletariat in Marx's sense of the term established in a politically and economically developed country, the Czechoslovak revolution of 1945 being the first proletarian revolution in a developed country to survive for more than two and a half years to the full extent of its original revolutionary base. Spontaneity of mass support gave this base its wide scope. Revolutionary nationalization was welcomed by a large majority. The strength of their support should not be discounted because the revolution was derived from the official doctrine and military victory of the Soviet Union. Nor should it be diminished because Marx's ideals were already completely perverted in the Soviet Union.

In brief, the DP was established in Czechoslovakia under almost ideal conditions. This is why the three years of the postwar history of a small European state become so important for the verification of Marx's entire theory that the proletarian revolution serves as a tool for the liberation of man and the formation of a classless society.

MODEL OF THE DP

Marx used the term "dictatorship of the proletariat" (DP) for what he planned and expected to be a democratic republic. Dictatorship of the proletariat is therefore interpreted as a misnomer, fully in line with the traditional conviction that democracy and dictatorship are incompatible, even mutually exclusive. However, the contradiction of the label can be easily overcome if we try to understand by dictatorship not government by decree (tyranny, despotism, autocracy and Caesarism, Fuhrerism, authoritarian government)[2] but what Marx probably had in mind: another specific state of power in human society, characterized by strong government (DP) that expropriates the expropriators, drastically changing the social structure.

I am not trying to simply define away one of Marx's problems. Therefore, even those who cannot fully accept the nontraditional definition of dictatorship to follow should try to do so temporarily, for the sake of argument; the results may be interesting. Having explained one of Marx's most controversial concepts, I shall show the built-in tension and instability of the power condition called dictatorship of the proletariat. This instability has relevant implications for real life. The revolutionary leaders, even if acting in good faith when making statements about their readiness to continue democratic procedures, wage an uphill struggle after seizing power. They cannot overcome, with the best intentions, the weakness of Marx's utopian solution called DP. The Czech Gottwald and the Chilean Allende learned this rather soon after their political triumph.

Besides our traditional treatment of dictatorship as government by decree, it is the "classical doctrine of democracy" (Schumpeter's term) that makes for the conflict. The emotional overtones, a consequence of the philosophical enrichment of democracy by elements totally unrelated to its substance, also helped to form the idea that democracy and dictatorship are incompatible. Thus, we shall have to redefine dictatorship, and at the same time realistically view democracy, in order to eliminate the incompatibility.

Let us start with the term "totalitarianism." I regard totalitarianism as the opposite of liberal teaching.[3] Liberal philosophy (such as Hayek) maintains the existence of a certain protected sphere of inalienable individual rights that cannot lawfully be abrogated by the state even when the common goals are involved, and that must be protected against interference from others. There are apparent exceptions in time of war, but these are only seeming exceptions because then the individual sphere is threatened even more significantly by the enemy. Naturally, the general view of what properly belongs to this sphere can change over time. Proof of this is development of liberal philosophy itself, starting with the Old Whiggism of the seventeenth century and ending with the contemporary neoliberalism, culminating in the most elaborate summation thus far by Hayek.[4] Nevertheless, recognition of the existence of the protected individual sphere is basic to the teaching of "paleoliberalism"[5] as well as neoliberalism.

This concept of totalitarianism differs from the current understanding of this term in the sense of a totalitarian state. However, it provides suitable means for delineating the term "dictatorship."
To summarize: Totalitarianism is a political conviction denying the existence of the protected individual sphere.

Let us now define the term "dictatorship." Dictatorship is here understood to mean the application of totalitarianism in political practice. Dictatorship is therefore a condition of society where, besides citizens who are "protected" (those enjoying a certain safety of the protected sphere), there exist "fair game" citizens whose protected sphere either does not exist (an especially drastic form of dictatorship) or is recognized and safeguarded to a much lesser degree. It does not matter how exclusive the power base in whose name the supreme holders of power implement the political doctrine of totalitarianism. What does matter is the size of the group of citizens to whom the government denies the real protection of the protected individual sphere. The larger the relative number of "fair game" citizens in a given country, the greater the extensity of dictatorship. The intensity of dictatorship is greater when the protected sphere is smaller. A simultaneous increase of both the extensity and intensity of dictatorship may be called the hardening of dictatorship.

The protected sphere has a practical significance in human life: It is of basic importance to the preservation of human freedom. However, this sphere is not synonymous with private ownership, and definitely not with the ownership of the means of production, even though private ownership plays a definite and important role. The above definition of dictatorship is somewhat unusual, for it does not stress government by decree. It is, however, extremely useful. We realize that the elements of dictatorship (as defined) can exist even under a democratic government: Lynch mobs in America are a classical historical example. However, only when dictatorship reaches a certain extensity (and intensity), and when it is associated with completely undemocratic political procedures, does it create the pernicious political system of modern history known as the totalitarian system.

Let us remember that the extensity and intensity of dictatorship may vary greatly. In one case, the "protected" citizens may be outnumbered and their "protected" sphere may be insignificant. In contrast elsewhere, the "fair game" citizens may be few and they may lack protection only in marginal aspects of life.

Let us now proceed to the concept of democracy. I conceive of democracy in Schumpeter's sense, as convincingly defined in his Capitalism, Socialism, and Democracy, chapters 21 and 22. There are several reasons why I consider his definition justified. One is his criticism of the weaknesses of the traditional so-called classical doctrine of democracy.

Against the criticized concept of democracy, stressing "will of the people" and "common good," Schumpeter juxtaposes a new definition. He does this even though he is aware of the prosaic sense and "godlessness" of the suggested definition, and of the quasi-religious and nationalistic associations that the classical concept of democracy evoke. According to Schumpeter, "The democratic method is that institutional arrangement for arriving at political decisions in which individuals acquire the power to decide by means of a competitive struggle for the people's vote."[6] Let us note: no will of the people, no lack of "common good"; however, also no protection of the minority,[7] no automatic guarantee of freedom of the individual, no self-understood general suffrage,[8] no unlimited rule by the absolute majority. I do not deny that democracy aids in realizing some of these values; nevertheless, it cannot be either described by them or identified with them.[9]

Our inquiry into the relationship between democracy and dictatorship may be minimized. Dictatorship and democracy are not mutually exclusive, since democratic processes can function under a dictatorship. Specifically, political competition can function in spite of the fact that the society includes people whose protected sphere is not fully safeguarded. In such a case, it is highly probable that democracy functions only within a narrow power base of the first-class citizens, those possessing full rights. However, it does not imply that all the second-class citizens (citizens deprived of influence in the selection of the supreme holders of power) must belong to the group of "fair game" citizens.

As an example, we can refer to the Swiss female citizen living in a canton where women have no local voting right: her protected sphere is fully safeguarded, even though she is a second-class citizen. In other words, she is free although she does not enjoy equal political rights. Moreover, her freedom aids her in gaining more political freedom (rights). Thus, recently all Swiss women won the right to elect national (Confederation) organs.

Another, somewhat more complicated example can be found in the Czechoslovak political situation of 1968. It demonstrates once more that the "fair game" citizens and the "second-class" citizens do not have to be the same group.

Thus, democracy and dictatorship are not mutually exclusive. However, if present in society simultaneously, they do not exist as two independent elements of the political system. It is here that the causes of instability of even democratic dictatorships lie. An overly restrictive democratic competition creates conditions for increasing the extensity of the dictatorship and may even increase its intensity. On the other hand, it is clear that an especially extensive and intensive dictatorship can transform the democratic competition slowly into an oligopoly or destroy it by transition to a monopoly, if I may use economic terms. (An authoritarian regime is, then, a "full monopoly" as contrasted with the democratic system.) The expression "totalitarian democracy"[10] should not be considered an intellectual extravagance but, rather, a serious danger to be constantly fought in even the most democratic society.

The dictatorship of the proletariat may now be defined. DP is a dictatorship that includes within the group of the protected citizens (persons whose protected sphere is fully safeguarded and respected) only members of the proletariat.

This definition has several advantages. First, it overcomes the sharp conceptual conflict raging in 1918-19 between Lenin and Kautsky because it leaves open the power base problem and does not attempt to solve the problem of the breadth and intensity of democratic procedures functioning upon the given power base. (In particular, it does not prescribe the extent of suffrage in a dictatorship of the proletariat.) Second, it draws attention to the circle of "protected" citizens and to the dynamics of this circle, with the attendant danger that it will become smaller and smaller during the revolutionary cycle. Third, this definition agrees completely with the concepts of Marx and Engels: It respects the basic function they ascribed to the dictatorship of the proletariat. This function was without doubt "the expropriation of the expropriators."

One more point should be stressed: Dictatorship of the proletariat is a power-political condition of society; it is not a problem of the social and property structure. Dictatorship is an instrument for change in the economic and social structure of society; it is not a definite phenomenon of this structure.

The substance of DP being clear, we may now look at Marx's postulate and expectation of a democratic dictatorship of the proletariat. He expected DP to be democratic because it was to appear first in developed countries, that is, in countries with a strong industrial proletariat, educated and politically experienced through decades of class conflict and even war. He demanded a democratic DP to start the process of mankind's final liberation. The instability of Marx's DP lies in its substance, the demand to restructure society through confiscation of the means of production, because even in the most developed countries the concentration of capital has not advanced enough to polarize society into masses of wage earners on the one hand and a handful of exploiters on the other. There remain, even in the most developed industrial countries, too many small businessmen and self-employed people who will not support the revolution. In addition, too many other people are not ready to support the revolution because of ideology (which is not dead!), personal antipathies and sympathies, and sometimes even convictions about the necessity for loyalty to their own past.

The basic problem is the conflict between the demands of a "strong government" changing the foundations of society through total "expropriation of the expropriators," and the demands of the population to keep democratic procedures alive. The more thorough the effort to restructure the property system, the narrower becomes the base of revolution on which the democracy may rest. The narrower the base, the greater the chances for hardening of the dictatorship. The more hardened the dictatorship, the narrower the basis of crumbling revolutionary support; that is, the less democracy even the most determined revolutionary leadership can afford. A snowball process may be started, stopped only when totalitarian conditions have been reached.

Special dangers emerge in countries where the proletariat is relatively small in numbers. Only the proletariat, which represents a small portion of the population, is treated as "protected." Under these conditions, the contradictions in the model of a proletarian dictatorship as conceived by the classics become even more apparent. The tension (which causes the instability of the power state of a proletarian dictatorship even in a highly industrialized country with a large number of wage earners) reaches such heights in an industrially underdeveloped country that the malignant growth of a dictatorship of the proletariat to a "dictatorship" over the proletariat becomes a very great threat.

SEIZURE OF MONOPOLISTIC POWER: FROM DP TOWARD DOP IN FEBRUARY 1948

On the whole, the Czechoslovak development followed the pattern of "malignant growth" just explained. The Soviet model of society forcefully fostered by the Communist Party of Czechoslovakia (CPC) lost much of its attractiveness in 1945-47. Decrease in the communist-inclined electorate, suggested by a 1947 public opinion survey, reflected a similar shift. These changes were taking place within the broad prosocialist base of the 1945 revolution, but were interpreted by partisans of the Stalinist creed, probably quite sincerely, as threats to the gains won by the working class.

The international situation toward the end of 1947 clearly did not help to prop up the stability of the Czechoslovak DP. In September 1947 Andrei Zhdanov proclaimed publicly Stalin's thesis of the division of the world into two hostile camps. Amid the rising wave of postwar Stalinism inside and outside the Soviet Union, far-reaching decisions were made (or, more correctly, a binding consent was given by the CPC leadership) to prepare for the monopolistic seizure of power in Czechoslovakia. The decision to go ahead with this plan was, of course, aided tremendously by assurances of Soviet support. The results of this action and the ease with which they were achieved were, however, due to domestic conditions (the case of Finland supports my thesis sufficiently). The power-state of the DP proved extremely unstable.

The takeover of monopolistic power by the Czechoslovak Communist Party in February 1948 is regarded in the West as a well-organized coup d'etat, successfully carried out by a militant minority. In contrast the official communist interpretation has not changed: that February 1948 marked the averting of a putsch by bourgeois forces hiding within noncommunist parties of the governing coalition, the so-called National Front of Czechs and Slovaks.

In truth, the putsch of February 1948 was not really an ordinary coup. It constituted a radical decrease in the number of citizens whose protected sphere would be assured by the government. Thus, there was a sudden increase in extensity of the proletarian dictatorship. It was a fatal increase. The "imported" Stalinist political climate took care of the intensification of the dictatorship: Suddenly human life was considered less significant in the political struggle.

For many people, all this was the logical continuation of the 1945 revolution and represented only a radical change in political structure. Later developments in the 1950s and in 1968 have shown how many people took an active part in 1948 in liquidating freedom in Czechoslovakia, wrongly believing that they helped to bring freedom to the masses. They were ready to accept the increase in extensity of the dictatorship, although less ready to accept its greater intensity, which was manifested in police terror, torture of detainees, political trials. This was understood to be the "consummation of the revolutionary process." They were ready to accept the destruction of the democratic process inside the revolutionary movement, and later within the victorious Party. This was interpreted as increase of "revolutionary discipline." The ideological factor played a strong role. But it was the institutional changes brought into the traditionally liberal-democratic Czechoslovak system, by establishing the DP of 1945, that prepared the ground for the fatal process, which began in 1948. There are not many "checks and balances" to stabilize the DP.

February 1948 can be regarded unequivocally as the beginning of the transformation of the dictatorship of the proletariat into a dictatorship over the proletariat.[11] Not only was there a radical decrease in the circle of citizens whose protected sphere remained safeguarded but the broad power base of the Czechoslovak revolution of 1945 was restricted. This process is typical for any postrevolutionary period. Nevertheless, it should not be omitted; it is intrinsic to the development that I call the "malignant growth" of the DP.

To summarize: When in February 1948 the Czechoslovak Communist Party seized absolute political power, allegedly in the interest of the proletariat, a process was started that totally enslaved the proletariat itself within a few years. However, the malignant growth of the dictatorship of the proletariat has tragic consequences for the entire society. All segments of society fall into deep bondage; even the nonproletarian, nonbourgeois elements, such as self-employed peasants, are affected. The historical role of the proletariat is thereby paradoxically fulfilled. According to the classics the proletariat, by liberating itself, liberates the entire society; the same happens in case of enslavement.

TESTING THE DP MODEL: CHILE, 1970-73

The Chilean developments of 1970-73 can be seen as completely analogous to the 1945-48 period in Czechoslovakia. The Chilean case is the second classical example of the establishment of DP in an economically and politically developed country—the level of development to be viewed, of course, from the point of view of Marx's insistence on an achieved level of industrialization and democratic procedures deemed necessary for a successful DP. The Chilean DP of 1970-73 proved to be a highly unstable system, just as the Czechoslovak case of 1945-48 was.

One remark is appropriate here. In considering the instability of the Chilean system I, of course, do mean somewhat deeper problems than the truckers' strike of 1972, for example. Phenomena of this type were mere reflections of the underlying tensions. The psychological prop received by the Chilean military from without— the CIA involvement, the American intervention, if of any substantial nature—cannot be blamed for the instability inherent in Allende's DP model. What is more important here is the relative lack of participation of Soviet neo-Stalinist forces in Chilean developments after 1970. The Chilean communists, probably under Moscow's directives, behaved in a very restrained way, as compared with, for example, the excesses in the countryside. This notwithstanding, the malignant growth of the DP developed nicely anyway.

The Soviet influence on the 1945-48 development in Czechoslovakia, as well as the U.S. impact on the Chilean case, cannot be negated. But the model of DP is a model for the real world, not for social experimentation in a political vacuum. Therefore, outside factors have to be taken into account. If they contribute to the instability of DP, the worse for DP —and Marx! In addition, the outside influence in both cases molded the outcome of the 33 to 34 months of malignant growth rather than the growth itself.

As stated, the Chilean DP proved highly unstable. Its unavoidable development through the malignant growth toward DOP was stopped only by the military coup of September 11, 1973. The malignant growth feature of DP has thus been confirmed in a non-Slavic milieu. The internal contradiction of the system of DP proved stronger than any cultural differences; the challenges in transforming the property structure of the Chilean society inside an overall nondiscriminatory democratic framework proved extreme.

On August 15, 1973, approximately one month before the military coup, I wrote:

> The conflict within the democratic model of the dictatorship of the proletariat is demonstrated fully in Chile. The political convulsions of the years 1972-73 express the instability of such a power condition. The radical elements forced a systematic broadening of the "unprotected" group. The maintenance of democratic competition (i.e., the method utilized to reach important political decisions), based upon a system that does not discriminate and includes all citizens, is becoming more and more difficult. First-class citizenship—still inclusive when regarded from the formally legalistic point of view—has not been thus far threatened in Chile. . . . The fact that . . . competition has thus far not changed to a political oligopoly shows—at least as I see

it—that President Allende tries not to liquidate this competition. Economic stagnation and a serious inflation are until now the main price paid by Chile for experimentation with the stability of the political system. It is interesting to note that even in Chile the original size of the group of "unprotected" citizens has changed. Together with foreign citizens (above all U.S. property owners), numerous if not all Chilean owners of the means of production have been affected. The "unprotected" sphere was until now only the sphere of private property rights. The future will show whether further hardening of the dictatorship . . . is inevitable.[12]

The Chilean military was obviously persuaded that the development—which I called hardening of the DP—was really inevitable. This is why they went ahead with their coup.

The buds of the malignant growth toward the DOP were clearly identifiable in Allende's Chile.[13] His attempt to change, by a constitutional amendment, the parliamentary system into a unicameral body and control it by a governmental majority was one. A replica of one Paris Commune feature, very much applauded by Marx, was being prepared: a strong government representing the fusion of legislative and executive power. (The abolition of the upper chamber of the Czechoslovak Parliament, the Senate, was one of the first demands of the communists, agreed upon by the exile coalition government long before the 1945 liberation.)

In August 1971, Allende's government attempted to buy out the remaining private sector of the paper industry; the suspected motivation was to gain control of the newsprint supply. (The danger for the free press was obvious, and the Czechoslovak experience after 1945 may serve as a warning.) By January 1971 Allende proposed—as part of the "reorganization of the judicial system," one of the Popular Unity program planks—the establishment of "neighborhood tribunals." Two locally elected officials from "labor or social institutions" and one government-appointed member were to be given the power to mete out sentences up to one year of "rehabilitative labor." (Experience with the neighborhood courts type of justice in countries establishing the DOP totalitarian system has been rather sad.) Much of the confiscated farmland was not distributed among individual peasants, and legal titles were withheld by the government. (Preparation for future collectivization of agriculture, an important elements of concentration of economic power, was suspected by the opposition.)

Unwittingly, as reported by Paul E. Sigmund, the "Lawyers' Association" of Chile identified the basic contradiction of DP, although exclusively on the legalistic level of analysis and without having the

DP model in mind.[14] Their declaration, issued toward the end of August 1973, asserted an "incompatibility between the institutional framework within which he [Allende] is supposed to exercise his office and the actions which he feels obliged to carry out in his program.

The Chilean right allegedly was afraid of the DP. If this was the case, it gravely misunderstood what the nation was experiencing. Chile of 1970-73 was already going through the DP. The dangers the Childean nation faced were dangers of the malignant growth into the DOP, into a neo-Stalinist regime. Allende's error, for which he paid with his life, was not this or that policy mistake or omission. It was much more serious: he did not draw the lesson from the East European experience of the post-World War II period. He took Marx and Engel's model too seriously, without identifying its intrinsic tension—which, again, proved stronger than the best motives and wishes. His "second model" of Marxism was a classical DP; he personally proved weaker than the dynamics of societal power. This all holds even if we—unlike his opponents—give Allende the benefit of the doubt, accepting at face value his statements about permitting democracy to survive in Chile.

Even the timing confirms my thesis about the instability of the DP. In Czechoslovakia the clash between the forces of DOP and their opponents, noncommunist though mostly socialist, took almost 34 months. In Chile—counting from November 3, 1970, the day of Allende's inauguration, to the day of the coup, September 11, 1973—the DP lasted 34 months and a few days. The instability of the DP simply "asks" for decision by means of a clash. (Of course, any future DP won't necessarily last exactly 34 months.)

There were other elements of striking similarity. For example, the Chilean Radical Party repeated the part the Social Democrats played during the Czechoslovak DP period. They first supported the DP regime, then split, realizing the dangers, and later tried to save what could be saved. The problems the DP poses are identical; the societal responses, therefore, are very similar.

In both cases, as already mentioned, foreigners were the first to become "fair game" people. Foreign owners of nationalized companies, mostly U.S. citizens and institutions, were the first to be denied full protection of their rights. The lack of protection related, however, only to property and only to foreigners, so the nation could applaud. Similarly, in Czechoslovakia of 1945, the millions of Sudeten Germans expelled from the country were only foreigners, although Czechoslovak citizens. The resentment due to atrocities committed by the Nazis in occupied Czechoslovakia may explain the attitude toward this expulsion. It should not, however, cover the facts.

The role of the military is another example that supports my comparability thesis. In Czechoslovakia the army was "neutralized"— partially by geopolitical considerations of the senior officers, partially by personnel policy (the 1948 minister of defense, L. Svoboda, was president of Czechoslovakia in 1968-75). In addition, the Czechoslovak army was educated in the spirit of not intervening in domestic political struggle; its record of 1918-38 was clean on this point. Nevertheless, there was an abortive attempt to organize a coup in 1948. Part of the hesitation of the Chilean army has been explained by a similar tradition, despite its political involvement in the 1930s.

SUMMARY

This essay has sought to prove that the system of political power called "dictatorship of the proletariat," conceived by Marx and Engels as a reliable tool for achieving a classless society through expropriation of expropriators, is a highly unstable system. The dictatorship of the proletariat was planned to be both democratic and discriminatory. The tension resulting from these postulates is the cause of instability. Most of the phenomena of malignant growth toward dictatorship over the proletariat observed during the 1945-48 Czechoslovak development could be later identified, mostly in nucleus form, in the second case of a classical DP: Chile of 1970-73. They were:

1. Tendency of the unprotected ("fair game") citizens to grow in numbers.
2. Tendency of the revolutionary power basis to crumble, increasing the number of "second-class" citizens in the population.
3. Tendency toward stronger and stronger executive control or efforts to control the legislature.

The primary reason for the failure of the DP to achieve the classless society without becoming totalitarian lies in a basic flaw of Marx's anticipated development of "capitalism." The concentration of capital, expected by Marx, did not advance enough, either in 1945 or in 1970, to polarize the developed societies into a mass of wage earners on the one hand, and a handful of exploiters on the other. Thus, the dangers inherently present in the DP model proved very strong in both Czechoslovakia of 1948 and Chile of 1973. In Russia after 1917 they were even stronger from the very beginning, for the number who (at least originally) were protected among the proletariat was negligible.

APPENDIX: DICTATORSHIP OF THE PROLETARIAT

In 1847 Engels attempted to clarify for the first time the meaning of DP. He declared that the socialist revolution would create "above all a democratic form of government and thus directly or indirectly the political rule of the proletariat."[15] The Communist Manifesto of 1848 talks about "seizure of the political power by the proletariat." Two well-known quotations from Marx claim:

> the class struggle necessarily leads to the dictatorship of the proletariat; and . . . this dictatorship itself only constitutes the transition to the abolition of the classes and to a classless society.[16]

> Between capitalist and communist society lies the period of revolutionary transformation of the one into the other. Corresponding to this is also a political transition period in which the state can be nothing but the revolutionary dictatorship of the proletariat.[17]

Most important, because of its concrete terms, is the example of the Paris Commune, which Marx saw as "the political form at last discovered under which to work out the economic emancipation of labor."[18] Engels is even clearer: ". . . the Paris Commune. That was the Dictatorship of the Proletariat."[19]

Using the historical example of the Paris Commune, only the following characteristics of the dictatorship of the proletariat could be accepted as indisputable: (1) the revolutionary political rule of the proletariat; (2) democratic form of government; (3) transition to a classless society in the transition from capitalism to communism.

What can be gained from the identification of the Paris Commune with DP? The following characteristics are emphasized by Marx:

> The Commune was formed of municipal councillors, chosen by universal suffrage in the various wards of the town, responsible and revocable at short terms. . . . The Commune was to be a working, not a parliamentary, body, executive and legislative at the same time.[20]

It is a historical fact that only about one-fourth of the usual number of voters took part in the elections on April 6, 1871. Many citizens either moved or simply did not cast their ballots because they were politically intimidated. Thus, although there are additional reasons, it is possible to agree with Trotsky that "the Commune was the living negation of formal democracy."[22] Nevertheless, elections of the representatives took place and were not a farce with a prearranged ending. Democracy in the Paris Commune actually functioned on a narrow base, while discriminating against those who did not vote; the representatives of the people were, however, elected and not co-opted.

The transition in the conception of what constituted usable power tools in the period of the dictatorship of the proletariat occurred during Lenin's lifetime. When he spoke in April 1917 about the dictatorship of the proletariat, he stressed: "There is no police, no army standing apart from the people, no officialdom standing all powerful above the people."[23] Several months later (August-September), he wrote in State and Revolution: "The 'special repressive force' of the bourgeoisie for the suppression of the proletariat . . . must be replaced by a 'special repressive force' of the proletariat for the suppression of the bourgeoisie (the dictatorship of the proletariat)."[24] The course of the repression is clearly set. The guarantees were not investigated. We can assume that laws were Lenin's guarantees (the repression of the bourgeoisie would have to be insured by discriminatory or so-called revolutionary laws, but laws nonetheless).

The change took place in the whirlpool of revolution. Before November 10, 1918, Lenin wrote in answer to Kautsky's work, The Dictatorship of the Proletariat,

> Dictatorship is rule based directly upon force and unrestricted by any laws. The revolutionary dictatorship of the proletariat is rule won and maintained by the use of violence by the proletariat against the bourgeoisie, rule unrestricted by any laws.[25]

Here, in this program of political arbitrariness, is the seed of all later development, culminating in 1921 in the establishment of the definitive dictatorship over the proletariat.

Let us now quote very briefly from the important controversy between Kautsky and Lenin concerning Marx's conception of the term "dictatorship of the proletariat."[26] Kautsky differentiated between dictatorship of the proletariat as a "political condition" (Zustand der Herrschaft) and dictatorship of the proletariat as a form of government (Regierungsform): "Dictatorship as a form of government means disarming the opposition, by taking from them the franchise and liberty of the Press and combination."[27]

In one sense Kautsky's vision of DP was somewhat black and white. He insisted on universal suffrage under DP. This provoked Lenin; he thought Kautsky denied the Russian proletariat the right to revolution, because of Russia's industrial underdevelopment.

To summarize: DP in the vision of the classics had to be a strong government "expropriating the expropriators" and combining executive and legislative powers. Democratic voting procedures should be continued, although on a narrow power base of proletarians. In my opinion, these are the two characteristics permitting the interpretation of DP as Kautsky's "political condition" rather than "form of government."

NOTES

1. Pravda, December 27, 1948.
2. International Encyclopedia of the Social Sciences, (New York: Macmillan and the Free Press, 1968), vol. 4, p. 162.
3. See F. A. von Hayek, Constitution of Liberty (London: Routledge and Kegan Paul, 1960), p. 103.
4. Ibid.
5. See R. Dahrendorf's lecutre in Was heisst Liberal (Basel: Friedrich Reinhardt, 1969), p. 71.
6. J. Schumpeter, Capitalism, Socialism, and Democracy (New York: Harper and Row, 1972), p. 269.
7. See, for example, Karl Kautsky, The Dictatorship of the Proletariat (Manchester: The Nation Labor Press, n.d.), p. 53: "under [democracy] minorities are . . . protected."
8. For the self-evidence of general suffrage, see ibid.
9. For example, the "Declaration of the Socialist International" of 1951 testifies to the vitality of the classical conception of democracy; see its Article I.3. Reprinted in M. Salvadori, ed., Modern Socialism (New York: Walker, 1968), p. 283.
10. See, for example, Jacob L. Talmon, The Origins of Totalitarian Democracy (London: Secker and Warburg, 1952); or chapter 14 of B. Jouvenal, Du pouvoir: Histoire naturelle de sa croissance (Geneva: Editions du "Cheval aile," 1945).
11. This expression—"dictatorship" over the proletariat— was used very soon after the October revolution of 1917 by T. G. Masaryk, first president of the Czechoslovak republic. J. Schumpeter employs this term, too, although in a somewhat different sense emphasizing its microeconomic aspect: "dictatorship not of but over the proletariat in the factory" (Schumpeter, Capitalism, p. 302).
12. See Lubos G. Hejl, The Road from Serfdom (forthcoming).
13. In this section I rely rather heavily on the information, although not the analysis, supplied by Paul E. Sigmund in his two Problems of Communism articles: "Chile: Two Years of 'Popular Unity,'" 21, no. 6 (November-December 1972): 38-51; "Allende in

Retrospect," 23, no. 3 (May-June 1974): 45-62.

14. See Sigmund, "Allende in Retrospect," p. 59.

15. In addition to the original sources, I used Wolfgang Leonhard, "Sovietsystem und demokratische Gesellschaft," Eine vergleichende Enzyklopadie, Band 1 (Freiburg-Basel-Vienna: Herder, 1966), pp. 1260-76.

16. "Brief an Joseph Weydemeyer vom 5 Marz 1852," in Marx and Engels, Selected Works in One Volume (New York: International Publishers, 1968), p. 679.

17. "Critique of the Gotha Party Programme" (1875), in ibid., p. 331.

18. "The Civil War in France," in ibid., p. 294.

19. "Introduction by Frederick Engels" to Karl Marx, Civil War in France (1891), in ibid., p. 262.

20. "The Civil War in France," in ibid., p. 291.

21. Roger L. Williams, The French Revolution of 1870-1871, (New York: W.W. Norton, 1969), p. 132.

22. Leon Trotsky, The Defense of Terrorism, ed. by H. N. Brailsford (London: Labor Publishing Company, 1921), p. 74.

23. "Letters on Tactics," First Letter; in V. I. Lenin, Collected Works (London: Lawrence Wishart, 1960-70), vol. 24, p. 46.

24. V. I. Lenin, State and Revolution (New York: International Publishers, 1932), p. 17.

25. V. I. Lenin, The Proletarian Revolution and the Renegade Kautsky (Peking: Foreign Languages Press), 1970, p. 11.

26. Kautsky, Dictatorship of the Proletariat; Lenin, The Proletarian Revolution. Kautsky's work was published first in Vienna in 1918; Lenin's work was written in the fall of the same year.

27. Kautsky, Dictatorship of the Proletariat, p. 45.

PART II
CENSORSHIP

CHAPTER 8

SOVIET PUBLIC COMMUNICATIONS IN THE POST-STALIN PERIOD
Gayle Durham Hannah

In a discussion of political communications in the Soviet context, one deals more with a Leninist model than a Stalinist one; it is from this perspective that the post-Stalin period should be viewed. Lenin's theories on the press were an integral part of his overall organizational strategy, and by implication and application they have been extended to other channels of information and socialization. They are still very much the basis for the organization and operation of the Soviet mass media and agitation-propaganda network. This early Bolshevik legacy has been quite noticeable in word-of-mouth patterns and underground communications as well. In the process of consolidating power and eliminating almost all opposition, Stalin naturally devoted a good deal of attention to channels of political communication, for through them an opposition group might express its views, try to crystallize public opinion, and mobilize support. His contributions to the nature of public communications reflected primarily his personal leadership style and overall goals rather than a specific strategy aimed at the media and official personal channels.

The most significant change that has occurred since the death of Stalin is the elimination of large-scale terror in society as a whole; naturally, this has affected the communications environment. Nevertheless, it is important to note that terror as a political weapon has never been discredited and it has frequently been used, albeit selectively, in the regime's efforts to inhibit the development of an oppositional or alternative communications network seeking to compete with the legitimate system. Limited terror is still very much a part of the public communications scene, more than in other areas of Soviet life.

Post-Stalin official Soviet public communications channels are still considered primarily ideological weapons with essentially the same purposes as before 1953: to convey Party directives and supply information on selected domestic and international political events; to disseminate the Party's interpretation of those events to officials and the public; to promote the acceptance of Party policies among the population; to mobilize the population for the implementation of policies; to transmit a small amount of information useful for everyday life (broadcast media schedules, weather forecasts). Most of these have a socializing function, promoting the legitimization and smooth operation of the political system.

While the public network has remained essentially the same in function, there have been some significant changes. These may be categorized as: (1) policies that have emerged as the result of direct, intentional elite initiative and (2) those that have been primarily responses to apparently unanticipated developments in the environment created by the intentional innovations.

CONTINUITIES IN PUBLIC COMMUNICATIONS

Before discussing the two types of policy changes and their implications, it will be useful to note certain basic features of the Leninist-Stalinist model that are still evident. The most significant is the continued importance of the network of official communications as the organizational axis for a highly politicized society. The media and agitation-propaganda apparatus are monopolistic and highly centralized, with control exercised by the Party at all levels. Second, this network is extremely bureaucratic and hierarchical. The Party's monopoly on organization, with a visible, stable, self-perpetuating apparatus, facilitates control over economic and technical resources, personnel, news sources, and a well-developed coercive organization for backing up persuasive techniques. Since the Party relies for its legitimacy on a systemic world view, the content of public communications is heavily prescriptive; news is interpreted so that the audience is clued in to the politically acceptable response. As the nerve structure of the Party, the communications system simultaneously transmits both esoteric messages to Party functionaries and exoteric communications to the public at large. The system also combines impersonal (mass media) with personal (the agitation-propaganda network) channels. The two are well coordinated and complementary. The official personal system has long been used to minimize uncontrolled interpersonal behavior and was a keystone of Stalinist control over the development of opposition. The flow of content is primarily from the top downward. There is some bottom to top "feedback," but this is selective and, again, highly controlled by the Party. Horizontal communications among groups and individuals below the elite level are severely restricted so that crystallization of opinions not centrally approved is prevented.

Obviously, this system is part of the authoritarian tradition, in which the state ranks higher than the individual, the apparatus is hierarchical, and the source of truth is restricted.[1] During the second half of the eighteenth century this view of public communications lost some popularity in the West; it was replaced by the libertarian notion that communication should serve the individual rather than the state, offer diversity rather than uniformity, contribute to change as well as continuity, and should have every right (even duty) to criticize the government in power. The official Soviet system of communication has been challenged in recent years by an assortment of dissenters who are, for the most part, adherents of the libertarian tradition[2] long accepted, if imperfectly achieved, in the West. This is why their underground communications system is such a fundamental challenge to the Soviet system.[3]

CHANGES IN THE POST-STALIN COMMUNICATIONS ENVIRONMENT

Considering the original intent of the regime, there are two major categories of change with regard to public communications. First, there have been dramatic and important changes instituted by the leadership as part of its overall political strategy. Second, policies initiated by the elite have created an environment in which unanticipated and undesired consequences have forced the adoption of policies in response to citizen-initiated behavior.

The most obvious change is the tremendous growth in the accessibility of the media. This "communications explosion" has meant an increase in technological capability and a message-spreading capacity far beyond that possible at the time of Stalin's death. The following figures illustrate the change:[4]

	1952	1959	1970
Copies of newspapers per issue (mil)	42	62	141
copies per 100 people (ages 10-69)		40	97
Total radio sets (mil)	17.5	53.9	94.8
per 100 people (ages 10-69)		34	60
Wired radio speakers (mil)	11.7	29.2	46.2
per 100 people (ages 10-69)		19	29
Wave radio sets (mil)	5.8	24.7	48.6
per 100 people (ages 10-69		15	31
Television sets (mil)	0.1	3.6	34.8
per 100 people (ages 10-69)		2	22

The Soviet audience has experienced a change from predominantly collective exposure to private access to the media. This has had several implications. The timing and nature of exposure to the media has been more flexible. One can read or listen at almost any time in the privacy of one's own family or friendship circle; the often unwanted interpretation of news by the official Party agitators usually present at collective readings or listening sessions is avoided. People can now share their private (sometimes unorthodox) reactions with others of similar opinions without official observation. Obviously, such communication among potential or actual skeptics might strengthen the development of interpretations other than what the Party is promoting. It also means that the function of propagandists and agitators, who had previously extended the scarce media (for example, by reading newspapers aloud during the lunch break at work), has been reduced to mere interpretation of the news, often to a more sophisticated and less interested audience. More private media exposure in a somewhat freer atmosphere also has increased opportunities for listening to foreign radio. A rising standard of living allows more people to buy the short-wave sets that best receive foreign broadcasts.

Official policy also has relaxed controls in certain areas. Jamming of foreign stations has been reduced, and for some has ceased altogether at times during the last decade. Consequently, the Soviet audience has had much greater choice of news sources. After being trapped in a relatively closed system and then allowed access to alternative, sometimes anti-Soviet viewpoints, the Soviet audience underwent important changes in awareness and expectations.

Greater access to Western sources of information and values has not been limited to foreign radio, of course. Printed materials, foreign tourists, Western journalists, all became more evident in European Russia and sometimes even made their way to Siberian cities. For a time Soviet publication of translated foreign-language (non-Soviet nationalities) belles lettres increased in volume. [5]

There is no way of knowing how many people who spoke other languages could obtain foreign literature through informal channels, but it is likely that they had greater access in the early and mid-1960s. During certain periods, handpicked Soviet tourists were permitted to visit East Europe and the West, although almost always with secret police surveillance. After the invasion of Czechoslovakia (1968), such travel was restricted considerably. These temporary contacts with the West brought increasing awareness of other values, worldviews, political norms. The rapid changes in the outside world were disseminated through official and nonofficial channels and dovetailed with the rapid and radical internal political changes that occurred during this time.

While the population became more exposed to both Soviet and Western media and contacts, and needed to rely less on the agitation-propaganda system, the system of Party schools producing speakers for that network was being diluted. During the late fifties and early sixties, the Party turned away from strict indoctrination of members for propaganda work and toward mass political education. This means that, while greater numbers of people were involved in Party education work, there was also less control over the operation by the elite, and therefore less orthodox presentations of the Party line through official personal channels. There was a tremendous increase in the number of students enrolled (from 6.2 million in the academic year 1957-58 to 25 million in 1964-65), and a simultaneous rise in the proportion of students who were not members of the Party (from 15 to 78 percent).[6] There was a shift away from the study of fundamentals of Marxism-Leninism; in 1963-64 less than a third of students were studying Party history, political economy, and philosophy, and younger people in particular were avoiding these subjects.[7]

Immediately after the ouster of Khrushchev, the new regime set about putting Party education "on a solid ideological foundation." Following a reorganization of the ideological apparatus,[8] the number of students registered dropped to 12 million and of these 75 percent were members or candidate members of the Party.[9] (By 1971 the total enrollment in Party education had increased to only 16 million.[10]) However, the slackening of discipline in Party education had already had its effect; people no longer felt such great pressure to attend political meetings, both because they could obtain their information directly from the media and because there was less emphasis on ideological purity in the propaganda apparatus. For outside events, even the elite sought and openly referred to foreign radio as a source of information. The Brezhnev-Kosygin team rapidly moved to correct what they saw as a dangerous laxity related to liberalization in Czechoslovakia. They feared "contagion" from East Europe, especially because Soviet intellectuals were following events there with great interest and referring to them in domestic ideological disputes. Pressure to attend political meetings was increased with the ideological campaign that began in March 1968; by this time speakers were much more orthodox in terms of Party affiliation and training than they had been under Khrushchev.

The development of sociology during the post-Stalin period significantly changed the communications environment by contributing to the open expression of political dissent. Public opinion polls, especially those conducted by the youth newspaper Komsomolskaya Pravda, made a great impact, especially among young people. By asking people what they thought, the polls helped to legitimize public opinion in contradiction to Leninist theory, which holds that the Party elite should lead the masses. While the polling techniques were unsophisticated at first, the net effect was to make people feel that their opinions, even less orthodox ones, were in some sense legitimate and worthy of consideration. Many of the poll results were not published, largely due to a publishing bottleneck that was most severe in the social sciences but also in part because many results did not confirm official mythology about Soviet society and the state of mass consciousness. Even among the published polls there were some obvious gaps between official myths and expressed opinions. [11] Some of these discrepancies had to do with attitudes toward the mass media. [12]

A significant amount of sociological research was carried out by centers on behalf of central newspapers and television stations in large cities. [13] Audience studies showed that people had rather serious complaints about the type and quality of news broadcasts. [14] There was a noticeable lack of enthusiasm for articles about economic life. Readers indicated they wanted more and better international news and greater attention to items relating to their personal lives: moral themes, practical information, consumer services. [15] Television, although considered by the regime primarily a didactic medium, was seen by the audience first of all as a means of entertainment; this gap in conception naturally led to a good deal of frustration at the programming. A study of the Tallin (Estonia) television audience indicated that, given a choice when seeking political news and commentary, the audience turned first to Finnish television, then to Estonian, and last to Moscow Central in Russian. [16] Intellectuals watched Finnish television more than any other group.

One of the most noteworthy features of the post-Stalin period, and one that has received too little attention in this context, is the return to civilian life of millions of former political exiles and inmates of prisons and labor camps. The significance of the dispersion of this group among the population is twofold. First, there has been a direct confrontation by the population in general with experiences of friends, relatives, and acquaintances who had disappeared. Perhaps more than all the official changes in the Party line during the post-Stalin period, the return of these people to tell the tale has most affected the legitimacy of the regime. These returnees also have spread among the population some of the political culture of the camps, especially communications skills useful in carrying on underground activities. [17] Facing these people has made it more difficult for the average Soviet citizen to dismiss questions about the integrity and legitimacy of the leadership. It has also given some people the sense that they have the duty to dispute the Party's interpretation or to speak out on political matters; the elite is no longer seen as infallible.

Increased leisure time also has been an important factor in changing communications behavior. With less time spent on political meetings, more access to the media, and the shortening of the work week in the early 1960s from six to five days, people have been able to engage in activities that are less political in content. A recent book on Party propaganda lamented the fact that most of the free time gained by workers goes not for ideological self-improvement but to such unworthy diversions as playing chess and dominoes.[18] There is much more time for informal discussion among friends and greater access to information providing material for speculation about political matters.

PUBLIC OPINION AND THE ROLE OF INTELLECTUALS

The more open communications environment, allowing for some discussion and crystallization of views other than the official version of reality (at times even an inconsistent official view), has created conditions for the development of what we have come to call public opinion. Hans Speier, in "The Historical Development of Public Opinion," has defined this as:

> . . . opinion on matters of concern to the nation freely and publicly expressed by men outside the government who claim a right that their opinions should influence or determine the action, personnel, or structure of their government.[19]

According to Speier, the existence of public opinion requires: an expectation that the government will publicly reveal and explain its decisions so people outside the government can think and talk about the decisions; that the government not deny the claim that the opinion of citizens on public matters is relevant for policymaking; and that there exists access to information on the issues with which public opinion is concerned. There is a series of implied assumptions about the population as well: that it possesses the financial means and skills for access to the media and that it has sufficient leisure time for discussion. In the Soviet Union today there is mere lip service paid to the above explicit requirements; however, the implied assumptions about the population concerning access and leisure are more true than ever before, especially for a certain broadening segment of the population: the specialists from among whom younger members of the Party elite and intellectuals are recruited. This is what Speier means when he calls public opinion "a phenomenon of middle class civilisation."

In contrast, Leninist theory on public opinion begins with the notion of "class consciousness." This can only be brought to the all-important class, the proletariat, from the outside since workers are imbedded in capitalist society, prey to its pressures, and insufficiently disciplined to develop more than a "trade union consciousness." The tightly organized revolutionary Party, composed for the most part of bourgeois intellectuals, earns its right to educate and lead the proletariat by its mastery of Marxism-Leninism. The Party elite must "elevate the spontaneity" of the masses; rather than merely testing the state of mass thinking, it must propagandize to actively influence it. The Party can learn from the masses in a tactical sense only; it can sense the right timing and form for political action, but does not assume its goals from the population.[20]

Obviously, these two concepts of public opinion are quite different in nature, particularly in the role they imply for the political elite and citizenry. The conflict between the two concepts has been the focus of much debate between the Party leadership and intellectuals, particularly those classified as "dissenters." It is their right to dissent, to create and maintain a public opinion of their own, that dissenters have brought into public focus; this is largely an indirect result of policies such as those we have discussed. Most dissenters, almost all of whom come from the specialist class,[21] point out the need for <u>glasnost'</u> or the open, free dissemination and discussion of ideas. They hope that by raising the informational level of thinking people they will increase a general consciousness of political factors; thus a renascent critical intellectual class or intelligentsia.[22] By emphasizing certain political trends and practices, this group hopes to promote the crystallization of public opinion on certain issues. It seeks to act as an opinion leadership group, coalescing and intensifying pressures growing among other segments of the population. All of this directly challenges the Party's monopoly on opinion leadership as set forth in Leninist theory, and puts dissenters in direct confrontation with the Party's rulers.

It is particularly relevant to consider the role of the intelligentsia within the emerging opinion leadership group. Although the intelligentsia was small in number during the early and mid-nineteenth century, its self-defined role as watchdog and critic of the political system made it influential in bringing about political change. Mainly through literature and literary criticism, it demonstrated that oppressive government could be opposed, albeit not without cost, and that a movement for change could be sustained and strengthened in the face of extreme repression. With increasing sophistication and ruthlessness, combined with the important moral and material assistance it received from outside the country, it played an important role in generating enough discontent and disorganization to undermine an already faltering political system. As victors in the revolutionary struggle, members of the Soviet elite are familiar with the power of underground communications networks and their recognition of the value of public demonstrations in awakening consciousness is based on a long tradition. The profound mistrust and class antagonism of Party bureaucrats toward the emerging critical intelligentsia in the post-Stalin period are part of an old Russian political pattern. Like the old intelligentsia in Russia, this new group is only a thin film on top of society, but like that group it also is nurtured by support from outside.

Moreover, the new more highly stratified class structure of Soviet society works to its advantage. Unlike the polarized class structure of tsarist autocracy, which left the critical intellectuals isolated from the masses, Soviet society is composed of a number of layers through which change may pass with ever-broadening repercussions. Very crucial in this structure is the group of highly skilled and educated people whose talents and training are needed by the nation and who therefore have some resources for bringing pressure on the elite, if they can operate in a cohesive manner.

The rapid development of mass media during the post-Stalin period has made high communications consumers of this group in particular, and because of their professions they are more in touch with the outside world than any other segment of Soviet society (except some members of the Party elite). Many have a working knowledge of a foreign language and some access to foreign printed materials relevant to their work; those who live in European Russia and the science cities come into direct contact with foreign colleagues.[23] They are uniquely qualified to perceive the relative isolation of Soviet society and the gap between reality as experienced in their own personal lives and seen through foreign channels on the one hand, and depicted in the Soviet media on the other. This intensifies a realization of their privileged position in Soviet society as well as a sense of deprivation of information and collegiality that is crucial both in maintaining their professional sophistication and in a realistic appraisal of the world.

Intellectual life is far more concentrated in the Soviet Union than in the West. More attention is focused on fewer cultural and intellectual events; information is spread very swiftly by word of mouth. There also is an unusual intensity of concern about intellectual freedom and professional working conditions. Politically imposed limitations exist because of the Party's concern about the potential development of opposition among intellectuals, but this becomes a self-fulfilling prophecy: It heightens antipathy toward the Party apparatus. It was the Prague Spring that made many intellectuals extremely dissatisfied with their situation by comparison; their frequent references to events in Czechoslovakia helped to convince the Soviet leadership that liberalization there would inevitably lead to serious problems in the Soviet system.

PATTERNS OF COMMUNICATION
AMONG INTELLECTUALS AND DISSENTERS

Soviet citizens use varied means, particularly intellectuals, to supplement the official system of information. We may think of these as a series of concentric circles relative to the central core of dissenters, who have especially urgent information needs not served by the Soviet system.

Intellectuals as a group, particularly the skeptical among them, lead a kind of double life in their communications behavior. They participate extensively in institutional and informal official networks. They have a high rate of exposure to the mass media, yet are most critical of them. The newspaper studies we mentioned earlier show that educated readers in general are "harder to please, more critical, more interested in problems of science and the humanities . . . the more educated are also more critical of newspaper and television materials pertaining to news and national and international issues." According to a Literaturnaya Gazeta readers' poll, those most dissatisfied with "discussion materials" are employees in the government bureaucracy, people in the arts, natural scientists, teachers of natural science, journalists, and professional people—all vitally involved in the social and political system. [24]

While these people seek information from official sources for their professional and personal activities, they supplement this with additional channels. They are among the most active users of "word of mouth." Nadezhda Mandelshtam, writing about the growing repression of intellectual life during Stalin's consolidation of power, called this phenomenon "linguistic dualism."[25] On the one hand, intellectuals are required to praise Party authority and incorporate its political symbolism in their work and professional-social intercourse; but among trusted friends they revert to the everyday language of the intellectual-professional class, speaking without Party jargon and often criticizing official authority. As a recent intellectual emigre put it, "After the Hungarian revolution the rule of the game became clear: you can speak as you like, but in private only."[26]

The extensive use of word of mouth in the Soviet Union has always been important but has assumed particular significance during the post-Stalin period. Subjects that do not illustrate the social and political processes that make up the official mythology are not treated in the media but a knowledge of them may be crucial. Among such subjects are: advance news about the availability of goods in short supply (such shortages are not usually publicly admitted); news of economic failures (bad harvests, scandals); accidents and natural disasters; information about poor living conditions or riots; political jokes critical of the regime; all sorts of political news such as advance warnings of personnel changes, background on political events and personalities, news of spontaneous citizen demonstrations or dissent activities; and information on the coercive apparatus (informers, arrests, punishments, camp conditions, and so on). According to many Soviet citizens, word of mouth is necessary to interpret news from official channels intelligently.

Contrary to popular conceptions about rumor, word-of-mouth information is known to be relatively efficient and reliable. The data reported out of the Harvard Project on the Soviet Social System as well as interviews conducted by a communications project at the Massachusetts Institute of Technology indicate the extensive use and credibility of this channel for most people.[27] Moreover, the fact that it has been deliberately used on several occasions by the Party to spread important and sensitive news would imply that the Party considers it trustworthy; for example, the ouster of Khrushchev was announced and explained only by word of mouth.[28] A group of sociologists in the Siberian division of the Soviet Academy of Sciences studying the readership of Trud (Labor, the union newspaper) in the late 1960s reported that the role of rumor was very active in times of crisis but even in normal times was "quite active." They found that "acquaintances" played a more important part as an information source among the best and worst educated people than among those in the middle.[29]

Different kinds of people use this source in various ways, according to their social and political position. The Harvard Project found that peasants, who are by tradition and experience hostile to the official system, use oral channels as a source for most news. Intellectuals, on the other hand, are closer to official sources but need more supplementary information in order to perform their professional duties and maintain a sensitivity to the political environment. They use word of mouth as an additional source rather than relying on it solely. This pattern seems to have continued and intensified during the post-Stalin period. Educated people are high media consumers in general, but often turn to word of mouth; this is especially true of the substrata called dissenters who, because of their skeptical attitudes and unorthodox activities, need extraofficial information more than most ordinary citizens.[30]

Even used privately, word of mouth can have a myth-busting function, helping to cut through official cant and extract facts from the politically orthodox context. It also produces interference for the official system by introducing more information and interpretation at variance with the Party line. Word of mouth is used heavily for the collection of information for, production, and distribution of samizdat publications, especially the journals that report on dissident activities and official responses. Much information is also transmitted by telephone, a natural extension of the oral network.

For decades foreign radio has been used as a supplement for official Soviet media. From it people can learn not only about things going on in the outside world but about events in their own country by reports sent out by Western newspeople and broadcast over European stations or back into the Soviet Union by special stations beamed at the Soviet audience. Certain stations have taken on the task of reporting to the Soviet population on the activities of dissenters and transmitting underground documents. In this role, Western reporters and foreign radio are for Soviet intellectuals and dissenters a transmission belt to the outside world and to their own cohorts across the Soviet Union, particularly professional colleagues or members of the same ethnic group (some nationalities have been forcibly dispersed throughout the country). Foreign media have thus become not only an alternative to the official network but an extension of the internal Soviet underground communications network. About 34 million Soviet radios can receive these foreign broadcasts on short wave and there are also well over 20,000 licensed (and several thousand more unlicensed) ham radio operators who listen to such broadcasts and pass on information. Most of these seem to operate in the European part of the country. For example, in August 1968, transmitters in the Ukraine informed Soviet troops in Czechoslovakia about the real circumstances and world reaction to the invasion, a view quite different from that presented to them by their commanding officers.[31]

Samizdat

Underground manuscripts circulating in typescript have been named samizdat (short for the Russian words for self-publication). The word was apparently first used in the early 1960s, although it may have existed in very narrow circles earlier than this.[32]

Lenin's own involvement in underground publication led him to form some of his own central organizational theories. He adapted the words of Wilhelm Liebknecht: "teach, propagandize, organize; only a party organ can and must be the central point of this activity."[33] During the early years of the Soviet regime, censorship existed in fact but was not formally reimposed until 1921. With the reinstitution of censorship, poems, novels, stories, and essays began to circulate in typescript. Nadezhda Mandelshtam vividly portrays the culture of this early Soviet self-publication (called "Underwood" after the make of typewriter) and poignantly describes the arrest and eventual death of Osip Mandelshtam for his anti-Stalin poem which circulated only by word of mouth or in private manuscript.

On the whole, post-Stalin samizdat was primarily literary in content at first. Literary intellectuals have a long tradition of using the written word for political purposes and working around censorship by using fables or indirect methods of political commentary. Long before Lenin arrived on the scene, they understood that "ideas are weapons." They also have had to confront censorship in their daily work even if they did not consider themselves primarily political in what they had to say or do. Later, scientific and technical people began to participate in producing dissident publications; one of the most influential was Zhores Medvedev's The Rise and Fall of T. D. Lysenko. Increasingly, political tracts, manifestoes, and reports of political events and trials have been included in the subject matter of underground communications. Dissent periodicals have become more and more important as regular sources of information about literary samizdat, political statements, and dissent activities and official reactions. The Chronicle of Current Events, the most widespread and best known of these, was published from 1968 to 1972, and began publication again in the spring of 1974.

The following list gives some indication of the range and type of materials known to be circulating in samizdat (items may appear individually or in journals):

1. Literary works
    a. Novels, stories, plays, poetry
    b. Memoirs, autobiography
2. News and Reports
    a. News notes on activities and persecution of dissidents at liberty in the USSR and manifestoes of support for the activity from abroad
    b. Stenographic reports and accounts of political events (searches, arrests, demonstrations, trials, meetings, "interviews" with KGB agents, psychiatric procedures, funerals of prominent literary people or dissidents)
    c. Reports from places of confinement: psychiatric hospitals, camps, and prisons
3. Appeals, declarations and letters to officials by dissenters and their supporters in the USSR or abroad
4. Analytic articles and philosophical treatises on various subjects (such as analyses of events in Czechoslovakia and Yugoslavia, the development of dissent, the position of Jews or Crimean Tatars, and so on)
5. Official documents (treaties, declarations, and pacts signed by the USSR, reprints from the RSFSR Criminal Code and Code of Criminal Procedure, texts of secret orders, and so on)

6. Pornography
7. Reviews of samizdat materials such as: collections of reviews of Solzhenitsyn's August 1914 and a review of a samizdat survey of the Soviet press from 1967 to 1971 on the Middle East (Our Middle Eastern Friends, mentioned in Chronicle of Current Events, no. 24) called Confrontation with Oneself (Moscow, 1972), also mentioned in Chronicle, no. 24
8. Miscellaneous
   a. Reviews of Soviet press on particular topics (to give readers some historical perspective on the official treatment of a given subject)
   b. Reprints of old newspaper articles of interest (for example, Julius Telesin mentions in Encounter (note 32) the reprint from Sovetskayaya Sibir' for 1938 of a report of a trial of local NKVD and procuracy officials who carried out repressive measures against 160 children
   c. Lists of cuts made by censors in legitimately published works
   d. Reprints of interesting passages published in legitimate works
   e. Reprints of articles published abroad, especially in Czechoslovakia, such as V. Skutina's "Prisoner of the President" from April 1968 issue of the Czech journal Reporter; for this article the author was persecuted and accused of calling Novotny a "tyrant, a scoundrel, and an idiot" (mentioned in Chronicle, no. 23)

It would be interesting to do a content analysis of samizdat materials and compare it with a similar content analysis of legitimate publications to determine the topics covered in each. We do have available a large number of samizdat publications in the West,[34] and can make some rough guesses at the most important areas of content in underground documents that have reached us. Since, for example, the Political Diary (1961-67) remained almost totally unknown to Westerners until after it ceased publication, it is risky to assume that what we do know of is at all representative. We can tell something about areas of interest, however, by what is available. A rough count of items in the Serial Register of the Arkhiv Samizdata (Radio Liberty, Munich) indicates that most of the material is directed at influencing public opinion or the official representatives of the regime (newspapers, government and Party officials and organs).

Categorizing the same materials by type of content, we find that the overwhelming majority are directly concerned with socialist legality or civil rights; the rest relate to these areas indirectly (against neo-Stalinism, on Czechoslovakia, nonofficial critiques of the socialist system or Marxism-Leninism). Judging by its printed materials, then, Soviet dissent is concerned mainly with trying to establish broader boundaries for the legitimate political culture and is designed to influence public opinion.

How does the samizdat network operate? Usually an author, editor (to whom a manuscript may have been submitted for publication), or friend comes into possession of a typescript. He makes a few copies and passes them on to friends, who either make more copies or find it useful for exchanging for another work in samizdat. Each person who gets a copy makes a few more, and by geometric progression hundreds of copies come into existence. The author of the original manuscript loses control over the number of copies made and no real knowledge of the impact of the work is fed back because contact with the manuscript is lost after one or two links in the chain.

Duplication is still done mostly by typewriter on thin sheets of paper. Photography also is used; since many Soviet people have this as a hobby, it is a useful method. An article in the samizdat journal Free Thought (no. 1, December 1971) extolled the virtues of photography and included detailed instructions on the type of equipment that should be used, price, and where it can be bought. [35] This method is rapid and many copies can be made at once; by contrast, the typewriter can make twelve or so copies, the last few often illegible.

An article by S. Topolev in Free Thought analyzes the disadvantages of the current organization and duplication method of samizdat for the dissent movement. [36] He mentions specifically the problems involved in getting committed, reliable typists; the fact that authors do not get much feedback and therefore have no sense of participation in an intellectual dialogue; and the duplication and scattering of intellectual energies. Storage of samizdat materials is a problem, yet people hoard copies of items they don't need in order to trade them for more desirable manuscripts, so samizdat has become its own kind of barter system. Topolev's solution to many of these problems is kolizdat (collective publishing): uncensored materials printed in journals with regular periodicity and a known list of subscribers, editorial boards, and the use of duplication equipment. The last suggestion is one of the most radical, since such machines are tightly controlled precisely for the purpose of preventing a proliferation of underground material. Topolev calls on scientists and engineers in the movement to solve this problem.

Symbolic Behavior as Political Communication

Public political rituals are patterned symbolic representations of various aspects of a political culture. Parades, Party congresses, and other such displays periodically reaffirm the legitimacy of the regime and its incumbents. The institutionalized roles of citizen and leader, linguistic formulas ("fascist beasts," "socialist legality") and physical representations (pictures of current leaders, military equipment) emphasize mutual expectations so that leaders and population can predict one another's behavior. The habitualization of such symbolic aspects of life to some extent relieves both of them from a continual reassessment of their position as a background to political interaction. In the Soviet Union, manifestations of rules and folkways of politics are subject to a high degree of control because of the high premium placed on citizen conformity and due to regime recognition of the socializing aspects of such rituals. One of the most important aspects of the dissenters' communications behavior is the adoption of public behaviors either at variance with official expectations of the citizen role or, in their more extreme forms, in direct violation of written or unwritten rules prohibiting certain types of communications behavior.

The most active and committed dissenters have adopted the technique of public demonstrations to communicate their views and a rejection of their clandestine status to the population and the authorities. This type of act has been very important in challenging the Soviet official monopoly on the control of public political behavior, pointing out the gap between rights as "guaranteed" in the constitution but in fact inhibited by the regime.

Several other kinds of acts have had great symbolic value since they represent behavior long beyond the pale in the Soviet Union. For example, Andrei Sakharov, at an international genetics meeting in 1970, picked up a piece of chalk and wrote on a blackboard "Academician Sakharov is soliciting signatures for the support of Zhores Medvedev [who had been arrested and incarcerated in a mental hospital several days earlier]."[37] His appeal attracted only a few signatures, but it was an act of unprecedented boldness. Several self-immolations in the Baltic republics, Kiev, and elsewhere surely represent the ultimate in symbolic expression of political views. Large gatherings of ethnic groups (Crimean Tatars in commemoration of the birthday of Lenin, Jews dancing outside the synagogue during a holiday) represent officially disallowed public statements of solidarity and commitment to non-Russian ethnic traditions; most such demonstrations are forcibly dispersed and many participants injured or arrested. The Chronicle, no. 22 (November 10, 1971) reported that on April 29-30, 1971, the yellow and blue flag of the Ukrainian People's Republic of 1917-20 appeared on a water tower in the town of Novy Rozdal.

In comparing the alternative communications network to the official one, its compensatory characteristics stand out clearly. In contrast to the official system, it is pluralistic, since no one person or group assumes the role of ultimate interpreter of the truth. It also is primarily descriptive and interpretive in content, although some political statements do border on the prescriptive. One notable feature of the Chronicle, for example, has been its dry, factual tone— in essence, a stylistic protest against the repetitious exhortations of the official media proclaiming formulalike interpretations. The alternative system is also multiform, employing many different kinds of symbolic and explicit communications to spread information and ideas. Because no one group has power, the network is non-hierarchical, and the flow of information is horizontal among groups and individuals. Within certain groups there may be hierarchical and indeed authoritarian tendencies, but they are not characteristic of the movement as a whole.

All of the forms of alternative or compensatory communications we have discussed play a consciousness-raising role, focusing attention on certain issues and circumstances that most people find more comfortable to overlook. People of like views find one another in such a system, and although they must overcome incredible obstacles to do it, they exchange ideas on political subjects, thereby stimulating analytic and critical thinking about Soviet society. The airing of opinions strengthens them, and common public action bolsters commitment to democratic or other ideas. Finally, the network constitutes a skeletal political organization through which political action not totally controlled by the regime can be initiated.

Perhaps one of the most important functions of the underground or alternative system in the USSR is the selection of content for public attention. Attention in these "media" confers a certain status on people, issues, and events that are not even shadows in the official system. This challenges the focus of the legitimate system by offering role models for a new type of political behavior and bringing attention to issues that have been glossed over or totally ignored throughout the Soviet period. This returns us to our basic point: that the Party's monopoly on what is important and true is challenged.

POLICIES DEVELOPED IN RESPONSE TO THE POST-STALIN COMMUNICATIONS ENVIRONMENT

The regime's direct, intentional policies, mentioned earlier, helped to create a milieu fostering the growth of a genuine public opinion; critical intellectuals have tried to create a particular role for themselves in leading this process. Some of the developments have not been limited exclusively to the post-Stalin period (the extensive use of word of mouth is an important example), but they have assumed special significance during this time. Dissent has become more organized and an impressive underground network has developed; this is inherently threatening to a regime that bases much of its organizational operation on the use of communications channels as a focus for public political life and needs to legitimize itself by a monopoly over those channels. Reactions of the regime have been predictably self-protective.

Word of mouth in the Soviet Union has long been the object of great attention from the security organs. Articles 58 and 70 of the RSFSR Criminal Code were designed to cut down on uncontrolled informal communication among citizens, and Articles 190/1 and 190/3 were added to reinforce the legal justifications for prosecuting people who openly criticize. These are in clear violation of the Soviet Constitution of 1936 (Article 125) guaranteeing freedom of speech, and the Universal Declaration on Human Rights of the United Nations (signed by the USSR). They are, however, consistent with the basic principle of Party organization, "democratic centralism"; since the Party is the model for all organizations and its political norms are the ultimate in operational guidelines, it is not surprising that this discrepancy is not taken seriously by Party officials. As dissenters have made a point of marking the logical inconsistency, officials of the KGB and other government bodies have openly acknowledged that the latter documents are "for people abroad" and not to be taken seriously. [38]

Foreign radio has been a bete noir for the system in its attempts to set limits on the flow of information into the Soviet Union from unauthorized sources. In Stalin's day there was routine jamming of stations considered taboo. In the post-Stalin years, foreign stations became an important, rapid source of information and music for intellectuals and young people in particular. Jamming has been used selectively since the early 1960s. It was ceased almost entirely on certain stations (excluding broadcasts from China, for example) from 1963 to 1968 with partial interference immediately following the ouster of Khrushchev in 1964. In the summer of 1968 jamming was reinstated with the invasion of Czechoslovakia. Recently it was relaxed again except for certain stations specializing in broadcasting news and samizdat to the USSR. There have been many Soviet press campaigns against foreign radio broadcasts, attempting to discredit the sources by disclosing their alleged espionage activities. [39] In 1964 the Soviet station Mayak (Beacon) was started as a rather obvious attempt to compete with foreign broadcasts; it carried news and music around the clock (most Soviet stations at the time did not broadcast late at night, during the peak hours for good reception of short-wave broadcasts from abroad) and broadcast on some of the same wavelengths as foreign stations, thus doubling as a jamming device. Nevertheless, the continued effectiveness of foreign radio as a news source has been so impressive that there have been rather concerted efforts to mount a counterpropaganda operation:

> In order to deeply analyze and more correctly plan all work in the battle with bourgeois ideology and inimical propaganda, there has been created . . . a Public Council on Ideological Problems [in its ranks are fifteen prominent specialists in the field of social science and propagandists]. Relying on the study of bourgeois propaganda materials the council makes recommendations on the thematics of counter propaganda broadcasts. . . . This allowed us to mount a broad counterpropaganda [effort] earlier than the bourgeois radio stations and at the same time <u>prepare listeners for a critical reception of falsified materials broadcast by them.</u> [Emphasis added.][40]

Obviously, Soviet propaganda specialists have become aware of the advantages of preparing the population for information or interpretations contradictory to the Party line. Foreign radio stations have made a clear impact on Soviet radio programming. As the above quotation indicates, they have realized the significance of the primacy effect by which the version reaching the audience first is more likely to be believed. This is one substantial adjustment a formerly closed communications system has had to make to cope with competition from outside.

Newspaper accounts of trials of dissidents are a rather weak means of trying to prepare listeners for foreign accounts of trials. These accounts have been consistently short, misleading, and tendentious in descriptions of the charges, and abusive with regard to defendants. In some cases the coverage has been so inadequate that it has backfired, for readers reasoned that if trial accounts really were aboveboard there would be more specific information.[41]

As the Soviet audience has become more educated and the agitation-propaganda apparatus less effective because of private media exposure and different patterns of leisure time, special attention has been devoted to training ideological workers. More specialized propaganda speakers called <u>politinformatory</u> ("political informers," although they have nothing in common with the usual Western understanding of that term) are trained to deal with people who have been better educated and have greater access to outside sources of information. Soviet media specialists have discovered two important facts about the Soviet audience of the 1970s: (1) it has experienced a rising level of frustration as it has gained access to some, but not enough, outside information, and (2) a two-sided presentation of events is more effective than a one-sided one (characteristic of the Stalin era) when people are better educated and likely to hear the opposite position from another source.[42] Intellectuals have been the particular concern of propaganda specialists, and periodic campaigns to involve them in propaganda work have been noted in the Soviet press; they seem quire resistant to such pressure.

The marked professionalization of Soviet journalism has accompanied these recent changes. Although this might have happened with the proliferation of the media (especially the broadcast media) anyway, it has assumed more importance in the face of competition with professionally trained media people from outside. The Party has needed to train more and more people who not only know how to communicate effectively but also are well schooled in the world view of Marxism-Leninism and can be trusted to put forth the correct interpretation. It also has had to establish an effective means of control over media personnel since they have become so numerous, with the expansion of the technical apparatus. Between 1956 and 1959, a new Union of Journalists was formed; its membership grew from 23,000 in 1959 to 47,000 in 1971.[43] By 1965 more than twenty universities throughout the country were preparing people for careers in journalism, with Moscow University's Faculty of Journalism emerging as the largest and most prestigious journalism school in the country.[44] There are many smaller schools where journalism is taught, and some journalistic training is provided through the Party education network as well.

The rise and spread of an active, organized dissent movement has prompted a number of reactionary responses on the part of the regime. Ordinary citizens are called upon in public meetings to sign petitions or publicly denounce the actions of people about whom they have little or no information except that given them by officials. Campaigns are waged in the agitation-propaganda system against particular individuals, such as Solzhenitsyn (both before and after his departure from the country) or Sakharov. Intimidation of the most active communications leaders takes many forms, including loss of residence permit to live in a major city, loss of union membership or job (this often is simultaneous), various attempts to harass friends and socially isolate people to weaken their views, and finally, the ultimate forms of isolation from society: arrest and imprisonment or incarceration in a mental hospital. In spite of worldwide protests against the use of mental hospitals to control dissent, they are still being used to intimidate even those whose major concerns are not especially threatening in political terms, except in the sense that they feel it important to speak out without sanction and sometimes in the face of official discouragement.[45]

Direct actions against underground means of communications, such as the arrest and imprisonment of people using ham radio stations to pass information on and those involved in the production of The Chronicle of Current Events and its imitator journals, have become well enough known to require only passing mention here. The publicity given thse actions by Western media, and the petitions and press conferences given by Soviet dissenters, have been ways of letting the world know about reactions of the regime and the seriousness with which it takes the threat. Finally, the use of the telephone to transmit information for the underground network has also become the subject of a decree,[46] confirming reports that it was an important link in the information-dissemination system for the Chronicle.

While all these responses have been important, the significance of official silence in the face of repeated petitions to Party and government leaders and organizations should not be minimized. This speaks eloquently of the refusal to allow underground communications, their subject matter and heroes, to enter the legitimate public political culture by dignifying them with direct replies and space in the official media.

CONCLUSION

The basic dilemma facing the Soviet system in the area of public communication is that the Leninist legacy of communications channels as central organization focuses remains basic but exists in circumstances radically different from when it was conceived. The Soviet government is no longer revolutionary, facing the demands characteristic of new political systems; it is one of the two major world powers and therefore must be part of a worldwide communications network in which it holds it own economically, technologically, and culturally. A controlled, authoritarian communications system designed to disseminate a systemic world view and perpetuate a circumscribed political culture intolerant of opposition cannot adapt to a libertarian tradition in which many voices speak, many views are presented, and ideas are forged in public debate. The demand for the latter has become so strong among intellectuals and professionals who possess skills and talents essential to the economy and society that it is hard for the regime to find acceptance for its communications policies among this group. The opening up of the system to outside influences, the need to compete not only technologically but in terms of form and content with sources external to the Soviet system, has intensified pressures not only from critical intellectuals but from a broader segment of specialists as well.

Coming to power on the heels of absolutism and isolationism, post-Stalin leaders have been faced with the essence of political control: how to maintain the basic quality of the system and yet become part of a worldwide communication system geared to a different tradition. Any modern authoritarian government faces this problem, of course, but none so powerful, so competitive, and so ambitious to control the lives of its citizens. Contact with the outside is bound to erode adherence to the basic conceptions of the functions of communications channels. The present regime has had to admit that persuasion has been unsuccessful in the game, and coercion has been necessary. Otherwise, the entire legitimacy of the Soviet system would be undermined. It illustrates the extent to which persuasion backed by coercion is such an integral part of the political system. As we have seen, Khrushchev's policies were relatively liberal and, although inconsistent, generally tended to increase contacts with the outside world and among Soviet citizens with varying political views. Because of the consequences of his policies, his successors have been much more preoccupied with control over these developments and more willing to use coercion in controlling the fundamental challenges to the system.

The question naturally arises as to how long this phase of gradual conservatization will last. Pressures will undoubtedly continue to build among the critical intellectuals even in the face of (and sometimes because of) severe reprisals and political exile. There may be pressure from liberal journalists and writers, but control by professional unions makes this unlikely.

Two points are important to bear in mind. First, whatever pressure comes, the name of the game is not the number of Soviet citizens supporting dissent or making demands for change, but who these people are and what power resources they possess for bringing pressure on the Party elite. Second, what is occurring now is a holding operation at best; leaders are frank about the use of coercion but cautious about the possibility of its spreading and boomeranging. We may expect limited and selected repression in the near future, with some long-range possibilities for liberal evolution, which is by no means inevitable.

The most optimistic view, then, would seem to be that, although there will continue to be restrictions in the short run, the events of the post-Stalin period have had enough impact on the upcoming generation of leaders that they will gradually come to tolerate more and more pluralism. This would mean, however, that they are breaking with Soviet political tradition in the most fundamental way.

NOTES

1. Hans Speier, "The Historical Development of Public Opinion," in Social Order and the Risks of War (Cambridge: M.I.T. Press, 1969), p. 323.
2. This is not to say that they are all liberal in outlook, however. There is an extraordinarily broad range of views expressed, ranging from conservative to liberal.
3. For a more complete discussion of communications theory and its relationship to Soviet dissent, see Hollander, "Political Communications and Dissent in the U.S.S.R.," in The Politics and Ideologies of Dissent, ed. Rudolf L. Tokes (Baltimore: Johns Hopkins University Press, forthcoming).
4. Sources: Broadcast media figures for 1952 and 1959, Narodnoe Khoziaistvo v 1962 godu (Moscow, 1963), p. 422; newspaper figures for those years, p. 604. Broadcast media figures for 1970, Narodnoe Khoziaistvo v 1970 godu (Moscow, 1971), p. 466; newspaper figures for that year, p. 678. Per 100 figures based on calculations from above and census data by age group from: 1959: Tsentral'noye Statisticheskoye Upravleniye pri Sovetye Ministrov SSSR, Itogi vsesoiuznoi perepisi naseleniia 1959 goda (svodniy tom) (Moscow, 1962), Table 12, p. 49; 1970: United Nations Demographic Yearbook, Statistical Office of the United Nations, 22nd ed. (New York, 1971), pp. 398-99.
Note: Per 100 figures are missing for 1952 due to the lack of comparable census data.
5. For all years, Pechat' SSSR v. . . . : table/page, published in Moscow the following year in each case: 1954, 15/57; 1957, 20/89; 1960, 19/85; 1961, 12/39; 1962, 11/43; 1963, 11/41; 1964, 16/49; 1965, 16/33; 1966, 16/33; 1967, 16/33; 1968, 16/33; 1969, 16/33; 1970, 16/33; 1971, 16/33.
6. For a complete discussion of the Party education network to 1967, see Ellen Propper Mickiewicz, Soviet Political Schools (New Haven: Yale University Press, 1967), p. 10.
7. Voprosy Parrtiinoy Ucheby (Moscow, 1966), p. 17.
8. See G. D. Hollander, Soviet Political Indoctrination (New York: Praeger Publishers, 1972), chapter 6.
9. A. Dmitryuk, "Nasushchnye voprosy Marksistko-Leninskoi ucheby Kommunistov," Politicheskoye Samoobrazovaniye 2 (1966): 85.
10. Brezhnev's speech at the 24th Party Congress, Pravda, March 31, 1971, pp. 2-10, in Current Digest of the Soviet Press, CDSP hereafter, 23, no. 14 (1971): 37.
11. To give but one example, a 1964-65 study of people in Gorkiy who had had their children baptized showed that, contrary to the

Party's assumption that unskilled and uneducated workers predominated in this group, 66 percent were skilled workers, the average monthly salary was higher than for most who had not had their children baptized, and the majority enjoyed good living conditions (their own house or apartment). Cited in Ellen Mickiewicz, "Policy Applications of Public Opinion Research in the Soviet Union, The Public Opinion Quarterly 26, no. 4 (Winter 1972-73): 574.

12. For example, Political Diary, no. 63 (December 1969) (an underground journal circulating among elite people) reports that a Literaturnaya Gazeta poll of readers was not published because the results of the study were so displeasing to the editors (A.S. 1010, Radio Liberty).

13. Most of these studies were done by the Sociological Research group under the Siberian Division. For a discussion of these studies, see Mickiewicz, "Policy Applications," and Problemy Sotsiologii Pechati (Novosibirsk, 1969 and thereafter). These sources indicate that the studies, done after the 1964 Party Plenum, were a result of the removal of restrictions on subscriptions to periodicals.

14. For more information on the audience research studies, see G. D. Hollander, Soviet Political Indoctrination; Nils H. Wessell, "The Credibility, Impact, and Effectiveness of the Soviet General Press" (doctoral dissertation, Columbia University, 1972).

15. See the report on the study of the Estonian newspaper Edazi (conducted over a ten-year period) in B. Firsov, "Massoviye kommunikatsiya," Zhurnalist 2 (1967): 50-52. A Literaturnaya Gazeta study showed that readers preferred only two of the topics occupying the most space in the newspaper: sports and trade union work.

16. Rut Karemyaye, "Kak tyazholiye pushki v boiu," Sovyetskoye Radio i televideniye 7 (1967): 30-35.

17. For references to these skills and techniques, see especially: Evgeniya Ginzburg, Journey into the Whirlwind (New York: Atheneum, 1967); Aleksandr Solzhenitsyn, One Day in the Life of Ivan Denisovich (New York: Praeger Publishers, 1963); Meyer Galler and Harlan Marquess, Soviet Prison Camp Speech (Madison: University of Wisconsin Press, 1972).

18. M. Dunchevska, "Svobodnoye vremya i organizatsiya propagandy," in G. L. Smirnova et al., Voprosy teorii i praktiki partiinoi propagandy (Moscow, 1971), pp. 1964-66.

19. Speier, "Historical Development."

20. Lenin, of course, tended to observe an increase in "mass consciousness" whenever people responded to his own propaganda appeals. Alfred Meyer, Leninism (New York: Praeger Publishers, 1962), p. 47.

21. Andrei Amalrik, in Will The Soviet Union Survive Until 1984? (New York, 1970), uses this term, pp. 17-25. See also Hollander essay in Tokes, ed., Politics and Ideologies.

22. Martin Malia, in "What Is the Intelligentsia?", in The Russian Intelligentsia, ed. Richard Pipes (New York: Columbia University Press, 1971), pp. 1-18, points out that there are two overlapping uses of the word: the "critically thinking" segment of the upper class, or those who were actively oppositional. Here, we mean "critically thinking," which by Soviet definition means oppositional because of Lenin's intolerance of sustained criticism.

23. In 1969 over 3000 foreign intellectuals visited Academgorodok, for example. See R. Tanovliy, "The Scientists's Ideological Convictions," Sovetskaya Rossiya, August 28, 1970—CDSP 22, no. 46, (December 15, 1970): 5; Zhores Medvedev, "Secrecy of Correspondence Is Guaranteed by Law," in The Medvedev Papers (London: Macmillan, 1971) for a realistic discussion of scientific correspondence with non-Soviet colleagues.

24. G. I. Khmara, "Pechat' v sistemye massovykh kommunikatsi," Problemy Sotsiologii Pechati 1 (1969): 209-10; and "Literaturnaya Gazyeta i yeyo chitatel'," Problemy . . . 2 (1970): 127-29, both mentioned in Mickiewicz, "Policy Implications." It also should be noted that the second least satisfied group were the workers who, according to the hypothesis of Ellen Mickiewicz, react critically to the discrepancies between their daily lives and the picture of workers' lives depicted in the media.

25. See Hope Against Hope (New York: Atheneum, 1970), p. 89.

26. Yuriy Glazov has called this "behavioral bilingualism." See Glazov, "Samizdat: The Background to Dissent," Survey 19, no. 1 (Winter 1973): 81-82.

27. See Raymond A. Bauer and David B. Gleicher, "Word-Of-Mouth Communication in the Soviet Union," The Public Opinion Quarterly 17, no. 3 (July, 1953): 297-310; for the MIT data, see Hollander, Soviet Political Indoctrination.

28. According to the Political Diary, no. 50 (November 1968) (AS1008), Anastas Mikoyan gave the following account: "When the Khrushchev issue was raised in the Presidium of the Central Committee, twenty-two people spoke in a business-like way, without abuse. Khrushchev defended himself. We did not make public the secret details about all this, not wanting to wash our dirty linen in public and not wanting to exaggerate it. We decided to inform the Party and the people by word-of-mouth." (New York Times, August 22, 1971.)

29. V. E. Shlyapentokh, ed., Chitatel' i gazyeta: Itogi izucheniya chitatel'-skoi auditorii tsentral'nykh gazyet, Informatsionny biulletin' 35 (Moscow, 1969).

30. T. Shibutani, Improvised News (New York, 1966), p. 62. In Shibutani's framework, distortion of messages is not a typical characteristic of rumor.

31. For a discussion of illegal ham stations, see Marianna Buten-Shoen, "Underground Airwaves Flourish Despite Officials' Strong Stand," Springfield (Massachusetts) Union, November 18, 1972.

32. Julius Telesin states that a Moscow poet used the term samsebyeizdat (I publish myself) in the late 1950s and later adopted samizdat ("I myself do the publishing," not necessarily of my own work). "Inside Samizdat," Encounter, February 1973, p. 25. It is an an acronym modeled on Gosizdat, the acronym for State Publishing House for Political Literature.

33. V. I. Lenin, Sochineniye, 4th ed. (Moscow, 1941-52), vol. 4, p. 200.

34. They have been collected by Radio Liberty and are available at several places in the United States and Europe. For a listing of items, see: Albert Boiter and Peter Dornan, The Radio Liberty Register of SAMIZDAT Material, Reference Handbook no. 76, February 1971 (with addenda to March 5, 1972); Albert Boiter, Five Years of SAMIZDAT; A Bibliography, Reference Handbook no. 77 (draft), Munich, April 1971; and Albert Boiter, Serial Register of the Arkhiv SAMIZDATA, June 15, 1972.

35. K. Glukhov, "Photography as a Method of Reproducing Textual Documentation," Svobodnaya Mysl', no. 1 (December 20, 1971), (AS 1180).

36. S. Topolev, "Ot Samizdata k Kolizdatu," Svobodnaya Mysl', no. 1 (December 10, 1971): 6-17. The first two issues of Seyatel' are available in Russian published by Possev Publishers in Frankfurt/Main: Vol'noye Slovo, Samizdat Izbrannoye, Dokumental'nyaya Seriiya, Vypusk 5. The first issue has been translated by Michael and Gretchen Brainerd in Intellectual Digest, January 1973.

37. The incident is described in A Question of Madness by the Medvedev brothers; and in James F. Clarity, "Soviet Dissent Is Not Unified, but It Proves to be Persistent," New York Times, June 14, 1970, p. 1.

38. Glazov reports that when Aleksandr Yesenin-Volpin, who was carrying a banner in the December 5, 1965, demonstration saying "Respect the Soviet Constitution," was asked by the KGB why he did this, he replied: "According to the Constitution, I am guaranteed the freedom to demonstrate." The answer he received was "Aleksandr Sergeevich, we are speaking to you seriously." In another instance, 149 Jews from various parts of the Soviet Union were conducting a hunger strike in the reception room of the Presidium of the Supreme Court (March 10-11, 1971). In answer to the remark that

the Soviet Union had ratified the convention on the abolition of all forms of racial discrimination and thus recognized the right of citizens freely to choose their place of residence, including emigration to another country, an official replied, "Didn't you know that this document has been approved for the sake of the outside world, but is not law on the territory of the USSR?" (The Chronicle of Current Events, no. 19 (April 1971, Moscow).

39. For examples of campaigns against foreign radio stations, see G. D. Hollander, Soviet Political Indoctrination, p. 114.

40. Ye. E. Vartanova, Chief Editorial Board for All-Union Radio, "Propaganda Marksizm-Leninizma po radio i televideniye," in Smirnova, Voprosy teorii.

41. For example, I. S. Kogan, writing to Chakovsky, then editor-in-chief of Literaturnaya Gazeta, remarked: "In Your 'Answer to a Reader' you asked "Why am I obligated to believe Litvinov?" And I, an ordinary reader, may ask "Why am I obligated to believe you, Aleksandr Chakovsky and the 'witness' Brocks Sokolov?" And here is my answer: The position of Litvinov is a principled one. . . . You say, of course, apparently possessing a short memory, "there is no reason not to trust the court." You readily have called and continue to call black white and white black, professing only one 'principle,' the preservation of your own position and the privileges associated with it. . . . That is why, lacking information about the trial, I believe Litvinov and do not believe you and Brocks Sokolov." Arkhiv Samizdata, no. 43 (March 27, 1968). See also "Excerpts from Proceedings of Trial in Moscow," New York Times, October 15, 1968.

42. See C. I. Hovland, I. L. Janis, and H. H. Kelley, Communications and Persuasion (New Haven: Yale University Press, 1953), p. 110.

43. Figures for 1971 are from the Yearbook for the Great Soviet Encyclopedia (1971), p. 35.

44. For more information, see Hollander, Soviet Political Indoctrination, pp. 34-37; Mark Hopkins, Mass Media in the Soviet Union (New York: Pegasus, 1969), chapter 4.

45. Recently a woman complaining of pollution (caused by her factory) to officials was seized in her plant's medical office and taken to a mental institution in spite of the fact that a health monitor at the plant had determined that the level of hydrogen sulfide there was five times that deemed permissible and that other dangerous pollutants were eight times in excess of established safe limits. "A Soviet Woman Tells of Ordeal," New York Times, August 6, 1974.

46. Decree no. 655 of the USSR Council of Ministers (August 31, 1972), Addendum to Article 74 on Regulations on Communications of the USSR, announced in Sobraniye Postanovleniye Pravital'stvza

SSSR, no. 19 reads: "The use of telephone links (intercity, city, and rural) for purposes contrary to state interests and public order, is prohibited."

CHAPTER

9

**LITERARY POLICY UNDER
STALIN IN RETROSPECT:
A CASE STUDY, 1952-53**
Edith Rogovin Frankel

In recent years Western scholars have been deeply interested in determining the nature and degree of change in the Soviet Union since Stalin's death. Numerous works have assessed the transformation of post-Stalin Russia: changes in economic policy, in the effectiveness of group pressures on policy making, in the use and role of terror, and in the area of public discourse, debate, and cultural creativity. But there has been relatively little effort to establish a reliable gauge to measure change. Detailed studies of specific areas of interest during the late Stalin years have been few and far between, so comparisons involving the Stalinist era have often been based not on well documented research but on generalizations. One exception has been Marshall Shulman's study of Stalin's foreign policy in the post-World War II period,[1] which emphasized its complexity and broad range of options.

It is the purpose of this brief study to investigate another specific field, literature, within a highly limited time span (the last year of Stalin's life) in order to examine the degree of uniformity prevailing at that time. Was the totalitarian regime as monochromatic as is often assumed? or was the literary field, too, of a complex nature?

The general view of internal Soviet politics in the early 1950s is that the increasing repression and prepurge tension were irreconcilable with a loosening of literary bonds. And yet an examination of the period shows that both trends—a policy of mounting intimidation by the state and an officially sanctioned "liberalization" in the

---

This article is based on a paper given at the International Conference of Slavic, Soviet, and East European studies held in Banff during September 1974.

literary sphere—coexisted in the Soviet Union in 1952.

Soviet internal policy at this time was characterized by a renewed attack on bourgeois nationalism, the instigation of the "Doctors' Plot," and the proliferation of the vigilance campaign. On the other hand, foreign policy provided a contrast—the broad alliance policy and the development of the peace movement after 1949 represented a "rightist" approach.[2] A similar absence of consistent correlation between all phases of Soviet policy had been seen at other times: In the mid-1930s, for example, the beginning of the Great Purge was coupled with an official veneration of law and order, with propaganda for the new constitution, and, in foreign affairs, with the pursuit of the Popular Front.

In 1952 the contrast was not limited to an emphasis "on 'peaceful coexistence' in foreign policy and strict ideological conformity at home."[3] A moderated policy was also to be seen in the field of literature. For approximately ten months an atmosphere of relaxation, albeit strictly limited, was felt in the literary world.

This modification in the firm attitude of the Party toward literature was first felt as early as February 1952.[4] Although prose was the object of some of the reforming criticism, the main brunt of the campaign was directed toward drama. There ensued a series of articles condemning the so-called no-conflict theory that had dominated postwar Soviet drama. The single most famous and most outspoken statement on the subject was made by the playwright Nikolai Virta in March 1952. In it he tried to explain his own role in the development of the theory:

> It arose as a consequence of "cold observations of the mind" on the manner in which those of our plays which contain sharp life conflicts passed through the barbed-wire obstacles of the agencies in charge of the repertoire. . . . Everything living, true to life, sharp, fresh and unstereotyped was combed out and smoothed over to the point where it was no longer recognizable. Every bold, unstereotyped word in a play had to be defended at the cost of the playwright's nerves and the play's quality. . . . Each of us accumulated a great deal of bitter experience in ten years about which, for some reason, it has been the custom to keep quiet.[5]

Virta placed much of the blame on people who killed plays, guided "not by the interests of Soviet art but by a wild rabbit fear of the hypothetical possibility of a mistake, mortal fear of taking any risk or responsibility for risk." His own initial adherence to the no-conflict theory had been the result of his search for "a creative way out." Perhaps, he had thought, the period of sharp conflicts in drama really had passed. But,

> no, this stupid and spurious theory did not arise because "everything was fine!" It is not because "everything is fine" that Pogodin writes a play about the beginning of the century, while Virta, who spent two years in a Russian village, wrote a play about peasants of the people's democracies!

Although, of course, the atmosphere of suppression described by Virta is not surprising, what is notable is that he expressed his views publicly—and in the way that he did. His candid remarks during what was assuredly an extraordinarily repressive period, his attack on problems of censorship and publication policy, and the fact that his statement was not a unique utterance but part of a concerted campaign in the press to revise established literary doctrine all make this a most noteworthy article.

What is interesting is not that a writer in the Soviet Union in the early 1950s should have felt bitterness and helplessness at his plight, nor necessarily that he should have committed these thoughts to paper, but that a publication such as Sovetskoe iskusstvo, of conservative leanings and quite orthodox editorial policy, should have published them. One can only assume that the editors—and there had been no recent significant changes of the board—deemed the article appropriate to the current literary mood.

Although Virta's article and others were subsequently attacked in the Soviet press,[6] the crusade against the no-conflict theory continued throughout the summer and into the fall, with concomitant demands for the portrayal of more well-delineated negative characters and for more and better comedies. It proceeded with varying degrees of fervor beyond the 19th Party Congress and extended to include not only drama but other prose forms as well.

Malenkov's speech at the 19th Party Congress in October did little to clarify the literary situation.[7] Nothing really new was said in the few paragraphs devoted to the subject. One thing that his speech did not do, however, was to put any further brake on the process of innovation that had been emerging since the previous spring. Literary events were apparently to proceed along their course without a strong directive from the top.

In January 1953, on the same day that the Doctors' Plot was announced in the press, I. Pitliar published an article demanding that more attention be paid to the material details of life: "What enormous artistic and editorial possibilities open up before the writer who is not afraid to be truthful in portraying the material conditions of people's existence. . . . Those writers who wave aside the so-called 'details of life' are sinning against the truth of life."[8] This sentiment, uttered at the beginning of a repressive swing in Soviet literature, would later be a central theme in the literary criticism of the early thaw.

A situation in which articles calling for conflict, for innovation, for a description of negative characteristics of Soviet life appeared simultaneously with attacks on nationalism in literature, with Great-Russian chauvinism, with virulent anti-Semitism and a campaign to induce mass paranoia was clearly anomalous. There was a build-up of fear and distrust, but there also was the other side of the coin, which cannot be ignored. Explaining it is by no means simple.

There are a number of possible explanations and there is probably some truth in each. First was the state of drama itself. It is certainly plausible that the attack on the no-conflict technique was nothing more than an attempt to cure the ills that had beset the theater for some time. Evidence of the low level of dramatic endeavor (half-empty theaters and the popularity of the classics over contemporary plays) is overwhelming, and it is not unlikely that a main goal was to raise the theater to the point where it could at least be a meaningful instrument of education or propaganda. Demands for more constructive criticism, for a reorganization of responsible committees, and attacks on dull and insipid plays all point in this direction.

If, however, one considers the period preceding Stalin's death as a whole, and not just in terms of literary development, one perceives other possibilities. Seeing the build-up of insecurity and tension throughout the year, reaching a frenzy early in 1953, one is struck by a certain similarity between the vigilance campaign and the attack on the no-conflict theory. The vigilance campaign, in essence, warned that no one was to be trusted, that subversive elements lurked in the background of Soviet society, that one should be on guard against every conceivable danger, whether from doctors, embezzlers, bourgeois nationalists, or petty criminals. Implied in the campaign against the no-conflict doctrine was the assertion that it was wrong to assume that Soviet society had reached the point of development where there was no sociopolitical danger left. Drama could not yet be written so that the only opposition present in a play was that between good and better. Evil remained in society and ought to be presented in the theater as it was, with the aim of rooting it out. In other words, in order to expose enemies the Soviet citizen had to know how to recognize them.

There is, finally, the possibility, which cannot be entirely discounted, that this "liberal" swing was simply to be used as a bait to draw out what Surov had referred to as the "keepers of silence"[9] from their lairs, with the ultimate intention of repression.

It is widely held that a major purge was in the offing on the eve of Stalin's death; perhaps this campaign was simply to be used as a mousetrap.

THE ROLE OF NOVYI MIR

Whatever the ulterior motives, the fact is that in 1952 writers and editors did find that they had somewhat more scope, more elbow room, limited though it still was. This became evident not only in the remarkable candor of some writers but also in the demands made by the writers as a group. The attack on the no-conflict theory permitted a less stereotyped publication policy. In order to demonstrate this point, it is instructive to look at the output of the literary journal Novyi mir, the most experimental journal in the 1950s and the one quickest to reflect a change of policy.

Two major works appeared in the pages of Novyi mir in the summer and early fall of 1952, as well as some lesser items, to distinguish that literary season from the Stalinist model. Almost predictably, Novyi mir was to be the object of a severe concerted attack by the Party press and the Writers' Union several months later.

In the July 1952 issue of Novyi mir, the first installment of Vasilii Grossman's Za pravoe delo (For the just cause) appeared.[10] Za pravoe delo was a lengthy novel centering on the Battle of Stalingrad; it followed a number of individuals and families whose lives were caught up in the war and whose fates were interrelated. Long sections were devoted to philosophical discussions on the causes of the war among soldiers, professors, and students.

It is indicative of the indecisive official attitude, and the amount of permissiveness, that the novel received some excellent, and at worst mixed, reviews at the end of 1952. Indeed, Za pravoe delo was virtually ignored in the beginning. Ilya Ehrenburg noted this in his memoirs, recalling that he considered this a positive development: "I have been looking through the files of Literaturnaya gazeta [1952]," he wrote. "Everything appeared most satisfactory. The paper noted that Grossman's novel Za pravoe delo . . . had appeared in Novyi mir, but the reviewers ignored it."[11]

In fact, as Ehrenburg clearly understood, the novel did contain sections that could well have been alarming to the Soviet reviewer. In the following excerpt an academic, Chepyzhin (one of the central characters), propounds his views in a conversation with Professor Shtrum:

> Look, imagine that in some little town there are people
> known for their learning, honor, humanity, goodness.
> And they were well known to every old person and child
> there. They enriched the town life, enlarged it—they
> taught in the schools, in the universities, wrote books and
> wrote in the workers' newspapers and in scientific journals;
> they worked and struggled for the freedom of labor. . . .
> But when night fell, out onto the streets came other people
> whom few in the town knew, whose life and affairs were
> dirty and secret. They feared the light, walked stealthily
> in the darkness, in the shadow of buildings. But there
> came a time when the coarse dark power of Hitler burst
> into life, with the intention of changing its most fundamental
> law. They started to throw cultured people who had illumi-
> nated life into camps, into prisons. Others fell in the strug-
> gle, others went into hiding. They were no longer to be
> seen during the day on the streets, at factories, at schools,
> at workers meetings. The books they had written blazed.
> But those who had been hidden by the night came out noisily
> into the light and filled the world with themselves and their
> terrible deeds. And it seemed that wisdom, science,
> humanity, honor had died, disappeared, had been destroyed.
> It seemed that the people had been transformed, had become
> a people of evil and dishonor. But look here, it isn't so!
> Understand that it isn't so! The energy contained in a
> people's wisdom, in a people's moral sense, in a people's
> goodness is eternal, whatever fascism might do to destroy
> it. [It continues to live, temporarily dispersed. It accumu-
> lates in nodes. It gathers around itself indestructible micro-
> scopic diamond crystals which can cut both steel and glass.
> And those popular champions who were killed transmitted
> their spiritual strength, their energy to others, teaching
> them how to live and how to die. And their strength was
> not destroyed together with the corpses of the dead, but
> continues to live in the living. I am convinced that the Nazi
> evil is powerless to kill the energy of the people. It only
> disappeared from view, but its quantity in the people has
> not diminished. Do you understand me? Do you follow my
> line of thought?] [12]

Chepyzhin then goes on to discuss the psychology of social change:

> You see, all sorts of things are mixed in man, many of
> which are unconscious, hidden, secret, false. Often, a
> man, living under normal social conditions, doesn't know

himself of the vaults and cellars of his soul. But a social catastrophe occurred, and out of the cellar came every evil spirit, they rustled and ran out through the clean, light rooms. [The flour fell and the chaff rose outside. It wasn't the relationship of things that changed, but the position of the parts of the moral, spiritual structure of man which was altered.] [13]

It is not at all surprising that, when the attack finally came, the critics singled out these passages. Chepyzhin, one wrote, taught an "idealist philosophy" that the author himself obviously espoused. [14]

It does not require great imagination to see Grossman-Chepyzhin's description of the coming of Hitlerism as a commentary on Stalinist Russia. Especially in the light of his later work, Vse techet (Everything Flows), [15] it is clear that Grossman was highly sensitive to, and understandably obsessed with, the evils committed in Soviet Russia during his lifetime. His concentration on the intelligentsia and their difficult fate was at least as applicable to the Soviet as to the German situation. This is a striking example of the not infrequent practice of political criticism by analogy, in which the dissenting writer attacks a feature of his own contemporary society through reference to tsarist times or to foreign and hostile countries. Of course, the official critics could not directly expose this type of invidious comparison, for to do so would be to admit that they, too, had recognized the forbidden parallel.

The critics in general—and the February article in Literaturnaya gazeta was typical—therefore had to confine their criticism within safe ideological bounds. Specifically, in the case of Grossman, they concentrated most of their fire on his universalist moralism, his apparent indifference to Marxist dialectics, and his preference for a class-free, science-based philosophy. "It adds up," said Literaturnaya gazeta,

to the idea that there is an eternal struggle of good and evil, and good is the personification of perpetual energy—whether the cosmic energy of the stars or the spiritual energy of the people. It is completely clear that these ideological, unhistoric fumblings of reasoning can in no way explain the existence of social phenomena. [16]

Chepyzhin, the article went on, spoke abstractly, and unhistorically, about fascism and war. He measured everything according to his "unhistoric categories" of the struggle of light and darkness, of good and evil. Shtrum, it continued, nodded agreement and not one of the main characters replied to this argument with a Marxist-Leninist explanation of the war and the nature of things. So one may assume that Grossman did not want Chepyzhin's reactionary philosophy refuted. Grossman, through Chepyzhin, seemed to follow the idea of the Pythagoreans that there is an eternal rotation of events, that "there is an eternal circulation of the very same beginnings, conditions, events."[17]

It should be noted here that when the novel was published in book form, as it was after Stalin's death and again in the 1960s, the two passages quoted above were considerably altered. Moreover, the entire dialogue between Chepyzhin and Shtrum was transformed. Although Chepyzhin's views were not essentially changed, only toned down and attenuated, Shtrum now emerged as an advocate of Soviet Marxist orthodoxy. For example, he now objected vigorously to the idea that Nazism was to be explained as the work of "a handful of evil men with Hitler at their head," arguing instead that it was the result "of the specific peculiarities of German imperialism."[18] Again, Shtrum now pointed out that Chepyzhin's theory of science and history if applied "not to fascism . . . but to progressive phenomena, to liberating revolutions . . . [implies that] the revolutionary struggle of the working class also cannot change society, also cannot raise man to a higher level."[19]

Besides the excerpts quoted here, many general features of Grossman's novel were attacked. Grossman had not "succeeded in creating a single, major, vivid, typical portrait of a hero of the battle of Stalingrad, a hero in a gray greatcoat, weapons in hand."[20] He "had not shown the Communist Party as the true organizer of victory."[21] A feeling of doom pervaded the work.[22]

The campaign continued unabated until a month after Stalin's death.[23] In fact, pressure became so great that several members of Novyi mir's editorial board—Tvardovskii, Tarasenkov, Kataev, Fedin, and Smirnov—publicly apologized for their "error" in publishing Grossman's novel.[24] It was a vain attempt to stem the tide of criticism directed at the journal. The climax was the admission by the editors that the fault lay with the editorial board—that is, with themselves—for not having gone into the work more thoroughly, for having failed to ferret out its ideological-artistic faults. They asked the secretariat of the Writers Union to "take measures towards strengthening the composition of the editorial board of Novyi mir." As for Grossman, he never made any kind of apology.[25]

The last major attack on Grossman's novel, and on the journal that had published it, was made by Fadeev at the end of March.[26] The focus of his criticism did not differ sharply from what had preceded it, except for a rather pointedly anti-Semitic undertone, but what is especially significant in terms of history is his account of the publication process through which the novel had passed.

According to Fadeev, the novel had been discussed for a number of years before its appearance in print, and there had been numerous objections to it. But the discussion did not reach the broad public.[27] "It was conducted in the narrow circle of the editorial board and the secretariat [of the Writers' Union], and only after the novel was printed did it creep into the Presidium of the Union of Soviet Writers—the body which should have decided these matters of principle."

Evidently, when the novel first came to the editorial offices of Novyi mir it had been strongly criticized by B. Agapov, then a member of the board.[28] As we know that Agapov left the editorial board of Novyi mir in February 1950, it is clear that the novel must have been under discussion for a minimum of two and a half years, and probably for much longer. It was when the new editorial board was appointed that discussion of the novel flared up again. The new editorial board, which brought out its first issue in March 1950, had been significantly changed. Tvardovskii took the place of Simonov as editor-in-chief. Agapov and Aleksandr Krivitskii were replaced by three new members: M. S. Bubennov (an abject conformist under Stalin—and afterward), S. S. Smirnov, and A. M. Tarasenkov.[29]

When the manuscript of Za pravoe delo was submitted for examination to the new board, Bubennov brought the issue to the secretariat of the Union of Writers. Fadeev reported: "The novel was changed many times. Discussion once more developed in the secretariat and the above-mentioned comrades held to their point of view."[30] Fadeev then asked why the novel had been published despite all the adverse criticism.

> Because a situation has arisen in the Union of Soviet Writers and in editorial boards in which the solution of many ideological questions—the evaluation of works, the formulation of one or another serious problem—very often depends on the opinion of a few leaders. We rarely apply the normal collegium principle in our work.

It must be assumed that, in the face of a good deal of opposition, someone on the Novyi mir board was keen on seeing Za pravoe delo published. The likelihood is, in view of his reputation and courage, that that man was Tvardovskii. Had he, as editor-in-chief, been unfavorably inclined toward the novel there would never have been a struggle to have it printed.

One cannot ignore the basic facts of the Grossman affair. First, the author was not an unknown. On the contrary, he had a reputation and, by official standards, a dubious one. Born in Berdichev in 1904, Grossman had been a war correspondent during World War II for both Krasnaya zvezda and Binekeit, the Yiddish-language journal of the Jewish Anti-Fascist Committee. His story "Narod bessmerten" ("The People are Immortal"), which appeared in Krasnaya zvezda 1942, was one of the earlier, more powerful works on the war. However his play Esli verit' pifagoreitsam (If We Believe the Pythagoreans)— written before the war, but only published in 1946—had been severely criticized by the press. After the war he had collected materials on heroic and tragic facts concerning Jewish victims of the Nazis. They were to have been published in what was to be called the Black Book, as a tribute to the Jews who had suffered during the war. The book, already set in type, was never published in the Soviet Union; the plates were destroyed in 1949, when the Soviet Jewish cultural community was closed down.[31] Grossman was hamstrung by Soviet criticism during the postwar Stalin years. Disliked by Stalin[32] and dogged by hack critics, Grossman never won the acclaim he deserved.

A second point is the undeniable fact that, as the novel had been under consideration for so long, the Novyi mir editorial board, members of the Writers Union and of the literary (and censoring) community must have been well aware of the objections to it. It was thus a conscious, not a random, decision to publish that particular novel by that particular author during the summer of 1952. It is quite clear that Tvardovskii took the step of publishing the novel then because he felt, correctly, that this was an opportune time, that the literary atmosphere warranted it.

Indeed, another remarkable aspect of this case is that Za pravoe delo, published during a period of mounting fear, under the unyielding influence of the Zhdanov tradition, was never republished in its original form in Russia. Passages published under Stalin were considered unfit to print in later years.[33] Furthermore, in spite of the pressure exerted on him and on Novyi mir, Grossman never confessed his "errors," never apologized. Nor did Part II of the book ever appear, even in the "best" of literary periods to follow. Grossman died in 1964, some six months after the manuscript of the second part had been confiscated by the secret police.[34]

All this indicates that the literary situation during 1952 was in a state of flux. The Virta statement provided one example of the subtle change that was evident; Novyi mir's publication of Za pravoe delo offered another. Whatever the motivation behind the campaign against the no-conflict theory, the end result was a different publishing policy.

SHIFTS ON AGRICULTURE?

One of the outstanding literary events of the 1950s was the 1952 publication in Novyi mir of Valentin Ovechkin's "Raionnye budni" ("District Routine"), the first of a series of sketches on contemporary kolkhoz life.[35] It was concerned primarily with Party work in a rural area and specifically attacked the complacent attitude of the district secretary, Borzov, whose sole aim was to see that the plan was fulfilled. Ovechkin contrasted him with the second in command, who was interested in the long-term goal of achieving communism and in treating fairly those kolkhozniki who did manage to fulfill their quotas. He supported the principle of incentive, if this would encourage the kolkhozniki to work harder and more effectively.[36] Ovechkin emphasized that these characters were not products of his imagination, but real people. The implication was that the Borzov approach was not uncommon and that the political direction of rural work was a real problem that the Party must solve.

It is significant that the sketch, far from being passively accepted, was warmly received in spite of the fact that it strongly censured the work of Party officials in the rural areas.[37]

Tvardovskii would later note the innovative nature of Ovechkin's sketch. In his article on the fortieth anniversary of Novyi mir, he called the appearance of "Raionnye budni" a literary turning point.[38] Noting that it had been published before the September Plenum of the Central Committee in 1953 (which had dealt with problems of agriculture), Tvardovskii said that its truthfulness and ideological orientation were only fully appreciated afterward. He pointed out that until then criticism had tenaciously attacked the slightest departure of prose writers from "conventionally accepted and, as it were, legitimized norms of interpreting of rural life in literature. It seemed that maintaining these norms of well-being in the reflected picture was more important than reality."[39] The fact is that "Raionnye budni" was to serve as a model for works on the rural scene throughout the mid-1950s and became symbolic of the "new approach" of thaw writing. Tvardovskii's other mention of "Raionnye budni" was in a letter to Fedin about Cancer Ward.[40] The letter, written in January 1968, came after the refusal to publish Solzhenitsyn's novel. Tvardovskii wrote: "Solzhenitsyn, incidentally, outstanding as he is, is not unique or unprecedented in our literature. We should not forget the courage of Ovechkin's "Raionnye budni," which appeared in Novyi mir as early as 1952 and marked a turning point."[41]

All indications—Tvardovskii's remarks, Malenkov's discussion of agriculture at the 19th Party Congress, which recognized both the "successes" and "shortcomings" in that sector of the economy, the very fact of the publication of Ovechkin's sketch, and an assertion that Stalin himself had called for it[42]—point to the fact that the ruling group had recognized the serious weaknesses of the agricultural situation and was seeking remedies. The coincidence of Ovechkin's first sketch and Malenkov's speech in the fall of 1952 indicate a coordinated introduction of what were to be forthcoming changes in agricultural policy. (In fact, however, agricultural problems and a corrective program were only to be dealt with six months after Stalin's death, in September 1953.)

Other items published in Novyi mir during the last year of Stalin's life contributed to the general atmosphere of moderation in publishing policy.[43] Thus, the Virta statement, along with the concerted attack on the no-conflict theory, the publication of Vasilii Grossman's novel and of Ovechkin's first sketch in the series, as well as the appearance of some lesser articles in Novyi mir, indicates variety in the Soviet literary scene, limited experimentation, and risk taking by the editors. Whatever was in the offing—and by January 1953 attacks on Novyi mir had already begun—the fact remains that an atmosphere of some give-and-take had existed in 1952.[44] Official policy did not on the surface proceed in consonance with the obviously repressive domestic environment.

CONCLUSION

We are thus confronted by some curious but, I submit, not random facts. The events described do present a cumulative image of literary life in 1952 that is far more variegated than is usually recognized. The year selected for examination is one generally assessed as oppressive to a degree at least typical of Stalin's postwar years. And there is no reason to doubt this overall judgment. On the contrary, indications do point to a vicious situation in the internal life of the Soviet Union, then headed toward a new phase of mass terror. But this should not lead us to the conclusion that there was complete uniformity in all aspects of Soviet life. Comparative studies covering both the Stalinist and post-Stalinist years—Ploss' work on agriculture, for instance, or Conquest's on politics[45]—have successfully shown in specific areas the intricacies and contrasts within the monolithic Stalinist system, thus providing a realistic basis on which to assess subsequent changes. Certainly, the literary life in the year examined here suggests that there, too, complexity was the norm.

There is often an assumption in Western writing, encouraged by the image of the totalitarian model, that the Stalin period must have been monochromatic. Thus, whenever one meets a clash of opinion, or an indication of variety or innovation in the post-Stalin period, the natural tendency is to assume that it is new. But the presence of terror did not necessarily mean an absence of variety. People willing to take a chance—and the risks were far greater then—could still manage, as Tvardovskii did with Grossman's novel, to find the means of publishing a particular work. And men like Grossman could still refuse to bow to official criticism, although his bravery could well have been suicidal had Stalin not died when he did. The examples provided were from the last year of Stalin's life, but detailed studies of other years would probably yield similar "anachronisms."

It is generally accepted that the thaw began in the late fall of 1953—after the September Plenum and after the 14th Plenary Session of the board of the Writers Union in October—and that the period was marked by a sharp break with previous literary life. In fact, signs of the post-Stalin relaxation were evident earlier. Ovechkin's second sketch in the series was published in Pravda in July 1953;[46] Tvardovskii's attack on literary restrictions in his poem "Za dal'iu dal'" (Horizon beyond Horizon) came out in Novyi mir the month before.[47] In September Mikhail Lifshits published an outspoken book review in Novyi mir.[48] The truth is that, while the atmosphere of the thaw was markedly different from the Stalinist era, many of its roots can be traced—despite the hiatus produced by the attacks on Novyi mir during the first months of 1953—directly to the preceding era.

Let there be no misunderstanding. The absence of arbitrary terror in the post-Stalin years made an enormous difference in the lives of people in all spheres—the difference between night and day, between madness and a measure of normality. But the absence of terror no more signals the existence of a "pluralistic" society than the fact of a "totalitarian" regime implies complete uniformity.

Certain people in certain fields were able on occasion to publish or say what was important to them even at the worst of times. The abandonment of the mass purge as a method of attaining compliance has not put an end to the coercive pressure enforcing conformity on the writer (or scientist, or lawyer). He is not at an opposite pole from his colleague of Stalinist times; he must still toe the line if he wishes to be published and paid. The writer who sticks his neck out is still taking a grave chance, even if it is not usually a chance of life or death. In the literary sphere, as in many other areas of Soviet life, the dichotomy between the Stalinist and post-Stalinist periods should not be taken for granted but analyzed and measured.

NOTES

1. Marshall Shulman, Stalin's Foreign Policy Reappraised (Cambridge, Mass.: Harvard University Press, 1963).
2. This is a theme to which Shulman devoted his book. He points out that, in order to find means of dividing foreign adversaries and maximizing influence, "the Soviet Union reintroduced tactical and ideological formulations that had been associated with earlier periods identified as 'Right' in Soviet terminology." Ibid., p. 7.
3. Ibid., p. 6.
4. A literary review criticized an author who "writes in only two colors—black and white. Her positive characters are good unto holiness, while from the bad character's very first appearance in the story he is completely unmotivated and a scoundrel." G. Kalinin, "Zhurnal i sovremennost'," Pravda, February 4, 1952, p. 2.
5. Sovetskoe iskusstve, March 29, 1952, p. 2; translated in Current Digest of Soviet Press (hereafter CDSP), 4, no. 11, pp. 6-7.
6. The first significant attack came in a Pravda editorial. It discussed the crisis in drama, but cautioned against overcorrecting the situation, then went on to criticize Sovetskoe iskusstvo for not taking a solid stand on the issue. See "Preodolet' otstavanie dramaturgii," Pravda, April 7, 1952, pp. 2-3.
7. Pravda, October 6, 1952, p. 6.
8. I. Pitliar, "About the 'Details' of Life as Handled in Literature—Let Us Discuss Questions of Craftsmanship," Literaturnaya gazeta, January 13, 1953, p. 3; translated in CDSP 5, no. 14, pp. 13-14.
9. Sovetskoe iskusstvo, March 12, 1952, p. 12.
10. Part I of the novel was published in four installments from July to October 1952.
11. Ilya Ehrenburg, Post-War Years: 1945-54 (Cleveland and New York: World, 1967), p. 293.
12. Novyi mir 7 (1952): 102. The section within brackets was omitted from later published editions.
13. Ibid. In later editions the section within brackets was omitted.
14. "Na lozhnom puti—O romane V. Grossmana, 'Za pravoe delo,'" Literaturnaya gazeta, February 21, 1953, pp. 3-4. See also A. Lektorskii, "Roman, iskazhaiushchii obrazy sovetskikh liudei," Kommunist 3 (1953): 106-15. Lektorskii wrote: "He sees the whole history of culture, all social phenomena, the history of peoples, through the antiscientific understanding of the idealistic-mechanistic philosophy of 'energetics' and the Freudian theory of the dark, subconscious instincts."

15. Vasilii Grossman, Everything Flows (New York: Harper and Row, 1972).
16. Literaturnaya gazeta, February 21, 1953, p. 3.
17. Ibid.
18. Vasilii Grossman, Za pravoe delo (Moscow: Sovetskoe izdatel'stvo, 1955), 137.
19. Ibid, pp. 139-40
20. Mikhail Bubennov, "O romane V. Grossmana 'Za pravoe delo,'" Pravda, February 13, 1953, pp. 3-4.
21. Ibid. This criticism echoed the notorious attack on Fadeev's novel The Young Guard. In fact, during the early 1950s Fadeev was rewriting the entire novel in order to give credit to the Party leadership, which, according to official doctrine, had been responsible for the war effort in the Krasnodon area. Grossman does not appear to have heeded the warning issued his colleague.
22. A. Fadeev, "Nekotorye voprosy raboty Soiuza pisatelei," Literaturnaya gazeta, March 28, 1953, pp. 2-4.
23. See also Marietta Shaginian, "Korni oshibok," Isvestiya, March 26, 1953, pp. 2-3.
24. "O romane V. Grossmana 'Za pravoe delo,'" Literaturnaya gazeta, March 3, 1953, p. 3. In this letter the editors also were apologizing for other published articles that had been severely criticized.
25. Grossman was criticized at least twice for failing to own up to his errors. See, for example, Literaturnaya gazeta, February 21, 1953, p. 3, which reported that at a meeting held at the Novyi mir offices on February 2, 1953, Grossman responded "scornfully" to the "completely justified" criticism made by various literary representatives.

See also "V Soiuze sovetskikh pisatelei," Literaturnaya gazeta, in which A. Perventsev expressed "general indignation" that Grossman had not replied to criticism.
26. The end of the campaign against Novyi mir—and against Za pravoe delo—was not simultaneous with the death of Stalin. Indeed, it is interesting to note that the literary campaign extended longer than other facets of the repressive onslaught characteristic of the last months of Stalin's life. Even after the official halt of the Doctors' Plot, articles criticizing Novyi mir works continued to appear. Ehrenburg discussed Fadeev's role in the publication of and later in the attack on Grossman's novel:

> In March 1953, soon after Stalin's death, I came across an article in Literaturnaya gazeta in which Fadeev sharply attacked Grossman's Za pravoe delo. This puzzled me because I had several times heard him speak well of this

novel which he had managed to get published. It had
aroused Stalin's displeasure and there had been some
scathing reviews of it. But Fadeev had continued to
defend it. . . . And now suddenly Fadeev had come out
with his article. [Emphasis added.]

Only by mid-April had the attacks on Novyi mir finally stopped.
Ehrenburg mentioned the continuation of the literary campaign in his
memoirs:

The announcement about the rehabilitation of the doctors
appeared: changes were obviously in the air. Fadeev
came to me without ringing the bell, sat down on my bed
and said: "Don't be too hard on me . . . I was frightened."
"But why after his death?" I asked. "I thought the worst
was still to come," he replied.

[Ehrenburg, Post-War Years, p. 166.]

27. Literaturnaya gazeta, March 28, 1953, pp. 2-4.

28. Agapov was a Simonov associate who followed him on and off a number of editorial boards, including a return to Novyi mir in the mid-1950s.

29. The only members remaining from the old board were the well-known writers Valentin Kataev, Konstantin Fedin, and Mikhail Sholokhov. But these three members were figureheads (or, as Soviet critics chose to call them, "wedding generals") and did not perform active roles on the journal.

30. Bubennov and Kataev objected to the novel, and Kozhevnikov joined them.

31. See Yehoshua A. Gilboa, The Black Years of Soviet Jewry 1939-1953, trans. Yosef Shechter and Dov Ben-Abba (Boston: Little, Brown, 1971).

32. See Ehrenburg, Post-War Years, p. 165.

33. See notes 12 and 13.

34. See, for example, Svetlana Alliluyeva, Only One Year (London: Hutchinson, 1969), p. 44: "In the U.S.S.R. one could expect anything: the search of one's home by warrant, the confiscation of books from one's shelves, of manuscripts from one's desk. In this way the government had confiscated the second part of Vasily Grossman's novel."

35. Novyi mir 9 (1952), pp. 204-22.

36. Ovechkin's sketches have frequently been described in Western studies. See, for example, Harold Swayze, Political Control of Literature in the U.S.S.R. (Cambridge, Mass.: Harvard University Press, 1962), pp. 95-97. Ovechkin's sketch was partially translated in Soviet Studies 4 (April 1953): 448-66.

37. See, for example, Marietta Shaginian, "Kritika i bibliografiia—'Raionnye budni,'" Izvestiia, October 26, 1952, p. 2; "Shirit' front boevoi publitsistiki!—V sektsii publitsistiki i nauchno-khudozhestvennoi literatury Soiuza sovetskikh pisatelei," Literaturnaya gazeta, January 17, 1953, p. 2; "Chitatel'skaia konferentsiia ob ocherkakh V. Ovechkina," Literaturnaya gazeta, February 19, 1953, p. 3.

38. A. Tvardovskii, "Po sluchaiu iubileia," Novyi mir 1 (1965): 3-18.

39. Ibid., p. 6.

40. Survey 69 (October 1968): 112-21.

41. Ibid., p. 113. For further discussion of the innovativeness of Ovechkin's "District Routine," see B. Platonov, "Novoe v nashei zhini i literature," Zvezda 5 (1954): 160-74; Gennadii Fish, "Na perednem krae," Novyi mir 4 (1957): 203-4. Fish wrote: "Already in 1952, in the days preceding the 19th Congress, when the adverse situation in agriculture, the disastrous condition of many kolkhozy and kolkhozniki was hidden under the froth of official reports of 'unprecedented' successes—the writer bravely, with precise, spare lines, showed the true picture of life of one artistically generalized agricultural region of Central Russia" (p. 203).

42. See Arkadii Belinkov's statement in The Soviet Censorship, Studies on the Soviet Union, vol. 11 (new series), no. 2 (Munich: Institute for the Study of the U.S.S.R., 1971), p. 17.

43. See, for example, V. Komissarzhevskii, "Chelovek na stsene," Novyi mir 10 (1952): 210-24, in which the author was relatively outspoken in extending the general lines of the attack on the no-conflict theory; N. K. Gudzii and V. A. Zhdanov, "Voprosy tekstologii," Novyi mir 3 (1953): 232-42, which discussed the censor's arbitrary destruction of texts in nineteenth-century Russia—a veiled comparison between that censor and his Soviet counterpart; V. Ognev, "Iasnosti!", Novyi mir 1 (1953): 263-67; E. Kasakevich, "Serdtse druga," Novyi mir 1 (1953): 3-125. Much of the criticism launched against Grossman was applied to Kazakevich as well, although the works were distinctly different and the Kazakevich story was far less ideologically interesting.

44. See, for example, reports of a conference of Maiakovskii in "Osnovnye voprosy izucheniia tvorchestva V. V. Maiakovskogo (Sovoshchanie v Soiuze sovetskikh pisatelei SSSR)," Literaturnaya gazeta, January 22, 1953, p. 3; January 24, p. 3; January 27, p. 3; and January 29, p. 3. What is striking about the record of the meeting is the atmosphere of pro-and-con discussion that seems to have prevailed. Ognev, for example, who was criticized there a number of times for his Novyi mir article and for oral statements, was quoted in Literaturnaya gazeta—both his own statements and his attacks on others present.

45. Sidney Ploss, Conflict and Decision-Making in Soviet Russia (Princeton: Princeton University Press, 1965); Robert Conquest, Power and Policy in the U.S.S.R. (London: Macmillan, 1962).

46. Valentin Ovechkin, "Na perednem krae," Pravda, July 29, 1953, pp. 2-3; Pravda, July 23, 1953, pp. 2-3.

47. Aleksandr Tvardovskii, "Za dal'iu dal'," Novyi mir 6 (1953): 59-83.

48. M. Lifshits, "Krepostnye mastera," Novyi mir 9 (1953): 220-26.

CHAPTER

10

INTELLECTUALS AND THE PARTY IN BULGARIA
Peter Raina

This essay does not analyze the theories of Marxist intellectuals in a communist society. Our purpose is the study of their role in such a society. This role is best described by Leszek Kolakowski in his well-known essay "Intellectuals and the Communist Movement." According to Kolakowski,

(a) Communist intellectuals have the responsibility to fight for the secularization of thinking, to combat pseudo-Marxist mythology and bigotry as well as religio-magic practices, and to struggle to rebuild respect for completely unrestricted secular reason.

(b) Communist intellectuals have the obligation, as well as the right, to bear the responsibility for the ideological development of the revolutionary movement.

(c) The Communist Party needs intellectuals not so that they can marvel at the wisdom of its decisions, but only so that its decisions will be wise. Intellectuals are necessary to communism as people who are free in their thinking, and [are] superfluous as opportunists.[1]

Most Marxist intellectuals take their responsibilities seriously and in the spirit described above; that is why they frequently run into difficulties with the Party hierarchy. The intellectual cannot afford to think dogmatically; he cannot be a dialectician or take a doctrinaire approach. The line of action taken by the intellectuals in East Europe has never been homogeneous: in the Soviet Union, it has been more or less underground, with a few exceptions; in Poland it has been traditionally consistent, open, and effective; in Czechoslovakia it reached a degree of explosiveness in 1968 and has disappeared since. Hungary should be classified somewhere between Poland and Czechoslovakia. In Bulgaria and Romania, Marxist intellectuals have been playing a distinct role since the mid-1960s.

We are taking Bulgaria as a case study to explore how active the intellectuals are. We believe that there is a specific group of intellectuals composed of philosophers, writers, journalists, and students that does influence the ideology of the ruling Communist Party. Within this group are some who defend the ideological dogma of the Party; they represent the orthodox point of view. Those who question this opinion we call dialecticians.

We would like to know if there is room for discussion in a system that is largely totalitarian and if the art of debating is peculiar to the post-Stalin era. To achieve our aim, we would have the actors present their own case on the stage of ideological discussion. We believe that the actors are well acquainted with their situation because they directly confront it. Our chief sources of information are the columns of the Bulgarian Party and literary press.

A serious and public debate among the Bulgarian intellectuals started with the fall of Vulko Chervenko, who was purged from the Politburo at the end of 1961.[2] He was supposed to have inflicted serious damage on the cultural front.[3] His disappearance opened up "creative possibilities to all people working in the arts and sciences"; this extended "their horizon," introduced "a breadth to their activities," and allowed "a true reflection of reality in life."[4]

MARXIST PHILOSOPHERS

Among Marxist philosophers, a major debate developed over Leninism and whether it is subject to revision. Sofia University philosophers (including Z. Zhelev, I. Dzhadzhev, and P. Uvakov) have been advocating the thesis that one should not dogmatically bypass the Leninist definition of matter as "objective reality," since it was not the key definition valid for all times. Lenin never sought such definitions. Lenin had not been concerned with one or another formulation but with the defense of the fundamentals of philosophic materialism.[5] Zhelev in particular felt that Lenin's dogma was no longer what it had been for previous generations. In the past people had been forced to regard his philosophy as incompatible with other philosophic currents. Today one saw Lenin as a scientist and theoretician who had always considered both Marxism and his own philosophy as a science that had to be developed under conditions of full freedom of opinion and debate. Lenin's ideas were no longer to be considered as dogma. Nobody should consider them final and definitive, only to be praised and quoted. They were to be viewed mostly as a starting point for new studies, debates, and discussions. There was no single idea in Lenin's philosophy that could not be debated or submitted to theoretical discussions.[6]

Todor Pavlov (honorary president of the Bulgarian Academy of Sciences and Politburo member since 1966) thought differently. He reprimanded the three Sofia philosophers for attempting to revise the "basis of all Lenin's philosophic conceptions."[7] P. Gindev, professor of dialectical and historical materialism at Sovia University, attacked Zhelev. Who (Gindev asked) had authorized "this champion of freedom to speak against Lenin on behalf of the young generation"?[8] Irresponsibility, pretentiousness, and sophistry, he wrote, were characteristic of articles like those of Zhelev. And these mistakes were not insignificant. The purity of Marxist-Leninist ideology was at stake. No one had the right to put ambition higher than concern for the purity and creative development of Marxist-Leninist theory. The ideological diversions would only serve the imperialist bourgeoisie in their anticommunist activities.

Marxist philosophers have been a source of constant irritation to the Party ideologists. There is a small but strong ideological opposition to dogmatists; these opponents are in no mood to make compromises. The theoretical organs of the Party are at times so afraid of meeting their adversaries in an open discussion that no risks are taken. To say that a debate on Marxism would lead to "chaos" is a weak argument.[9]

When some of the Sofia University philosophers praised Zhelev for his intellect and courage, Filosofska Misal (no. 5, 1965) called this action "disquieting." The journal failed to understand why so many members of the Party had criticized the Party's decision to "justly" punish Zhelev for his "anti-Party" attitude. The journal's editors were disturbed that young Bulgarian authors had been guided by neopositivism in their methodology and scientific work, had disregarded the principle of Party loyalty in esthetics, and had called the leading role of the Party the dictatorship of theoretical monotheism. The editors of the journal, however, confessed that unsolved and unexplained theoretical problems could be cleared only through scientific argumentation. It was not enough to accuse some of dogmatism and others of revisionism or idealism. When false views were not scientifically defined, then the Marxist-Leninist ideological front would end in chaos, thus aiding the anticommunist forces in the struggle against Marxism-Leninism. The editors further suggested that they were prepared to publish the views of critics, if such views were scientifically enlarged and devoid of personal insults. And one can only support the thesis advocated by Krustyn Goranov, professor of esthetics, that "unwillingness to understand one's opponent is not a good quality in a scientific dispute."[10]

WRITERS AND LITERARY CRITICS

The Party leadership is the group that most fears the intellectuals. On March 14, 1969, when Todor Zhivkov, first secretary of the Bulgarian Communist Party, addressed the Sofia City Komsomol Organization, he admitted that the cultural intelligentsia of the nation was being threatened by an "imported illness." "What is surprising," he said, "is the fact that our literary critics, who on many occasions in the past have successfully intervened in the struggle against the more serious illness, have recently seemed less effective, both in taking preventive measures and in effecting cures. This is already creating a danger of epidemics." Literature and art belonged to the arena of the class struggle, and the Party looked upon artistic creation as an "inseparable part of all-Party, all-proletarian and all-national work." For, "a pair of defective shoes is just a pair of defective shoes and nothing else. They can only deform the feet of a single person. On the other hand, if an artistic work is defective, it can deform tens of thousands and even hundreds of thousands of human minds." Power over art was power over the human mind.

Stoyan Daskov (another orthodox Party member) criticized the "deheroizing and primitivism" of some Bulgarian intellectuals. They were untouched by social revolution; they did not want to "swallow the bait called partiinost"; they took care that their minds did not "fall under the influence and encroachments of party-mindedness."[11] Daskov felt this would help the subversive centers, whose aim it was to divide the creative forces in Bulgaria. Thus the enemy could also create conditions for counterrevolution in his country.

At a Party meeting of the Bulgarian Writers Union in 1969, the chairman, Georgi Dzhagarov, stated that some Sofia University lecturers were having a bad influence on "young creative workers." They were being led toward "alien ideological meridians."[12] The secretary of the Party organization of the Writers Union, Nikolj Zidarov, condemned the literary critics for showing fascination toward "structuralism" and for failing to demonstrate the "obligatory class-and-Party approach toward literary facts." This had caused the Party serious concern.

The Party daily, Rabotnichesko Delo (February 7, 1969) criticized Assen Ignatov, an assistant professor at Sofia University, for his recent work Sorrows and Impulses of the Epoch, which discussed, among other things, the problems of alienation. The daily labeled the book "in complete disharmony with Marxist-Leninist principles, especially those concerning the problem of ideological purity and the class principle regarding journalistic and scholarly works." Ignatov was further accused of having been influenced by such bourgeois ideologists as Karl Jaspers and Martin Heidegger.

Writers do not usually answer these charges directly. They take refuge in satire. Radoy Rolin, a prominent Bulgarian satirist, made these comments about Bulgarian society:

He who is honest has a hard time.

He who is right can't find a way out.

Bulgaria, Bulgaria, you anguished Bulgaria!
I know you from yesterday and the day before—
You, the land of all clumsy careerists.

How long shall this dreadful stupidity still rage at this land of our forefathers?

Indeed, Rolin has his admirers. Writing in the literary magazine Plamak, the young Bulgarian poet Mikhail Berberov noted the following on Rolin's satire: "This is the mastery of being able to create on the sound basis of contemporary ethics. The social and personal morals of the satirist Radoy Rolin are connected with the highest human principles. The communist ideal, which has always been the starting point of his poetry, determined the direction for this brave and courageous talent."[13]

This view is not shared by the dogmatists. In an editorial, Literaturen Front (November 21, 1968) firmly stated that socialist progress could be achieved only by "waging a merciless struggle against the powers of obscurantism, which have crazy, monstrous plans to weaken and eliminate socialism itself." The satire, we are told, had a place in "our literature" only if it unmasked imperialism and its ideology in "all their acts and manifestations." In "our satire there are sometimes certain makeshifts that deal with petty themes; these are colorless, helpless, and often ideologically misleading little works that artificially attribute great significance to peripheral phenomena, or obviously point the spearhead of their criticism in the wrong direction." "The authors of these scribblings—rhymed or unrhymed—manifest, without a vestige of shame, their political and esthetic backwardness, their complete lack of understanding of the basic principles of our method"—the method of socialist realism.

Aphorisms of Georgi Tikholov and Kouch Grosev have been labeled "slanderous lies." The cartoonist Boris Dimovsky has been criticized because of his "deviations" from the principles set forth by the Party in the field of humor and satire. Arbitrary generalization, we read in the editorial of Literaturen Front (November 21, 1968), betrayed the ideological position of a pessimist. The ambiguity of satire was being used to hide this position. Ideological ambiguity was ideological duplicity. Truth did not need the assistance of ambiguous allegory. The Party (advised the editorial) needed a satire "with the conscious aim of serving as a Party weapon in the historic struggle we are waging for the bright future of humanity."

The editors of Literaturen Front failed to observe that allegory was not necessarily an escape into ambiguity. It is a class of writing with its own place in literature.

There is yet another aspect of allegory, and this is political. When one makes insinuations, there is a reason: fear of censorship, imprisonment, or both. The editors of Literaturen Front put forward the claim that the very existence and development of socialist society were based on the fact that truth and reality were taken into consideration. If such is the case, why should the editors abuse the satirists? Who should decide what is true or false in satire—the editors, the Party hierarchy, or the author himself? The high quality of aphorism lies in its direct proportionality to sincere human feelings. Literaturen Front would not tell us why Rolin has been very popular with the Bulgarian masses[14] or why his satire is so appealing.

In 1962 a Sofia theater staged Improvisation, a satire ridiculing the vices of the Red bourgeoisie. This play had been jointly written by Rolin and Valery Petrov. It was a great success. Zhivkov was furious, and the play was banned. On April 15, 1963, Zhivkov referred to Improvisation in his speech to the Central Committee. He warned the writers in these terms: the Party cadre "should not be abused in such a manner; our apparat as a whole should not be painted in dark colors; it should not be generalized in such a way." The works of some authors, he said, were intended against those who were leading the nation's struggle for communism. "We cannot agree with such a satiric-line."[15] Novo Vreme (no. 5, 1963), the theoretical monthly of the Party, called Improvisation a "distorting mirror."

THE FUNCTION OF WRITERS

Writers have debated continuously about their proper role as ideologists in a communist society.

In January 1968 Georgi Karaslavov, a writer,[16] was interviewed by Rabotnichesko Delo (January 7, 1968). Karaslavov was asked how he evaluated the artistic reflection of socialist construction upon Bulgarian literature. The positive changes in Bulgaria, he said, were so impressive that even the blind could see them. There were still outdated but ingrained habits of bourgeois social structure, longings for a philistine way of life, for bureaucratic comfort, civic inaction, and social indifference present in people's minds. Karaslavov further complained that "some" Bulgarian writers had allowed themselves to be enticed by unsound theories and formalistic researches. They had deviated from reality, which was the sole source of material for writing. These writers had become guilty of national nihilism, pessimism, and cosmopolitanism. In this way the trends of imperialistic ideological erosion were permitted to seep through literature. It was the duty of Bulgarian literary critics, Karaslavov asserted, to unmask every trace of ideological infiltration and to prevent the authors from allowing misunderstandings, unhealthy fancies, and wrongly understood modernism to creep in.

Karaslavov's interview provoked a long comment from the editors of Literaturen Front (January 18, 1968).[17] The Bulgarian writers, we read, were marching firmly (along with the Party) against obscurantism, misanthropy, and pessimism. The fact that the bourgeoisie was making efforts to infiltrate the intelligentsia ideologically should in no way cause panic. It was well known that the enemy had been sowing the seeds of disbelief among the "unified and harmonious ranks of the socialist intelligentsia." But it was a pity that the ideological condemnations that "appear in articles and statements, are not always the result of vigilance but are more frequently motivated by private animosities and partialities." The editors stated that they had been disappointed with the "menacing conclusions" and "menacing evaluations" in the Karaslavov interview. "When you read these peremptory political sentences, you have the sensation of feeling something very old and very repugnant, something of that stuffy atmosphere of mutual observation and mutual distrust which the April plenum[18] of our Party decisively and definitely banished from our life, while paying no attention to the nostalgic cries of some people."

Criticism from abroad is thought to be an interference in the "internal affairs" of Bulgarian writers. We are told that this "assistance, unceremoniously offered," was unwanted and that Bulgarian writers "have learned and are still learning from the wise words of the Party."[19] What we are not told is that those who have followed only the "wise words of the Party" have remained obscure even in their homeland.

On November 27, 1968, the Administrative Council of the Bulgarian Writers Union summoned a conference to discuss the contemporary character of Bulgarian literature. There was little talk of literary theories. The conference was haunted by the events in Czechoslovakia. The sole purpose of the meeting, Nikolai Ziderov told the delegates, was to wage a struggle against ideological "saboteurs who have repeatedly tried to undermine our cause in this or that sector of the socialist bloc, have attempted to initiate a more serious battle in Czechoslovakia against the Communist Party and its theory and practice."[20] Stoyan Iliev denounced lyricism as "one of the most biased arts" because it was subjective in character and therefore did not serve socialism.[21] "The escape from oneself in lyrics is simultaneously an escape from reality." Iliev would have wanted the poets to be "in the vanguard of engaged Party literature" and to commit themselves to the strengthening of the "authority of socialism." He wrote, "The Czechoslovak events have proved again that every poet should remember that the basic contradiction in our contemporary world is between capitalism and socialism. That is why our society must be protected against counterrevolutionary manifestoes like Two Thousand Words; private, personal, illusory freedom should not be allowed to hinder that social development whose goal is universal freedom." Poetry not committed to socialist realism was irresponsible.

It is common knowledge that obscure minds produce obscure thoughts. We would have had no great poetry or lyric verses if poets had learned their art from Iliev. We must hasten to add that no Bulgarian poet of merit shares his views. Iliev himself is a writer of no distinction in Bulgaria. These incompetent writers, ruled by jealousy, take pleasure in supporting the administrative measures of the Party against those of talent, imagination, and courage. The results are disastrous. Chavdar Dobrev admitted to the delegates at the November 1968 meeting that he could not "point to major works of socialist belles lettres dealing with contemporary subjects which could be considered milestones in development of our artistic thought."[22] But he did not say how much the Party inquisition was responsible for the lack of major works in the country.

During the late 1960s, one prominent poet, Blaga Dimitrova, was criticized by the orthodox thinkers. In an interview with the Komsomol daily <u>Narodna Mladezh</u> (November 21, 1969), Dimitrova complained that "heroism" had been "overused." Contemporary man had to get rid of egotism. And although society influenced the individual, his subjective character also was important. "We have already built up Bulgaria," Dimitrova commented. "Now we must build up ourselves." One had always to be ready to answer the question: "Are you a human being or an egotist? . . . The human being is what is left after one has lost everything."

Dimitrova was criticized soundly by Stoyan Daskalov (Dimitrov Prize laureate) in a letter to <u>Narodna Mladezh</u> (January 7, 1970). She was accused of advocating a philosophy of subjectivism, of the individual's isolation from society, and of "creating heroes outside our socialist society." Criticism also had been voiced against her twelve poems, which appeared under the title "For the First Time" in the literary monthly Septemvri (November 1969). These poems are unique in that they express the individual transient experiences and intuition of the poet. The Komsomol fortnightly Puls (December 23, 1969) felt that Dimitrova's verses were a violation of socialist realism and Marxist-Leninist philosophy. The verses were supposed to be abstract, chaotic, and uncommitted. Moreover, her heroes were alienated. The verses expressed "persecution mania" and moods of depression. Perhaps such is really the case. Perhaps the verses do reflect the conditions prevalent in contemporary Bulgaria.

Under the despotic chairmanship of Georgi Dzhagarov, many talented writers chose to keep silent rather than cooperate with the Writers Union. This group of writers came to be called the "silent minority." And if the Party leadership wished to win back the alienated writers, Dzhagarov had to be replaced. This actually happened on June 8, 1972, only a few months before the second congress of the Writers Union. Panteley Zarev (also a conservative) became the new chairman. But a change of policy also took place. The writers subjected to severe Party criticism during Dzhagarov's time reappeared in a favorable light. Such writers as Vesselin Andreev, Ivan Dinkov, Blaga Dimitrova, Emil Manov, and Valeri Petrov were rehabilitated.[23] When Blaga Dimitrova's new novel Underground Sky appeared in 1972, it was well received by the local critics.[24] At the same time, criticism of the deposed chairman of the Writers Union heightened. The poet Mladen Issaev now hoped that the "principle of collective discussion" in solving important problems would be observed and that blunt "subjective decisions" would no longer be taken "without the knowledge and consent" of the members of the Writers Union.[25]

The dogmatic policies of Dzhagarov seemed to have gone so far that they had almost killed satire in Bulgarian literature, as noted earlier. A known literary critic, Lyuben Georgiev, complained that Bulgarian satire had disappeared by publishing "unsatirical satire."[26] Georgiev called the satire of Vassil Tsonev a "gray output," a "most banal and primitive writing," and an insult to the Bulgarian language. Tsonev was further condemned for his lack of "courage." Georgiev asked, "Why has there not been a single literary-satirical type in this country for about three decades?" Why had the most common negative heroes disappeared? Where was today's shady hero, who should "serve as a counternorm, as an edifying example"? Perhaps the Bulgarian writers should follow the advice given them by Lada Galina (at the second congress of the Writers Union (October 22-23, 1972), to widen their horizons and travel abroad.

JOURNALISM, PUBLIC CRITICISM, AND
THE ROLE OF MASS MEDIA

In June 1968, Bulgarski Zhurnalist (a monthly of the Union of Bulgarian Journalists) published an article on the journalist's responsibilities. The author, Chankov, a member of the executive board of the Journalists Union, made a comparison between socialist and bourgeois journalists. The bourgeois journalist, he wrote, was a paid hireling working for a monopolistic publishing house; he sold his pen to his employers for his daily bread and for the comforts of a modern consumer society in the capitalist world. The socialist journalist, on the other hand, fought for communism, was a citizen of his socialist country, took upon himself the difficult and noble task of serving his nation and socialism through his pen. Every Bulgarian journalist should be proud that his pen served the Party's cause and that he was fighting to translate its ideas into reality. The bourgeois theory of an "independent press" and "independent journalism" was merely cheap demagogy. Such freedom soon turned the information and propaganda media into the "monopoly of groups lacking any sense of responsibility, into an instrument of blackmail and moral terrorism, into a purveyor of anti-Party and antisocialist misinformation. . . . We cannot be misled by attempts, in the name of freedom, to incite the journalists of the socialist press to oppose the ideological and political harmony within the Bulgarian Communist Party that was realized under the Central Committee's leadership on the basis of the Leninist principle of democratic centralism." Chankov's article appeared at the very time that Czechoslovak journalists were fighting for the right to criticize the Party hierarchy publicly.

In its editorial column, Bulgarski Zhurnalist (November 1968) made it clear that there could be no full freedom of the press. The press was an ideological weapon and could control the selection of materials. The question was, what kind of selection would be made and what kind of social and class interests would be served? Referring to the Czechoslovak thesis on "selection," the editorial asserted that the struggle of the Czechoslovak press against "selection" had become a struggle against the communist ideological orientation of the press.

Another orthodox view held that the democratization of socialism was a revisionist concept. Petko Russev (editor-in-chief of Partien Zhivot and chairman of the Press Commission of the Union of Bulgarian Jurists) expressed the opinion that the rejection of the leading role of the Party would result in "our giving up positions" to the bourgeoisie and to its propaganda centers, and in finally losing the battle.[27] In the current ideological struggle, Russev continued, it was not possible for anyone to be politically noncommitted. Honesty in personal relations was a great thing. In politics, however, if honesty led to passivity and indifference and if it served as a base for foreign propaganda, it immediately became treason. "Such 'honesty' might bring counterrevolution into your house."

During the last several years, much self-criticism has been exercised regarding the efficacy of ideological campaigns. At a joint Soviet-Bulgarian theoretical conference in Sofia at the end of May 1972, Venelin Kotsev (a candidate member of the Politburo) recommended measures necessary for the ideological struggle. One could not seal the ears of the people, he said. "We can successfully oppose our enemy only if we succeed in creating a powerful radio-TV base, and, along with this, in unceasingly improving our radio programs."[28] Kotsev complained that the organs of propaganda were not efficient enough. The present structure of the press was not satisfactory. The newspapers looked as alike as "two drops of water." If the Party was to struggle against bourgeois ideology, revisionism, and conservatism, then the Bulgarian mass media would have to be more efficient.

Georgi Bokov (a member of the Central Committee Secretariat, chairman of the Union of Bulgarian Journalists, and editor-in-chief of the Party daily, Rabotnichesko Delo) was very annoyed at Kotsev's remarks. Bokov refuted them in these terms:

> Our press, radio, and TV are developing successfully and are following the right path. We decisively reject the groundless and subjectivist attacks that have recently been persistently made, especially on our press. We cannot agree with statements alleging that the newspapers look alike as two drops of water, that they are boring, that they do not contain information, that their language is primitive. We reject such ill-conceived evaluations.[29]

Krustyn Goranov, a young professor who teaches history and theory of literature and fine arts, was of a different opinion. In an article, "Qualitatively new requirements of the ideological struggle," Goranov stressed that the ideological struggle today was "becoming more and more complicated and requires a cultural approach, flexibility, and an effective offensive," and that this precluded all dogmatism.[30]

In May 1973 Bulgarski Zhurnalist published readers' reaction to journalism in Bulgaria. Two views were symptomatic. Professor Panayot Gindev (deputy director of the Institute of Philosophy at the Bulgarian Academy of Sciences) pointed out that too many journalists were not well informed, "probably because of lack of first-hand information or lack of knowledge of a foreign language, or because they are too lazy to do proper research. . . . We do ourselves no service when we publish incompetent ideological material." A similar stand was taken by the writer Vera Mutafchieva. She said, "The press is still suffering from an insufficient amount of information. One often turns the pages of a newspaper and within a few minutes gets a feeling of frustration." The press lacked dynamism. She therefore suggested that conflicting opinions be published in the press.

Even Party leader Zhivkov has come out for greater public participation in working out general concepts and in political decision making. "There is an urgent need," Zhivkov reported to a Central Committee plenum (December 11-13, 1972), "to create a system of information from below upward which will not modify or polish the opinions of the people. Only if we secure timely, comprehensive, and reliable information about the opinion and the mood of the people, will the Party, state, and economic agencies be able to make decisions which best correspond to the interests of the people and take their ways of seeing things into account."[31]

PEACEFUL COEXISTENCE AND IDEOLOGICAL STRUGGLE

Party dogmatists have rejected peaceful coexistence on the ideological front. According to Professor Ruben Avramov (director of the Institute for Contemporary Social Studies), peaceful coexistence did not mean that the clash between socialist and bourgeois ideologists was at an end.[32] Imperialism was expected in the future to undertake diversions of a far more flexible but equally perfidious kind. Therefore, kindheartedness and complacency, political and ideological disarmament were absolutely unacceptable.

On July 3, 1972, the Central Committee of the Bulgarian Communist Party met especially to discuss "the further strengthening of the struggle against bourgeois ideology." The main report was delivered by Dimitar Dimitrov, head of the Agitprop section. The primary task of the Party, he asserted, was a "firm, systematic, irreconcilable, offensive struggle against bourgeois ideology and against deviations from Marxism-Leninism."

Mihail Benliev (head of the propaganda department of <u>Otechestven Front</u>) was more specific.[33] When East-West contacts and exchanges of ideas were constantly increasing, he wrote in <u>Rabotnicheska Delo</u>, ideological isolation was an absurdity under the conditions of a scientific-technological revolution. This led to "sharpening of the ideological struggle—a trend that cannot be and should not be opposed."

The Party would have to be careful of right- and left-wing opportunism. "Our ideological opponents noisily proclaim" ideological struggle unnecessary, but "in practice they are waging it with all their might and all their resources."

A more sensible and constructive proposal came from Professor Krustyn Goranov.[34] The orthodox device of "caricaturing the opponent," he held, could no longer be used because it did not reduce one's antagonist to less dangerous dimensions. The Bulgarian ideologists, he thought, were not well qualified. They lacked a "profound knowledge of both Marxism and their opponents' theories." Goranov suggested that the Bulgarian cadres should be trained to "fill in the ideological vacuum in the West," especially among leftwing university students. Vast opportunities existed in Western countries to lecture on Marxist philosophy, sociology, and esthetics, and these opportunities ought to be exploited by scholars in the socialist countries.

THE YOUTH

The Party hierarchy has been finding it more and more difficult to bring the younger generation under control. The Party's Central Committee hopes that overemphasis on patriotic education, accompanied by compulsory military training, will solve the problem.[35] The exact meaning of patriotism is nowhere defined but is generally understood as love for the Soviet Union, fidelity toward the native Communist Party, and repugnance for the West.

The Bulgarian Komsomol often has expelled "inactive" and politically "unreliable" members. Its official organ, Narodna Mladezh, complained (October 3, 1968) that a large number of Komsomol members did not work actively or participate in the sociopolitical life of the organization. The Komsomol Central Committee weekly, Studentska Tribuna, announced (December 18, 1968) that it was its duty to cleanse the Komsomol ranks of students who displayed manifestations "foreign to our socialist reality and morality."

The 1968 Czechoslovak events had alarming effects on Bulgarian society, and youth in particular. In an article in Rabotnichesko Delo (September 15, 1968), Lt. Gen. Mircho Spassov (first deputy-chairman of the Committee for State Security) admitted the following:

> If we really want to draw a timely lesson from the events in Czechoslovakia . . . then we must . . . reassess our own attitude toward certain manifestations in our own country which have already come to the surface and which

betray unmistakable traces and characteristics of hostile ideological diversion. These manifestations, even if only isolated instances, do, however, fully resemble all that led up to the counterrevolution in Czechoslovakia. We must not permit an unnecessarily naive and tolerant approach to such brazen manifestations, which occur here and there. Persons who either overtly or covertly rejoiced and are still rejoicing over the successes of the counterrevolution in Czechoslovakia must be prevented in good time from doing harm and spreading this hostile poison. . . . There is no place for a middle course or for hesitation, just as there is no place in our country for those who serve some kind of abstract "humanism" and want to be on good terms with all.

The Bulgarian army also has become susceptible to "subversive ideological activity of imperialism," and the political department of the army has warned of the dangers of bourgeois ideology.[36] A series of special lectures were made compulsory for political officers of the army. These included" Anticommunism is the main ideological weapon of imperialism"; "The bourgeois theory about contemporary industrial society"; "The ideological diversion of imperialism, vigilance, and discipline."

Criticism was voiced against the Interior Ministry as well. Damjan Obreshkov, a journalist, wanted to know whether the militia ought to take administrative measures against Sofia youth wearing rags and uncombed long hair "obviously trying to ape some Western behavior."[37] Even officials at the Interior Ministry believed that questions of fashion and taste were complicated and delicate matters. A person's ideas were by no means determined by the way he was dressed, and to blame the bourgeois influence for insignificant matters was to miss the most important point, namely, the exploitative nature of the bourgeois system: "It would be far wiser to inculcate sound esthetic tastes and criteria in young people, to teach them to distinguish between real and false value, instead of trying to regulate people's tastes by administrative measures." In order to create the atmosphere of a socialist nation, Obreshkov suggested, Bulgarian songs, films, newspapers, magazines, clothes and shoes, and many other things "must surpass foreign ones in quality." He added, "Those who make poor movies, write bad songs, and manufacture ugly shoes render the greatest service to bourgeois influence." Obreshkov hoped that the Interior Ministry would "act with care and tact, thus respecting their own dignity as well as the dignity of others."

Another ideological problem was discussed in a series of articles by Radoslav Radev (deputy editor-in-chief of <u>Narodna Mladezh</u>).

> For more than two decades, communist ideology has been
> dominant in our country, for more than two deacades Marxism-
> Leninism has been studied in both high schools and uni-
> versities, and has been propagated throughout the press.
> Why, despite all the efforts to create a Marxist-Leninist
> outlook among the people (especially among the young
> people) are the results rather far from what they should be?
> . . . I question some aspects of the system, by means
> of which for years we have been trying to heighten the
> interest of young people toward ideological (mainly philo-
> sophical and economic) problems. . . .
> Why should we say that manifestations which have
> accompanied mankind since the humanization of monkeys
> (such as stealing, careerism, toadyism, etc.) are a direct
> result of bourgeois influence? Would it not be more correct
> to say that these manifestations have not yet been overcome
> due to various reasons—reasons which exist in our country
> and not reasons imported from abroad? . . . Of course it
> is easier, more suitable and safer to put the whole blame
> on bourgeois influence instead of on ourselves. But there
> it is—if something does not fit our pattern of bourgeois
> influence, then we should have the courage to look for its
> roots elsewhere.[38]

Not many, it seems, cared for Radev's suggestions. Writing in Narodna Prosveta (no. 3, 1968), a critic, N. Cholakov, listed three types of ideological diversion of imperialism infiltrating into the country: (1) influx of foreign magazines, films, and music; (2) increased activity of religious groups, especially the Catholic Church; (3) international tourism. These diversions were meant to sow the seeds of disbelief in the Party among the youth and the intelligentsia.

We are not told why Bulgarian youth has been feeling alienated, hopeless, disillusioned.[39] Why has youth lost confidence in both the Komsomol and the Party? "You did nothing but lose our confidence," wrote an 18-year-old high-school graduate to the editor of the Komsomol organ.[40] Why are they fed up with the kind of patriotism preached by the Party hierarchy? "Our patriotism," said Zhivkov in a speech at the 9th Congress of the Bulgarian Communist Party, "is inseparable from our love and respect for the Soviet Union and its great Communist Party."[41] This view has been echoed by Georgi Atanassov, first secretary of the Komsomol.[42]

The result of such propaganda has been just the opposite: Bulgarian youth is becoming more internationally minded and pro-Western. This enraged Zhivkov. At the 9th Party Congress he shouted: "We should mercilessly burn with a hot iron all manifestations of admiration for what is foreign, of a nihilistic attitude toward our country, toward the past achievements of our motherland and people."[43]

Despite Zhivkov's threats, the situation remains unchanged. Two sociological surveys carried out in 1972 and 1973 demonstrate this. In 1972, of 123 high-school students interviewed, 66 expressed preference for foreign goods; 53 (out of 96) preferred Western-made cars. A "large majority" (no number was given) thought that the West was far ahead in scientific-technical achievements. Uchitelsko Delo (a publication of the Ministry of Education and the Union of Bulgarian Teachers), which published these statistics (September 26, 1972), complained that the young people were unaware of the big difference in the level of economic development between capitalism and socialism. For 114 students did not know how long the United States had been in the capitalist stage of development and 57 were unable to name fields in which the Soviet Union had overtaken the United States. Many did not even know the Bulgarian economic rate of development.

In 1973, some 3,800 university students were interviewed; of these 70 percent expressed great interest in Bulgarian publications that "devoted most of their pages to a wide variety of news items about the West." Western magazines were most eagerly looked for and circulated from hand to hand. Little interest was shown in domestic politics. University students did not conceal their preference for anything coming from the West.[44]

It would be wrong to emphasize that students are only Western-oriented, for the student trials of 1971 revealed that there is a group ideologically opposed to the Party dogma. On July 16, 1971, Radio Sofia reported that a "radical" and "subversive" youth movement had been crushed and the "instigators" put on trial.[45] Sofia University seems to have been the main center of action. At the trial, one student claimed that there were "definite moral and ethical motives" behind their movement; another said, "the Czechoslovaks acted prematurely, but that was their only fault"; and a third said, "I want to awaken the desire for struggle against the Party and the Soviet Union, for full equality and—above all—for democratic communism."

What caused all this? It was held that the Komsomol had been practicing outdated methods of working with the youth. Sociologist Georgi Belev appealed for a "well-organized and flexible system of information." Poet Mladen Issaev was more explicit. "Let us not," he wrote, "excuse ourselves by talking about the remnants of the past and foreign ideological influences. These influences would never have found fertile soil in this country had we not ourselves made it easy for them to do so. Our own inadvertence and inability to use the media for exerting ideological influence on the masses have caused us to lose control over youth."[46]

CONCLUSIONS

We have tried to show in the present essay:

1. That not all Bulgarian intellectuals are dogmatic in their analysis of Marxist ideology,
2. That as long as the intellectuals do not directly challenge the Party leadership, it is possible to criticize Party policies publicly.
3. That these intellectuals are evolutionary, and not revolutionary in their thought; that is, they aim at changing their social environment through evolutionary and not revolutionary means, and this mode of thinking distinguishes them from the New Left in the noncommunist world,
4. That there is a certain tolerance for ideological flexibility.

The last point needs further explanation.

The Party leadership seems to have realized that it cannot pursue a stringent policy toward the intellectuals. It would not be in the Party's interest to alienate or isolate them.

Dr. Lilia Todorova makes a very fine distinction between the terms "leading" and "managing," so far as the role of the Party is concerned.[47] She prefers the term "leading." This, she believes, would enable the Party to maintain a "flexible approach" on cultural affairs. She notes the apathy among the intellectuals, who had isolated themselves in their "own narrow circles, escaping from life and contemporaneity," which needed to be overcome. Here the literary circles had a special role to play. But, she warned, one must not confuse the "functions of the creative organizations with those of the state and Party agencies or substitute one for the other."

These are sensible words from a sensible scholar. The Party leadership would do well to pay serious attention to what Dr. Todorova has suggested, if it does not want to alienate the intellectuals further. The dogmatists are doomed to failure in the long run. And the Party cannot afford to be anything but "flexible" in any future ideological debate.

NOTES

1. Leszek Kolakowski, <u>Marxism and Beyond</u> (London: Pall Mall, 1968), pp. 178-92.
2. For an excellent analysis of the cultural situation during the 1950s and 1960s, see "Frost and Thaw in Bulgarian Culture," in

J. F. Brown, Bulgaria under Communist Rule (London: Pall Mall, 1970), pp. 240-62.
  3. Novo Vreme, January 1962.
  4. Literaturen Front, December 7, 1961.
  5. J. Jelev, I. Djadjev, P. Uwakov, "Uber die philosophische Bestimmung der Materie," Deutsche Zeitschrift fur Philosophie no. 5 (1964).
  6. "Zum Schluss mochten wir sagen, dass man mit der leninschen Bestimmung der Materie als objektive Realitat nicht dogmatisch umgehen darf, da sie keine Schulbestimmung ist, die fur alle Zeiten Gultigkeit hat. Bestimmungen solcher Art hat Lenin niemals gesuch." In ibid., p. 635.
  7. Septemvri, no. 1 (1965).
  8. Filosofska Misal, no. 3 (1967).
  9. Filosofska Misal, no. 5 (1965).
  10. Narodna Kultura, January 27, 1973.
  11. For some of the speeches delivered at the conference of the Party organization of the Bulgarian Writers Union held on January 31, 1969, see Literaturen Front, February 6, 1969.
  12. Ibid.
  13. Plamak, no. 7 (1967): 73-74. Rolin's satires have appeared in book form: Bezopasni igli (Sofia, 1960).
  14. As early as 1957, Andrey Goulyashky, then secretary of the Party organization of the Bulgarian Writers Union, stated that Rolin had become well known among the people for his anti-Party aphorisms and epigrams. See Literaturen Front, no. 52 (1957).
  15. Rabotnichesko Delo, April 24, 1963.
  16. Karaslavov was born in 1904, became full member of the Central Committee of the Bulgarian Communist Party in 1958, received the Dimitrov award in 1959, and became a "Hero of Socialist Labor" in 1964.
  17. Karaslavov also was on the editorial board of Literaturen Front.
  18. Reference is to the Plenum of April 1956, when Stalinism was publicly denounced in Bulgaria.
  19. Bogomil Raynov, chief editor of Literaturen Front, in the June 6, 1968, edition.
  20. Literaturen Front, December 5, 1968.
  21. Ibid.
  22. Ibid.
  23. Valeri Petrov was expelled from the Party because he refused to join in a protest action against Solzhenitsyn's Nobel Prize.
  24. Zdravko Petrov, a known critic, praised Dimitrova in Otechestven Front, September 17, 1972.

25. Literaturen Front, September 14, 1972. Similar views were expressed by Lilyana Stefanova, editor-in-chief of Obzov, October 19, 1972.

26. Literaturen Front, September 14, 1972.

27. See Russev's article in Bulgarski Zhurnalist, November 1968.

28. For the details, see Politicheska Prosveta, July 1972.

29. Pogled, July 24, 1972.

30. Narodna Kultura, July 21, 1972.

31. Rabotnichesko Delo, December 14 and 17, 1972. See also R. N., "CC Plenum Decisions on Standard of Living," RFE Research, Bulgaria, March 2, 1973.

32. Otechestven Front, July 2 and 4, 1972.

33. See Benliev, "The ideological struggle is a feature of our time," Rabotnichesko Delo, August 4, 1972.

34. Narodna Kultura, July 21, 1972.

35. This problem was first discussed at a Politburo meeting in October 1967: Rabotnichesko Delo, November 21, 1967. See also an article by Lt. Gen. V. Palin, head of the main political department of the Bulgarian army, "The Military-Patriotic Education of Youth," Novo Vreme, March 1968.

36. See Christo Ivanov, Narodna Armia, January 9, 1968.

37. Pogled, September 25, 1967.

38. Uchitelsko Delo, July 25 and 28, August 1, 1967.

39. See the results of the poll conducted in 1964 by the Komsomol organ: "A self-portrait of the generation," Narodna Mladezh, January 24 and 25, 1964.

40. Liubomir Peicher (from the town of Russe) to the editor of Narodna Mladezh, June 19, 1967.

41. Rabotnichesko Delo, November 15, 1966.

42. Speech at the 14th plenum of the Komsomol Central Committee, Narodna Mladezh, December 21, 1966.

43. Rabotnichesko Delo, November 15, 1966.

44. Literaturen Front, November 7, December 6 and 13, 1973.

45. See R. T., "Higher Education in Bulgaria," RFE Research, Bulgaria, November 9, 1972, p. 17.

46. M. Issaev, "Alarm in the name of the future," Literaturen Front, March 1, 1973.

47. Filosofska Misal, no. 2 (1973): 49-57.

PART III
NATIONALITIES

CHAPTER

11

SOVIET HISTORIOGRAPHY AND THE NEW NATIONALITIES' POLICY, A CASE STUDY: BELORUSSIA AND UKRAINE

Stephan M. Horak

The study of Russo-Ukrainian-Belorussian relations in terms of common interests, origins, ties, and confrontations represents an important chapter in the history of the USSR as well as in general historical studies of these Slavic peoples.

The topic as such as been of greater interest to Soviet scholars than to Westerners, who until recently paid little attention to this particular question. However, it generated more response among Ukrainian and Belorussian emigre scholars, who were the first to recognize the Soviet political and ideological interest in that area of historiography.[1] American East European specialists, while essentially aware of the existence of the problem only during the 1960s, have increasingly turned their attention toward this rather complex issue. In addition to several Ph.D. dissertations dealing with Belorussian and Ukrainian histories and a sprinkling of articles in various professional journals,[2] Lowell Tillett's recent study focuses exclusively on Soviet historiography of the non-Russian nationalities.[3] Several other studies produced in the last decade are either of a general nature or concentrate on political or economic facets of the question.[4] Such negligence did not result from a scarcity of material, which in fact is in abundance, including the large Soviet output of the last five decades. Rather, such factors as expediency, linguistic obstacles, and political considerations have limited research and interest.

This survey is a revised version of a paper presented at the International Conference at Banff, Alberta, September 4, 1974, under the title: "Non-Russian Nationalities in Tsarist Russia and in the USSR: A Comparison?"

Other difficulties stem from the time factor (spanning four centuries), as well as the inherent emotions accompanying historical meetings from the time of Medieval Rus' to the present.

Precisely these reasons suggest the necessity of selective methodology, topic restriction, and even analytical generalizations, with the assumption that the specific background knowledge is either self-evident or to be obtained from the available pertinent literature.

Historical ties, and ethnological, cultural, religious, and linguistic similarities affecting these three peoples have led to various myths, interpretations, serious disagreements, and created a suspicion that lingers even today. Nationalist ambitions and hostilities have flourished in this triangular intercourse for centuries. The oppressive Russian nationalism of the tsarist age did not wither away in 1917. There is strong evidence of its presence under the Soviet regime, as there are of separatist nationalist manifestations by Belorussians and Ukrainians (especially the latter), today as in the past. Indeed, one should speak of similarities, repeating cycles, and continuity.

Utilizing all elements that contribute to the similarities among Slavic peoples, Moscow encroached upon the national identities of the non-Russian Slavic peoples with the aim of increasing Russian potential at the expense of Belorussian and Ukrainian human, cultural, and economic resources and separatist ambitions. Gradually, the pluralistic composition of the former Russian empire was to become a monolithic society or just Russified, a process interrupted in 1917 but quickly renewed in the late 1930s and again after World War II.

Here an attempt will be undertaken to demonstrate the continuity of Russia's traditional policy, which underwent several changes and adaptations after 1917, increasingly serving more the Russian national interest than the Marxist ideological concept. After a brief experimental period, Soviet nationalities policy is now unmistakably on the course of transforming the non-Russian peoples into societies of only geographical identity (like "Siberians"), speaking the language of the master nation—Russian. At present, emphasis is on the formation and existence of "one Soviet people" or, as Soviet historian G. B. Starushenko, adapting Lenin's views to the 1960s, bluntly stated: "In this manner, the basic aim which the Marxists pursue, bringing forward the principles of self-determination, is to bring nations closer, to adjust the tightest political, economic, and cultural relations among them in the present and gradual amalgamation of nations in the future."[5] This clear formulation of intentions has since been narrowed even further through the promotion of bilingualism among Belorussians and Ukrainians, favoring Russian as an all-Union language, and the concept of so-called "supranational pride" and "Soviet nation," lending priority to Russian culture and history.[6]

The gap between Piotr Valuev's decrees prohibiting publishing of books in the Ukrainian language and eliminating the Belorussian language (in 1863 and 1867, respectively) and current Soviet policy is closing rapidly, thus departing from the period of relaxation from 1906 through the 1920s, including Lenin's attempt to please Belorussian and Ukrainian nationalists and the Russian Marxists equally.[7]

When suggesting that the desire to achieve a monolithic structure remained a common goal of the tsarist and Soviet regimes, however, one must not overlook some significant differences.

The official tsarist Russian policy, initiated by Peter I and supported by Russian nationalists and conservatives in the nineteenth century, denied any individuality to the other two Slavic peoples. Nicholas I's pillars of the Russian empire—autocracy, orthodoxy, and nationalism, fortified by Valuev's orders and extended by Alexander II's ukaz of Ems of 1876—were designed to erase any national identities, including historical and territorial ones, and to implement the myth of "one indivisible Russia." The renaming of the territories (which fell under Russian rule only during the seventeenth and eighteenth centuries) into "West Russia," composing mainly the Belorussian ethnographic territory, and "Little Russia" for the Ukrainian lands, also suggests the complete absence of any willingness to compromise with forces that would or could challenge the policy of Russian Gleichschaltung. Not until the 1905 revolution would the tsarist regime relax its oppressive measures, testifying only to the necessity of its own destruction in order to allow the two other nations to exist. Russia failed in its policy of ignoring the Belorussian and even more the Ukrainian emerging national rebirth and of responding with terror rather than searching for a compromise. An ironic twist of history resulted in the collapse of the tsarist regime and the culmination of Ukrainian and (to a limited degree) Belorussian political aspirations.

By 1917 a new approach and a new solution were bound to appear. A multinational empire in an age of nationalism and social radicalism with almost 50 percent non-Russian peoples (including approximately 35 million Ukrainians and 9 million Belorussians), plagued with heavy war losses and a pressing need for socioeconomic reforms, had little chance to survive a great upheaval. In such a situation, a total disintegration or a fundamental restructuring to meet the emerging processes were the only two reasonable alternatives. What followed immediately, however, was only a mixture of the two—with new confusing results. The brief period of Russian democracy revealed, if only fragmentarily, the basic unwillingness of the Provisional Government to resolve the national question on terms acceptable to all involved. Some guarded promises to Ukrainians would not have restored the status quo of the Ukraine as specified by the terms of the Pereiaslav Treaty of 1654. What was offered was in essence a limited cultural autonomy in a limited part of the historical as well as ethnographic Ukrainian territory. The case of Belorussia was never even considered in Petrograd, despite the advances by the Belorussian cultural and national movement.

What followed within the framework of the national minorities of former Tsarist Russia under the new Soviet regime has already been skillfully discussed by Richard Pipes, in addition to several other monographs, including those from the Soviet Union. [8]

In Soviet writings and historiography it became customary to claim credit for having finally resolved the national question. From Lenin to the Resolutions of the 24th CPSU Congress of 1971, it is categorically pronounced that only Marxism and the Soviet system are capable of solving national conflicts, removing discrimination, and restoring freedom for all nations, large and small. This claim of exclusive infallibility, proclaiming the realization of a pax Sovietica on the foundation of Marxist-Leninist theory and practice, has been noted by Tillett: "The new historical myth differs from the old ones both in kind and degree. Never before have the proponents of myth made such claims for the 'scientific' bases of their theories."[9]

Within the realm of historiography, the magic key unlocking the absolute—the "only truth and the scientific interpretation of history"—has been identified with historical dialectic. The first and foremost generally recognized Soviet Marxist historian, Michael N. Pokrovskii, who accepted most seriously this axiomatic diagnosis, became the first victim. He and his school did not long survive, for he was unaware of new changes within the USSR and did not fully realize that two other factors were singled out by Lenin and Stalin as the prevailing and determinant Soviet policy. To Lenin, Marxism was not a dogma but a guide for action; the methodology of interpretation, which Stalin named Leninism, offered him in turn a handy reference and excuse for all his actions, including his interference with linguistics and historiography. [10] The national histories of Belorussia and Ukraine could not escape the consequences of continuous revisionism and rewriting of history. Their share during the Stalinist period of physical and intellectual annihilation was at least partly revealed by Soviet Ukrainian historian O. K. Kasymenko:

> Immeasurable harm has been done the study of history in the Ukraine by the [Stalin] cult; as a result of Stalin's tyranny in the handling of important historical events, his biased interpretation of the role of his person, and the cultivation of subjectivity in works on the history of the Ukraine, he is responsible for all sorts of distortions of historical truth. The struggle for the establishment of the

Soviet system in the Ukraine was reduced to the thesis: "Stalin was the creator of the Soviet Ukraine." Furthermore, Kaganovich, Stalin's emissary to the Ukraine, was personally responsible for numerous sufferings of the people, of the party, and of the intelligentsia.[11]

As for Belorussia, "at the end of the second purge, the Belorussian national and cultural leadership was almost completely destroyed,"[12] and the study of Belorussian history for the remaining years of the 1930s became irrelevant and restricted to only a few insignificant articles.

A critical review of the most recent historiographies of these two nations not only reflects some significant changes within the USSR but also offers a better insight into the implementation of Soviet policy affecting non-Russian peoples. In a way, their historiographies project the past, present, and future. While some developments are characteristic for the whole of the USSR, several underlying problems seem to involve these two Slavic peoples to a greater extent than any of the others.

Although general trends have been sufficiently identified in the past by several authors,[13] some poignant questions remained on the sidelines and have only recently been connected with the trend affecting the two republics. The problems best illustrating these changes relate to such issues as the ethnogeny of all three Eastern Slavs, the insistence on the theory of a common origin from the "ancient Russian nationality" (drevnerusskaia narodnost'), the succession to the Kiev Rus' state, the introduction of the idea of a "voluntary reunification with Russia," and the determined pronouncement of the fusion of the nationalities into one "Soviet nation" as a cover for the forcible policy of Russification. The very nationalistic nature of all those crucial historical problems suggests a substantial change within Soviet historiography, for in Pokrovskii's era none of them was of any particular significance apart from casual reference as compared with the emphasis placed upon economic and socioeconomic factors. For instance, in chapter 9 of his Russian History this orthodox Marxist writes: "Feudalism was generally indifferent to national distinctions; nationalism appeared only during the subsequent stage of social development. . . . What was considered by the historians as the religious frontiers was in fact the social frontier, and there was no religious struggle in western Rus' as there was no national struggle."[14] This same economism is present in Pokrovskii's treatment of Ukrainian history in the chapter entitled, "The Struggle for Ukraine,"[15] in which Russia's drive to the south is characterized as a colonial clash with Polish colonialism.

Pokrovskii's terminology is of special importance within the context of Russo-Belorussian-Ukrainian relations. In this regard he followed M. Kostomarov's scheme. Accordingly, the first Eastern Slav state of the tenth to thirteenth centuries was Ancient Rus', split in the fourteenth to seventeenth centuries into Moscow Rus', Western Rus' (Belorussia), and South-West Rus' (Ukraine), which became during the eighteenth and nineteenth centuries, Russia, Belorussia, and Ukraine. In the absence of an elaboration on the formation of national identities of all three peoples, including the linguistic differentiations as they progressed through the fourteenth to nineteenth centuries, it can be suggested that Pokrovskii remained unimpressed with the importance of this aspect of history.

However, it was Pokrovskii who had seen tsarist Russia as "the prison of nations." He wrote:

> It does not matter that Witte through his own ignorance included Ukrainians among Russians and even called them "Little Russians." . . . What does matter is that even Witte ought to have properly written the name "Russia" in quotation marks, as I am writing it now; for the "Russian Empire" was not at all a national Russian state. It was a collection of several dozen peoples, among whom the Russians constituted a clear minority (about 47 percent), peoples who were united only by the general exploitation on the part of the ruling clique of landowners, and united moreover through the help of the most brutal oppression. . . . Even the Muscovite State of the seventeenth century, in spite of the opinion of bourgeois historians, was no longer a national state of the Great Russian tribe.[16]

Indeed, this negative reflection on Russia's history was the cause of only a partial rehabilitation of Pokrovskii after 1953; he was described as "one of the former Marxist historians, whose works cannot be used at the present time as textbooks for students of history. . . . Soviet historiography in the meantime has made great progress."[17]

The restoration of Russian nationalism in Soviet historiography inescapably made Pokrovskii's works suspect and obsolete, due to emerging analogies between his portrayal of tsarist Russia and the contemporary state of affairs in the USSR. His dethroning coincided with several important events of far-reaching significance in Ukrainian and Belorussian history. The revival of the idea of statehood at the expense of previously stressed internationalism helped Stalin not only to build socialism in one country but also to establish a personal dictatorship that provided the opportunity to intervene in all spheres of life. On the level of the republics, these changes led to the suppression of local nationalisms, to an end to the policies of Ukrainization and Belorussianization, opening the way to more and deeper inroads for the Russian elements at the expense of the national interests of those nationalities. In the realm of historiography, the destruction of nationally oriented histories, represented by such outstanding scholars as Michael Hrushevskyi, Michael Dovnar-Zapolskyi, Vasyl Picheta, and others signaled disaster ahead. The subordination of Belorussian and Ukrainian historiographies to the dictates of the CPSU and the USSR Academy of Sciences resulted first of all in a new interpretation of the origin of all three respective nationalities. While the first steps to eliminate Hrushevskyi and Dovnar-Zapolskyi's historical schools were taken in 1934[18] and renewed by S. Kovalov in 1946,[19] the campaign has continued to the present. The most recent Soviet position was stated in response to the writings of Ukrainian national historians in the United States, especially in response to Mykola Chubatyi's study on the emergence of eastern Slavs.[20] Chubatyi dismissed as false the official Soviet version of a common origin from a mysterious "ancient Russian nationality" and of Kiev Rus' being the cradle of all three peoples. The Soviet historian B. Grekov insisted that "the history of Ancient Rus' was not a history of the Ukraine, nor of Belorussia, and not yet of Great Russia alone. It was the history of a state that enabled all three to mature and gain strength."[21] Yet in his terminology people of that state were "Russians" (russkie), and not as in Ukrainian national terminology Rusyny, Rusychi, or Ruthenians in Latinized usage, names under which Ukrainians were known for centuries. Exactly this linguistic confusion or the absence of a clearly defined terminology in Soviet as well as Russian national historiographies is the subject of Chubatyi's dispute and Hrushevskyi's earlier criticism.[22] Both favored a separation of the processes of formation of all three peoples within their ethnographic-territorial bases from the earliest stage to the present, an approach that rejects the Russian historical scheme promoted before 1917 and the contemporary Soviet position.

Defense of the Soviet official interpretation was assigned again to a Soviet Ukrainian historian, M. F. Kotliar. In a lengthy article, Kotliar concluded that by the sixth to ninth centuries eastern Slav tribes living within the Kiev-Chernyhiv-Pereiaslav triangle, known also as Rus'ka zemlia, developed a sense of unity, as evidenced by the formulation of a common language, state loyalty, and an economic life pattern.[23] This "ancient Rus'ian nationality" became in turn the common ethnological precedessor of three eastern Slav peoples: Russian, Ukrainian, and Belorussian, whose ultimate identities and differentiations emerged only in the fifteenth century. On the question of terminology, M. N. Tikhomirov, if consulted, could have helped

Kotliar to learn that the names Rossiia and Rossiiskoe gosudarstvo appear in historical annals at the end of the fourteenth century; only in the seventeenth century did the first Russian state, Muscovy, begin to call itself Russia.[24] Another Soviet Ukrainian historian, M. Iu. Braichevsky,[25] recently relieved of his teaching position at Kiev University, explained the formation of Russian nationality as a result of a mixture of Slavic tribes with Finno-Ugrian autochthons.

From among historians representing the Belorussian SSR, a non-Belorussian, M. Ia. Grinblat, was commissioned to defend the Soviet scheme. In his work, written in Russian,[26] Grinblat found his main target in M. Dovnar-Zapolskyi and "hostile Belorussian emigres," accusing them of "distortion and refusal to recognize the existence of drevnerusskaia narodnost." His attempt to prove that the Drehovychi, Kryvychi, and Radymychi tribes were aware of their Rus'ian nationality lacks concrete evidence such as the existence of a commonly used conversational language, a socioeconomic structure of life and of prevailing loyalty to one center, person, or institution.

On the other hand, research and writing related to the pre-Rus' age as well as to the Kiev Rus' state is almost exclusively reserved for Soviet Russian historians and the USSR Academy of Sciences. The only Soviet Ukrainian historical journal, Ukrains'kyi istorychnyi zhurnal, has not published a single article on the ancient history of Ukraine during the last five years. In Belorussia the situation is even worse, for there is no historical journal.

In addition to the late B. Grekov, and M. N. Tikhomirov, V. A. Rybakov and V. P. Shusharin belong to the group of Soviet Russian experts on Rus'. Shusharin took it upon himself to debate extensively several Ukrainian national historians of the past and present on the question of ethnogenity of eastern Slavs and claims to Kiev Rus'.[27] He spoke of Ukrainian national historiography as the greatest Soviet enemy, saying it continues to promote Ukrainian separatism from ancient times to the present and is, therefore, undermining the "everlasting union of brotherly peoples united by history and fate."

The Soviet theory of the common origin not only is in line with the Kremlin's internal policy but also provides the necessary background for the next historical stage of meetings among Russians, Ukrainians, and Belorussians. This comprises events of the seventeenth and eighteenth centuries related to Muscovy's expansion to the West and South, prolonged periods of conflicts and wars with Poland, and the question of incorporation of Belorussians and Ukrainians into the expanding Russian empire. At this stage of historical development, the idea of a common cradle became a handy tool for Russia's rulers and, subsequently, for Russian and Soviet historians.

For that particular period, the "reunion" of the formerly "single nationality" disintegrated into three different peoples as a result of foreign conquests—Tartar-Mongel, Lithuanian and Polish, during the fourteenth to sixteenth centuries. The term "reunification" preserved this same functional meaning in contemporary Soviet as well as in formerly tsarist Russian political and historical vocabulary. It gained an almost religious meaning in historiography, describing prolonged and complex events traceable to the rise of Muscovy and completed only in 1945 with the final incorporation into the USSR of Western Belorussia, West Ukraine, and Carpatho-Ukraine.

Pursuing the policy of "reunion of all Rus' lands," Muscovy-Russia seemingly emerged not as conqueror, as Pokrovskii held, but as rectifier of the original unity that had been destroyed by foreign enemies. Hence, not economic, military, or purely imperialistic motives guided Moscow but an exclusively altruistic policy of liberating kindred peoples from "foreign oppressors" (Lithuanian, Polish, Turkish, with Austrian and again Polish in 1939 added later on). For this reason, Soviet historical literature either minimized or just ignored the fact that the fate of the Belorussian and Ukrainian peasantry as well as the chances for the development of national cultures worsened under Russian occupation.[28] V. Ihnatouski, the Belorussian national historian, could not detect in the union with Russia any historical necessity or justification, for a union with Moscow would have proven still more disastrous (than with Poland-Lithuania) for the people, whose way of life was "completely and inherently incompatible with the social structure and moral climate of the Muscovite state." And according to I. Liastouski, "bitter reminiscences of the past turn the Belorussian away from both [Poland and Russia], with an equal disgust."[29] Nevertheless, the rewriting of history in the USSR resulted in a quite different interpretation. Another Russian-language book recently published by A. P. Ignatenko suggests that the Belorussian people have struggled for more than a century to be reunited with Russia.[30] Belorussians are told that "toward the end of the eighteenth century an ancient dream of the Belorussian people had been fulfilled. Belorussia was reunited with Russia. This event took on great importance in the further economic, political, and cultural development and opened new possibilities for a steady intercourse of the Belorussian people with the Russians and other peoples of Russia."[31]

This trend of gravitation toward Russia penetrates the structure and projection of the latest <u>History of Belorussia</u>, a five-volume work in process.[32] Chapter 12 of the first volume, entitled "Belorussian War of Liberation and the Struggle for the Reunification with Russia, 1648-1667," ties the uprisings in Belorussian with the Ukrainian Cossack revolt against Poland. Both movements shared, however, the desire for "reunification with Russia to which Russia responded favorably." Yet, despite the inclusion of Belorussians into the original "ancient Rus'ian nationality," chapter 6 of the second volume significantly narrows this partnership. It defines Belorussians as "latecomers," who only during the age of feudalism began to emerge as a people and only during the seventeenth and eighteenth centuries developed as a nation. Thus, in the 1970s Belorussians were relegated to the position of junior partner from the previously offered equal partnership. Belorussia's "reunification with Russia" came about not as a result of the Belorussian "struggle for unification" but only after Poland's partitions, 1772-95. This act of Russian, Prussian, and Austrian aggression also found a new interpretation in the newest Soviet History of the USSR:[33] "As far as Belorussian and Lithuanian lands are concerned [the partitions of Poland] are justifiable ones, which cannot be said, however, about Prussia's and Austria's robberies of Polish lands."[34] The logic of the reasoning of Soviet authors is that Russia's reunification of "former Rus'ian lands" was an act of justice even at the price of Poland's disappearance from the political map.

The most celebrated "reunion" in Russian as well as Soviet historiography is the Pereiaslav Treaty of 1654 between the Muscovite Tsar Alexis and the Hetman of Ukraine, Bohdan Khmelnytskyi.[35] This originally defensive alliance of two sovereign states with provisions guaranteeing political autonomy of the Ukraine and a certain measure of independence in foreign affairs, soon disregarded and ignored by the tsars, became the model for the future formulation of Russo-Ukrainian relations—with the understanding that union with Russia amounted to a renunciation of the idea of an independent Ukraine. To remind Ukrainians of their relinquishment of sovereignty and to restate Moscow's position on Russo-Ukrainian relations, this act of 1654 was commemorated in 1954, on its tercentenary, with the incorporation of the Crimea into the administrative frontiers of the Ukrainian SSR and with numerous political and historical publications.[36] Ukrainian Soviet historians, as well as the political establishment, had to reassure Moscow once again of their loyalty, express gratitude for making possible all Ukrainian achievements, and show their disapproval of writings by Ukrainian national historians.

> The bourgeois-nationalist historians' position on the reunification of the Ukraine with Russia was negative. They denied that the reunification was the result of an ancient friendship between Ukrainian and Russian peoples, and that in that period the economic, political, and cultural ties between these two peoples grew closer, and that Khmelnytskyi from the very beginning of his rising against Poland worked toward reunion with Russia, and that the reunification had a progressive impact upon the economic and cultural life of the Ukrainian people.[37]

None of the works on the tercentenary of the Pereiaslav Treaty elaborated on the negative aspects of the subsequent Russian policy in the Ukraine, resulting in the total elimination of autonomy, incorporation into the Russian empire, and suppression of the national movement including the very names Ukraine and Ukrainians. Subsequently, reunion became synonymous with Russification and the colonial-type influx of Russian nationals into Ukraine. The Prussianization of Germany served as a model not only to the Russian nationalistically minded Panslavists but also to the court in Petersburg and to the present Soviet leadership; this is reflected in M. S. Dzhunusov's article, "On Soviet Autonomy and Remnants of Nationalism," which summarizes well the state of affairs and the prospects for non-Russian nationalities:

> The numerical growth of the Russian nation is progressing not only as a result of natural increase but also as a result of a voluntary assimilation of the non-Russian nationalities. . . . The statistics show how intensively this process of assimilation progressed. There is no reason to assume that in the immediate future this process will slow down. On the contrary, it will become even more intensive.[38]

The article suggests that acceptance of the Russian national identity is a progressive act, a predetermined trend of the future, and an indicator of the emergence of an intensified period of Russification, sometimes presented as the building of a Soviet nation. The article's title also seems to indicate that remaining a Belorussian national symbolizes backwardness, while becoming a convert is in line with the "final destiny of history." Indeed, Russian Panslavists of the nineteenth century, together with Valuev and the "Black Hundreds," would be pleased with Dzunusov's reasoning.

Another development characteristic of changes within the USSR and promoted in Soviet historiography is the idea of "supranational pride" of the Soviet man. According to V. H. Korolko, this represents a new trend in the spiritual life of the socialist nations. It is reflected in the desire to be identified with "one fatherland, one destiny, one historical fate, and is being expressed more and more by all nationalities of the USSR."[39]

The process of achieving exclusive oneness is accompanied by intensive Russianization of the Belorussian and Ukrainian languages in addition to the policy of Russification penetrating every level and area of national life of those two nations. The trend favoring the Russian element, nationality, history, and language initiated by Stalin after World War II began to move in the 1960s to the next stage—exclusive domination of all vitally essential areas. Non-Russian elements, while tolerated on lower levels in society in such areas as folklore, elementary education, and language of only regional application, have been left with only a limited existence. Moreover, it has already been determined which way to move in order to recreate the ancient single nationality that passed through the process of reunification, adaptation, and sovietization. For to reunite on contemporary Soviet terms implies renunciation of linguistic, cultural, as well as historical differentiations. The prototype of the future society reveals the exclusiveness of the "grand Russian language," the final fusion (zlienie) of nations, and the transformation of the present republics (which still symbolize national and political stratification and identities) into only regional-administrative functions, thus creating psychological allegiance to only one state (rodina), with Moscow not only the exclusive power center but also the symbol and mirror of a new monolith—Soviet man, Soviet people, with "Russia" and "Russian" the only acceptable substitute and reference.

After several decades of experimentation, confusion, and promises, Soviet policy is returning to das ewige Russisch.[40] This, in final analysis, is an inescapable conclusion based on a survey of contemporary historiography exposing quite clearly all changes of the past and rapid adaptation to the present.

However, "it is too early to determine whether the new Soviet history, with its strong emphasis on the friendship of Soviet peoples in the past, will make the desired contribution to the reduction of nationalist tensions among the peoples of the Soviet family."[41] Imprisoned Ukrainian historian Valentyn Moroz, together with many other Ukrainian intellectual dissidents, has already begun to challenge and to correct the writing of the history of Ukraine and its relations with Russia, past and present. It was Moroz who assured his accusers that "the national rebirth is the deepest of all spiritual processes."[42]

NOTES

1. As exemplified by such works as Nicholas Chubaty, "The Ukrainian and Russian Conceptions of the History of Eastern Europe," Proceedings of the Historical-Philosophical Section of the Shevchenko Scientific Society, vol. 1 (1951), pp. 1-16; A. Varonic, "The History of Belorussia in the Works of Soviet Historiography," Belorussian Review, no. 2 (1956): 73-97; Dmytro Doroshenko, "A Survey of Ukrainian Historiography," and Olexander Ohloblyn, "Ukrainian Historiography, 1917-1956," in The Annals of the Ukrainian Academy of Arts and Sciences in the U.S., vol. 5, no. 4(18); vol. 6, nos. 1, 2 (19-20), New York, 1957; Oleksander Ohloblyn, Dumky pro suchasnu

ukrains'ku istoriohrafiiu (New York: OOChSU, 1963); Borys Krupnytskyi, Ukrains'ka istorychna nauka pid sovietamy (Munich: Institute for the Study of the USSR), 1957.

2. Nicholas P. Vakar, "The Name 'White Russia,'" The American Slavic and East European Review 8, no. 3 (1949): 201-13; Jaroslaw Pelenski, "Soviet Ukrainian Historiography After World War II," Jahrbuecher fuer Geschichte Osteuropas 12, no. 3 (1964): 375-418; Stephan M. Horak, "Ukrainian Historiography 1953-1963," Slavic Review 24, no. 2 (1965): 258-72; Lubomyr R. Wynar, "Ukrainian-Russian Confrontation in Historiography," Ukrainian Quarterly 30, no. 1 (1974): 13-25.

3. Lowell Tillett, The Great Friendship: Soviet Historians on the Non-Russian Nationalities (Chapel Hill: University of North Carolina Press, 1969).

4. Such as Erich Goldhagen, ed., Ethnic Minorities in the Soviet Union (New York: Praeger Publishers, 1968); Edward Allworth, ed., The Nationality Problems (New York and London: Columbia University Press, 1971); Robert Conquest, ed., Soviet Nationalities Policy in Practice (New York: Praeger Publishers, 1967); George Schopflin, ed., The Soviet Union and Eastern Europe: A Handbook (New York: Praeger Publishers, 1970).

5. G. B. Starushenko, Printsip samoopredeleniia narodov i natsii vo vneshnei politike Sovetskogo gosudarstva (Moscow, 1960), p. 54.

6. M. S. Szunusov, "O sovetskoi avtonomii i perezhitkakh natsionalizma," Istoriia SSSR, no. 1 (1963): 18; F. S. Martsinkevich, "Iekanamichne razvitse Belarusi u sastave Soiuza SSSR," Vestsi Akademii navuk BSSR, Serya hramadskikh navuk, no. 6 (1972): 16; V. H. Korolko, "Pro zahalnonatsionalnu hordist' radians'koi liudyny," Ukrains'kyi istorychnyi zhurnal, no. 3 (1974): 14. See also N. Vakar, "Soviet Nationality Policy: The Case of Belorussia," Problems of Communism 3, no. 5 (1954); Stephan M. Horak, "Belorussia: Modernization, Human Rights, Nationalism," Canadian Slavonic Papers 16, no. 3 (1974): 403-23; John Kolasky, Education in Soviet Ukraine: A Study in Discrimination and Russification (Toronto: Peter Martin, 1968), and his Two Years in Soviet Ukraine (Toronto: Peter Martin, 1970); Ivan Dzyuba, Internationalism or Russification (London: Weidenfeld and Nicolson, 1968); Vyacheslav Chornovil, comp., The Chornovil Papers, introduction by Frederick C. Barghoorn (New York: McGraw-Hill, 1969); Michael Browne, ed., Ferment in the Ukraine, forward by Max Hayward (New York and Washington, D.C.: Praeger Publishers, 1971); Serhii Mazlakh, On the Current Situation in the Ukraine, ed. Peter J. Potichnyj, introduction by Michael M. Luther (Ann Arbor: University of Michigan Press, 1970); Yaroslav Bihun, ed., Boomerang: The Works of Valentyn Moroz (Baltimore: Smoloskyp, 1974).

7. Lenin's views on nationalities policy are well documented in Alfred D. Low, Lenin on the Question of Nationality (New York: Bookman Associates, 1958).

8. See Richard Pipes, The Formation of the Soviet Union: Communism and Nationalism, 1917-1923 (Cambridge, Mass.: Harvard University Press, 1954). Selected works in English: Nicholas P. Vakar, Belorussia: The Making of a Nation: A Case Study (Cambridge, Mass.: Harvard University Press, 1956); Ivan S. Lubachko, Belorussia Under Soviet Rule, 1917-1957 (Lexington: University Press of Kentucky, 1972); Basil Dmytryshyn, Moscow and the Ukraine, 1918-1953: A Case Study of Russian Bolshevik Nationality Policy (New York: Bookman Associates, 1956); Jurij Borys, The Russian Communist Party and the Sovietization of Ukraine (Stockholm: the author, 1960); Robert S. Sullivant, Soviet Politics and the Ukraine, 1917-1957 (New York: Columbia University Press, 1962); Jurij Lawrynenko, Ukrainian Communism and Soviet Russian Policy Toward the Ukraine: An Annotated Bibliography, 1917-1953 (New York: Praeger Publishers, 1953).

On the Soviet side, Lenin's Collected Works, available by now in five different editions, remain essential to all authors discussing the nationalities question. The most recent interpretation is offered by A. K. Azizian, Leninskaia natsionalnaia politika v razvitii i deistvii (Moscow: 1972); M. I. Kulichenko, Natsionalnye otnosheniia v SSSR i tendetsii ikh razvitiia (Moscow, 1972); M. P. Kim, Sovetskii narod—novaia istoricheskaia obshchenost' (Moscow, 1972).

9. Tillett, The Great Friendship, p. 4.

10. On this aspect of Soviet historiography, see C. E. Black, ed., Rewriting Russian History: Soviet Interpretations of Russia's Past (New York: Praeger Publishers, 1956); Konstantin F. Shteppa, Russian Historians and the Soviet State (New Brunswick, N. J.: Rutgers University Press, 1962); Klaus Mehnert, Weltrevolution durch Weltgeschichte: Die Geschichte des Stalinismus (Stuttgart: Deutsche Verlags-Anstalt, 1953); Anatole G. Mazour, The Writing of History in the Soviet Union, Hoover Institution Publications no. 87 (Stanford, Calif.: Hoover Institution Press, 1971).

11. Ukrains'kyi istorychnyi zhurnal, no. 3 (1963): 140.

12. Lubachko, Belorussia, p. 115.

13. Tillett, The Great Friendship; Ohloblyn, "Ukrainian Historiography," Annals; Pelenski, "Soviet Ukrainian Historiography," Jahrbuecher; Horak, "Ukrainian Historiography," SR; Varonic, "The History of Belorussia," BR.

14. M. N. Pokrovskii, Russkaia istoriia s drevneishikh vremen (Leningrad, 1924), p. 137.

15. Pokrovskii, Russkaia istoriia, vol. 2, chapter 9.

16. M. N. Pokrovskii, Russia in World History: Selected Essays by M. N. Pokrovskii, edited with an introduction by Roman Szporluk (Ann Arbor: University of Michigan Press, 1970), p. 109.

17. From O. D. Sokolov's introduction to new edition of Pokrovskii's works, M. N. Pokrovskii, Izbrannye proizivedemiia, 4 vols. (Moscow, 1966), vol. 1, p. 71.

18. O. P. Ohloblyn, "Burzhuaznaia istorychna shkola Dovnar-Zapols'koho," Zapysky Istorychnoho instytutu Vseukrains'koi akademii nauk (1934), pp. 157-225.

19. S. Kovalov, "Vypravyty pomylky v osvitelli deiakykh pytan istorii Ukrainy," Kultura i zhyzn, no. 3 (1946); Pelenski, "Soviet Ukrainian Historiography," Jahrbuecher, pp. 377ff.

20. Mykola Chubatyi, Kniazha Rus'-Ukraina ta vynyknennia triokh skhidnoslovians'kykh natsii, Zapysky N. T. Sh., vol. 178 (New York: ODFFU, 1964).

21. B. Grekov, Kiev Rus (Moscow, 1959), p. 12.

22. On Hrushevskyi's scheme of Eastern Slavs' history, see Doroshenko, A Survey of Ukrainian Historiography, pp. 264-65; Horak, "Michael Hrushevsky: Portrait of Historian," Canadian Slavonic Papers 10, no. 3 (1968): 341-56.

23. M. F. Kotliar, "Proty burzhuazno-natsionalistychnykh perekruchen spilnoho mynuloho rosiis'koho, ukrains'koho ta bilorus'koho narodiv (IX-XV st.)," Ukrains'kyi istorychnyi zhurnal, no. 8 (1973): 3-14.

24. N. N. Tikhomirov, Rossiiskoe gosudarstvo XV-XVII vekov (Moscow, 1973), pp. 16-17.

25. M. Iu. Braichevs'kyi, Pokhodzhennia Rusi (Kiev, 1968), pp. 193-94.

26. M. Ia. Grinblat, Belorusy: Ocherki proiskhozhdeniia i etnicheskoi istorii (Minsk, 1968).

27. V. P. Shusharin, Sovremennaia burzhuaznaia istoriografiia Drevnei Rusi (Moscow, 1964).

28. Tadeusz St. Grabowski, Rus'-Ukraina i Bialorus pod rzadami Rosji, 2 vols. (Cracow, 1916); Vakar, Belorussia, pp. 30-33.

29. Quoted from Vakar, Belorussia, p. 64.

30. A. P. Ignatenko, Borba velorusskogo naroda za vossoedinenie s Rossiei (vtoraia polovina XVII-XVIII v.) (Minsk, 1974), p. 5.

31. Ignatenko, Borba bel. naroda, p. 168.

32. Historyia Belaruskau SSR u piatsi tamakh, AN BSSR, Instytut historyi (Minsk, 1972- ; three volumes published as of 1973).

33. Istoriia SSSR s drevneishikh vremen do nashikh dnei v dvukh seriiakh v dvanadtsati tomakh, AN SSSR, Instytut istorii (Moscow, 1966-).

34. Istoriia SSSR, vol. 3, p. 527.

35. For background material, see Tillett, The Great Friendship, pp. 298-99, 336-37; Pelenski, "Soviet Ukrainian Historiography," Jahrbuecher, pp. 381-89; Horak, "Ukrainian Historiography," SR, pp. 260-62.

36. Vossoedinenie Ukrainy s Rossiei, 1654-1954 (Moscow, 1954); Ivan Krypiakevych, Bohdan Khmelnytskyi (Kiev, 1954); Dokumenty ob osvoboditelnoi voine ukrainskogo naroda, 1648-1654 (Kiev, 1965); Nerushimaia druzhba bratskikh narodov SSSR: K 300-letiiu vossoiedineniia Ukrainy s Rossiei: Sbornik bibliograficheskikh i metodicheskikh materialov dlia massovykh bibliotek (Moscow, 1954); 300-richchia vozziednannia Ukrainy z Rosiieiu (1654-1954). Bibliohrafichnyi pokazhchyk (Kiev, 1953).

37. Krypiakevych, B. Khmelnytskyi, p. 10.

38. M. S. Dzunusov, "O sovetskoi avtonomii i perezhitkakh natsionalizma," Istoriia SSSR, no. 1 (1963): 19.

39. V. H. Korolko, "Pro zahalnonatsionalnu hordist' radians'koi liudyny," Ukrains'kyi istorychnyi zhurnal, no. 3 (1974): 24.

40. Mehnert, Weltrevolution, p. 29.

41. Tillett, The Great Friendship, p. 422.

42. Valentyn Moroz, "Zamist' ostannioho slova," in Shyroke more Ukrainy: Dokumenty samvydavu z Ukrainy (Paris and Baltimore: Smoloskyp, 1972), pp. 197-202.

CHAPTER

12

MODERNIZATION, POPULATION CHANGE, AND NATIONALITY IN SOVIET CENTRAL ASIA AND KAZAKHSTAN

Robert A. Lewis
Richard H. Rowland
Ralph S. Clem

Since the conquest of the area now known as Soviet Central Asia and Kazakhstan by Russian troops during the eighteenth and nineteenth centuries and the incorporation of the several major nationalities indigenous to that territory into the tsarist empire, a series of dramatic political, economic, and social changes have occurred in the region. The purpose of this essay will be to describe and explain the historical, demographic, and socioeconomic trends in Central Asia and Kazakhstan since the late nineteenth century, and to assess the benefits that have accrued to the Central Asians and Kazakhs as a result of the modernization of their homelands and their membership in the multinational Soviet federation.

Throughout, we use the term Central Asia or Soviet Central Asia to connote the Kirgiz, Tadzhik, Turkmen, and Uzbek republics. Kazakhstan, of course, coincides with the Kazakh Republic. The terms Central Asia and Central Asians will be understood to exclude Kazakhstan and Kazakhs, and to include the titular nationalities of the Central Asian region (the Kirgiz, Tadzhiks, Turkmens, Uzbeks, and Karakalpaks).

Our approach will be to examine the impact of Russian and Soviet rule in Central Asia and Kazakhstan within the framework of the concept of ethnic stratification. Ethnic stratification refers to the hierarchical ranking of nationalities along socioeconomic lines, which

---

This research was supported by grant HD 05585 of the Center for Population Research of the National Institute of Child Health and Human Development, and the International Institute for the Study of Human Reproduction, Columbia University.

seems to be a universal characteristic of countries including more than one ethnic group; this, incidentally, means most countries.[1] In this sense it is important to note that our approach explicitly assumes that the ethnic situation in the Soviet Union can be understood by reference to general concepts that seem valid for all multinational cases; the USSR, in other words, is not necessarily unique.

Systems of ethnic stratification are established after different nationalities come into contact, either through immigration or, as in Central Asia and Kazakhstan, through military conquest. The hierarchical rankings or status of nationalities within systems of ethnic stratification are arrived at through a gradual process wherein the relative power and cultural traits of the various groups result in a consensus as to which groups will enjoy the privileges of higher status and which will be consigned to subordinate positions. Once the system of ethnic stratification is established, sanctions and ideologies tend to perpetuate the order and change is only reluctantly accepted. Finally, visible differences in physical features, such as skin color, may serve to delimit further the cleavages in society.[2]

Of all aspects of social change, the process known generally as modernization has had the greatest impact upon human society. By modernization we mean the complex of economic, social, demographic, and psychological changes that began in Western Europe in the late eighteenth century and eventually spread to Central and Eastern Europe, Anglo-America, Australia, Japan, and the USSR. The primary effects of modernization are reflected in such tangible changes as economic development, industrialization, urbanization, lower levels of fertility and mortality, higher levels of education, a redefinition of the status of women, and also a number of more subtle and difficult to define changes involving personal aspirations, values, and attitudes.[3]

Within multinational countries, the effects of modernization are not experienced equally by all ethnic groups. It seems to be a universal fact that some nationalities enter the modernized sectors earlier than others, with the result that certain groups attain higher levels of modernization than others, as measured by socioeconomic and demographic indicators. The principal reason for these differential levels of modernization among ethnic groups appears to be twofold: (1) the system of ethnic stratification, with its sanctions against minorities, facilitates the entry of the dominant nationality into the modern sectors and inhibits the integration of the minorities and (2) certain ethnic groups appear to achieve high levels of modernization despite minority status because of facets of their culture that might be characterized as "achievement-oriented."[4]

With these very general remarks in mind, it is our intention to examine, in turn, (1) the historical and geographic basis of Russian rule in Central Asia and Kazakhstan; (2) the impact of modernization in the area; and (3) the implications of these forces for the future Soviet society. First, it would be in order to mention briefly the derivation of the data that form the basis of our investigation.

Although substantial census data exists for the area comprising the present-day Soviet Union, problems of area comparability and definitional consistency have rendered rigorous empirical research over time almost impossible. About ten years ago we began an extensive project through which we hoped to arrive at a solution to these problems and ultimately to derive a set of data in comparable geographic units and employing consistent definitions.[5] Essentially, what we have done is to reorder data from the tsarist census of 1897, the Soviet censuses of 1926, 1959, and 1970, and a large number of censuses from surrounding countries (necessary because of changes in the national territory of the USSR) into nineteen territorially comparable regions (the Soviet economic regions of 1961).[6] Thus, we now have available a time series of consistent data beginning in the tsarist era in the late nineteenth century (1897) through the early years of communist power (1926) and into the postwar (1959) and present-day (1970) Soviet periods. To supplement these census figures, we have calculated several other indexes from aggregate data on education and work force.

THE HISTORICAL AND GEOGRAPHIC BASIS OF RUSSIAN RULE

The history of Russian imperial expansion into Central Asia and Kazakhstan is well known and will only be summarized here. When Russian contact with the Kazakhs and Central Asians began in earnest in the early eighteenth century, the various nationalities of the area, although frequently engaged in internecine warfare, formed a defensive system in depth, with the steppe and semidesert expanses to the north and desert to the west shielding the agricultural oases to the south and east. In order to conquer the entire area, the Russians first had to break through the nomadic Kazakhs, a task that they accomplished by establishing lines of fortified posts to the north, east, and then south of the steppe.[7] By the middle of the nineteenth century, the Kazakhs had been effectively neutralized by this encirclement and Russian attention turned toward the Muslim khanates of Bukhara, Khiva, and Kokand to the south.

Contrary to their earlier expectations, the Russians found on closer contact with the khanates that the Muslim states possessed little in terms of military power and political organization. Once they appreciated this fact, the tsarist forces overwhelmed the remainder of what is now Soviet Central Asia in short order. Only sixteen years elapsed between the fall of Tashkent in 1865, a landmark event that foretold the end of the khanate's independence, and the climactic battle with the Turkmens at Gok Tepe in 1881, which for all intents and purposes signaled the completion of tsarist expansion in Central Asia.[8]

A number of reasons have been proposed to explain the expansion of the Russian empire into Kazakhstan and Central Asia. The more tangible reasons cited include the desire to obtain new trade routes and trading partners, secure frontier settlements against nomad attacks, the need for agricultural land, and the aggressive, often unilateral actions of frontier commanders. Less tangible reasons that have been proposed include a spirit of manifest destiny, the enhancement of Russian prestige abroad, and the desire to counter growing British pressure from further south in India and Afghanistan. It appears likely that all the factors cited here, and possibly others, at one time or another played some role in Russian planning.[9]

Whatever the motivations for the territorial expansions of the empire, the conquest and pacification of Kazakhstan and Central Asia by the Russians and the incorporation of the area into the tsarist state led to significant social and demographic changes. By far the most important consequence of tsarist rule in the regions was the inmigration of Russians, Ukrainians, Tatars, Armenians, and other nationalities. With regard to this aspect of population change, it is necessary to discuss the cases of Kazakhstan and Central Asia separately, because the migration to the Kazakh steppe was considerably larger and of a different character than that to Central Asia.

The vast majority of migrants to Kazakhstan during the tsarist period were agricultural settlers, and the bulk were ethnic Russians. The earliest Russian penetration of the Kazakh steppe was that by the Ural Cossacks in the sixteenth century; eventually the Cossack regiments occupied territory along almost the entire northern and eastern boundaries of the Kazakh lands. Numerically, however, the major influx of Russians to Kazakhstan during the tsarist era did not take place until the late nineteenth century and the first decade of the twentieth century.[10] This migration involved principally Russian and some Ukrainian peasants and resulted from a set of push-and-pull forces such as the poor rural conditions in European Russia and the promise of good agricultural land in Kazakhstan.[11]

Our data indicate that by the first tsarist census in 1897 there were over 772,000 Russians within the borders of the present-day Kazakh SSR, and by 1926, in the first years of Soviet rule, this figure had grown to over 1,355,000 (see Table 9). In addition to the Russians, there were over 100,000 Ukrainians in Kazakhstan in 1897, and well

TABLE 9

Total Population by Russians and Other Eastern Slavs
in Kazakhstan and Central Asia, 1897-1970
(in millions)

	1897	1926	1959	1970
Kazakhstan				
Russians	.77	1.35	3.99	5.55
Ukrainians	.13	.86	1.12	.94
Belorussians	.00	.02	.11	.20
Total eastern Slavs	.90	2.23	5.22	6.69
Central Asia				
Russians	.12	.48	2.28	2.97
Ukrainians	.03	.11	.26	.29
Belorussians	.00	.01	.02	.36
Total eastern Slavs	.15	.60	2.56	3.62
Central Asia and Kazakhstan				
Russians	.89	1.83	6.27	8.52
Ukrainians	.16	.97	1.38	1.23
Belorussians	.00	.03	.13	.56
Total eastern Slavs	1.05	2.83	7.78	10.31

Note: These figures do not incorporate the territorial exchange between the Uzbek and Kazakh SSRs in the Golodnaya Steppe. This exchange did not have great demographic significance, especially since much of the originally exchanged area was returned to Kazakhstan by the time of the 1970 census.
Sources: See note 6.

over three-quarters of a million in 1926. In 1897 the Russians alone accounted for 16 percent of the population of Kazakhstan; if all eastern Slavs (Russians, Ukrainians, and Belorussians) are considered jointly, they amounted to almost 19 percent of the population. By 1926 the Russian share of the population had increased to 22 percent, and that of all eastern Slavs to 36 percent.

The in-migration of Russians and other outsiders to Central Asia was of considerably less magnitude. By 1897 only about 120,000 Russians and about 10,000 Ukrainians were living in this region. In 1926 the figure had risen to 480,000 Russians and about 110,000 Ukrainians. Yet by 1926 the Russians accounted for only about 6 percent of the population of Central Asia, as contrasted with 22 percent for the Russian share of the population of Kazakhstan at the same time. Since migration during this preindustrial period was closely tied to agricultural resettlement, the lesser volume of migration to Central Asia (compared to Kazakhstan) can be attributed primarily to the scarcity of available farmland. Agriculture in Central Asia is based upon intensive cultivation of irrigated plots in a desert environment, whereas the open steppe to the north required no irrigation systems. Furthermore, the prime lands in the south were already densely occupied by the indigenous Central Asians, and due to the high costs involved in expanding irrigated acreage, little accommodation could be made for Russian agricultural settlers.[12]

THE IMPACT OF MODERNIZATION

By the beginning of the Soviet period, the Russians had already established their presence numerically in Kazakhstan and Central Asia, as the foregoing figures illustrate. The major demographic and socioeconomic impact of Russian rule was yet to come, however, and this impact was to be occasioned by the rapid economic development and industrialization that began in the Soviet Union in the late 1920s. As in the preindustrial period, the Russian influence was to be much greater in Kazakhstan than in the four republics to the south.

The extremely fast growth of extractive and manufacturing industry in Kazakhstan during the pre-World War II and postwar periods is characteristic of the expansion of Soviet economic power in general. The Kazakh SSR is particularly well endowed with the mineral resources necessary for heavy industries, the industries emphasized in Soviet economic plans. Major coal basins at Karaganda and Ekibastuz, iron ore at Kustanay, copper deposits at Dzhezkazgan and Balkhash, major reserves of nonferrous metals in the Altay Mountains, and petroleum along the littoral of the Caspian Sea have facilitated the establishment of major industrial centers in Kazakhstan.[13] The growth of heavy industry in the republic also was prompted by the shift of manufacturing plants to eastern regions of the USSR in advance of the German invasion in World War II.

The economic development of Kazakhstan is dramatically reflected in the growth of cities in the republic during the Soviet period. Between 1926 and 1939 the average annual growth of the urban population in Kazakhstan was almost twice the rate for the entire Soviet Union.[14] Only one other region of the USSR (the Far East) had an urban growth rate higher than that of Kazakhstan during the 1926-39 period. During the period 1939-59 the rate of urban growth in Kazakhstan again was almost twice that of the Union-wide rate, exceeding all other regions of the USSR. Finally, between 1959 and 1970 the percentage increase in the urban population of Kazakhstan was higher than in all but two Soviet regions (Moldavia and Belorussia), both of which benefited in this particular measure because of relatively small base figures.

The immediate impact of this tremendous industrialization and urban growth has been the in-migration of Russians and other outsiders into the urban areas of Kazakhstan. By 1959 there were almost 4 million Russians in the Kazakh SSR, an increase of 2.6 million over 1926. The vast majority of this Russian increase took place in cities; between 1926 and 1959 the number of urban Russians in Kazakhstan grew by over 1.6 million, whereas rural Russians in the republic increased by about 960,000. The growth of urban Russians in Kazakhstan was even more pronounced between 1959 and 1970, amounting to almost 1.3 million, or over 87 percent of the total increase for Russians in the republic during this period (1.5 million).

In 1959 Russians comprised 42.7 percent of the total population of the Kazakh SSR, and in 1970 they totaled 42.4 percent. These percentages represent a large increase from 1926, an increase that can be partially accounted for by a significant loss in the Kazakh population, largely as a result of economic disorganization. The Kazakh population of the USSR, most of whom live in the Kazakh SSR, declined from almost 4 million in 1926 to barely more than 3 million in 1939. Taking natural increase into consideration, the total loss in population was about 1.5 million people. The slight relative decline in Russians between 1959 and 1970 is largely the result of a very high rate of natural increase among the Kazakh population.

In contrast to Kazakhstan, the four republics of Central Asia have not experienced such a high rate of industrial or urban growth. The Central Asian republics do not possess a mineral resource base equal to that of Kazakhstan, although their deposits of petroleum and natural gas have figured prominently in economic development under the Soviets. The average annual rate of urban growth between 1926 and 1939 was below the Union-wide rate, and during the period 1939 to 1959 only slightly exceeded the Soviet average.[15] The rate of growth of urban areas in Central Asia has increased more recently, as evidenced by the fact that the percentage increase in urban population between 1959 and 1970 for this region was exceeded only by Moldavia, Belorussia, and Kazakhstan.

As of 1970 there were slightly more than half as many Russians in Central Asia as in Kazakhstan. Between 1926 and 1959 the number of Russians increased from 480,000 to over 2.2 million, and during the period 1959 to 1970 the figure rose to almost 3 million. In 1959 Russians comprised 16.4 percent of the population of Central Asia, and in 1970 they totaled 15.1 percent. Once again the relative decline is the result of a very high rate of natural increase among Central

Asians. The largest increases in the Russian population have taken place in Central Asian cities. Of the increase of more than 2.5 million Russians in the four Central Asian republics since 1926, over 70 percent, or almost 1.8 million, has been in the cities.

In summary, tsarist and Soviet rule in Central Asia and Kazakhstan has resulted in a heavy influx of Russians and others into the area. In the tsarist and early Soviet period this influx was primarily agricultural in nature, although numerous Russians also moved to cities. During the Soviet industrialization drives of the pre-World War II and postwar periods, large numbers of Russians moved to Kazakhstan and Central Asia to take jobs in the rapidly expanding urban sector.

IMPLICATIONS

The in-migration of Russians into Central Asia and Kazakhstan and the consequences can best be understood by reference to the previously mentioned concept of ethnic stratification. The Russians, as military conquerors of the area, have, as is usually the case in such situations, preempted the more desirable lands and sectors of society. During the preindustrial tsarist period, Russian agricultural settlers seized grazing lands and migratory routes from the nomadic Kazakhs, much as pioneers and livestock ranchers occupied Indian lands along the expanding American frontier, and English settlers annexed territories from the Maori in New Zealand. In all these instances, the superior military power of the outsiders forced the indigenous groups to accept this radical alteration of the status quo, but only after a long and bitter struggle. The uprising of the Kazakhs under Kenesary Kasim between 1837 and 1847 parallels the Indian wars in the United States and the Maori wars in the early 1860s in New Zealand.

With the onset of modernization in Kazakhstan and Central Asia, particularly as this process is manifested by urbanization and industrialization, the Russians continued to preempt the more desirable sectors of society, although now their attention turned to the expanding urban and manufacturing sectors. Because of the existence of an ethnic stratification system, the entrance of Russians into the modernized sectors was facilitated and that of the indigenous peoples was impeded.

As noted above, after 1926 the influx of Russians to Kazakhstan and Central Asia was directed mainly to cities, this move in turn being related to industrialization. Because of the dominant status of the Russians, cities and industry became Russian in all but geographic location. Karl Deutsch, in his well-known study of modernization and its relationship to nationality, suggested that "social communication"

TABLE 10

Level of Urbanization by Russians and Major Nationalities
of Central Asia and Kazakhstan, 1970
(census definition of urban)

Nationality	Percentage Urbanization
Russians	68.0
Kazakhs	26.7
Kirgiz	14.6
Tadzhiks	26.0
Turkmens	31.0
Uzbeks	24.9
Karakalpaks	30.5

Source: 1970 Soviet census (see note 6).

links were particularly important in determining the extent to which the individual could integrate into advanced segments of society; language is of major importance in providing or inhibiting access to more desirable fields.[16] A Soviet demographer has essentially confirmed this hypothesis in a study of the ethnic composition of the work force at two modern enterprises in the Tadzhik SSR, in which he attributed the overwhelming presence of Russians and dramatic underrepresentation of indigenous Tadzhiks to a lack of industrial skills and poor command of the Russian language (which is used in the plants) on the part of the Tadzhiks.[17] The fact that Russians do have the necessary skills and that the Russian and not the Tadzhik language is used in the modern economic sector is a reflection of the early modernization of Russians and the dominant position of Russians within Soviet society.

The question now becomes: What effect has this influx of outsiders had upon the social and economic development of the indigenous Kazakh and Central Asian nationalities? Clearly, as measured by available socioeconomic and demographic indicators, the effect of ethnic stratification has been to limit the participation of the non-Russians in modernized society. Perhaps the best single indicator of modernization is the level of urbanization of a group or country (the percent of the population residing in urban centers). Although the Soviet Union is generally regarded as a modernized country, with over one-half of its population residing in cities based upon the census definition of urban (56 percent in 1970), all of the Central Asian nationalities and the

Kazakhs are below one-third urban; the Kirgiz, the group with the lowest level of urbanization among the Central Asians, are only 15 percent urban (see Table 10). Although international comparisons are only approximate because of definitional differences, it is nevertheless interesting to note that the 1970 levels of urbanization for the Central Asians and the Kazakhs are about equal to the levels in such developing countries as Liberia, Zambia, Paraguay, and West Malaysia.[18]

The most important explanation for the low level of urbanization of the Kazakhs and Central Asians is simply that Russians and other outsiders moved into the regions to take the industrial and service jobs in expanding urban areas, largely because of the relatively low levels of education and training of the indigenous peoples.[19] Thus, Central Asians and Kazakhs have been impeded from moving to cities in their own homelands. This contention is borne out by data on the ethnic composition of urban areas (census definition of urban) in Central Asia and Kazakhstan (see Table 11). In 1970 Russians accounted for a high of 58 percent of the urban population of Kazakhstan and a low of 29 percent in the Turkmen SSR. Russians comprised 45 percent of the total urban population of Central Asia and Kazakhstan combined in 1970, and the Central Asians and Kazakhs accounted for 34 percent. Put another way, in 1970 there were roughly 1.5 million more Russians in cities in Central Asia and Kazakhstan than there were Central Asians and Kazakhs.

The Russian domination of urban areas in Central Asia and Kazakhstan is mirrored in the ethnic composition of the capital cities of the various Union republics in the region, as shown in Table 11.

TABLE 11

Russians as a Percent of Urban Population in
Central Asia and Kazakhstan, 1970
(census definition of urban)

	Urban Population	Capital City Only
Kazakh SSR	58.4	70.3 (Alma-Ata)
Kirgiz SSR	51.4	66.1 (Frunze)
Tadzhik SSR	30.0	42.0 (Dushanbe)
Turkmen SSR	29.0	42.7 (Ashkhabad)
Uzbek SSR	30.4	40.8 (Tashkent)

Source: 1970 Soviet census (see note 6).

TABLE 12

Level of Urbanization by Russians and
Turkic-Muslims, 1897-1970
(15,000 and over definition)

	1897	1970	Percentage Change
Russians	13.0	56.3	43.3
Turkic-Muslims	5.0	22.8	17.8

Sources: See note 6.

In all these ostensible centers of the nationalities' political and economic life, Russians outnumbered the titular ethnic groups. In the most extreme cases, there are about six times as many Russians as Kazakhs in Alma-Ata, and about five times as many Russians as Kirgiz in Frunze. The ethnic balance between Russians and the titular nationalities in the other three capitals, Tashkent, Dushanbe, and Ashkhabad, is much closer.

With regard to historical trends in urbanization, data available on the Union-wide scale reveal that the Russians have benefited from modernization to a much greater extent than the Central Asians and Kazakhs. We have calculated the relative difference between the levels of urbanization for the Russians and the Turkic-Muslim nationalities (excluding Tatars) of the Russian empire and the Soviet Union for each census year, using a consistent urban definition (see Table 12). The majority of the supranational Turkic-Muslim grouping is comprised of Central Asians and Kazakhs, although the Azeri, some other Caucasus groups, and a few nationalities of the Volga region also are included. Importantly, Tatars, because of their unique status, are not included in this grouping. In 1897 the difference in the level of urbanization between the Russians and the Turkic-Muslims was 8 percentage points, but by 1970 the difference had increased to 33.5 percentage points. This is, of course, a reflection of the fact that the Russians urbanized at a faster rate during this period than did the Turkic-Muslims.

In a recent study, Leslie Dienes demonstrated that significant differences remain in the level of economic development among regions of the USSR, despite Soviet pronouncements regarding the desirability of a uniform pattern of growth.[20] In another study, Gertrude Schroeder presented data indicating that the four Central Asian republics and Kazakhstan are below the Union-wide average on four indicators of living standards: personal income; retail sales services; expenditures on health, education, and culture; and urban housing space.[21] Important as these regional inequalities are, indicating as they do that Central Asia and Kazakhstan have not yet benefited from membership in the multinational Soviet federation to the extent that other, primarily Russian, areas have, the crucial fact is that within Central Asia and Kazakhstan themselves the indigenous nationalities are deprived relative to outsiders.

Data available on other aspects of participation in advanced sectors substantiate the fact that the Russians have modernized to a greater extent than the Central Asians and Kazakhs. Figures available on the Union-wide levels of education (see Table 13) indicate that the percentage of the population of each of the nationalities attaining higher or secondary education remains lower for the Central Asians and Kazakhs than for the Russians, and in fact the disparity increased between 1959 and 1970. Data on students in higher education, standardized for age (see Table 14), reveal that the rate for Russians remains higher than for the nationalities of Central Asia and Kazakhstan, but, interestingly, in this index the Central Asians (with the exception of the Turkmens) and Kazakhs gained ground relative to the Russians between 1959 and 1970. Finally, figures for participation in the

TABLE 13

Educational Levels by Russians and Major Nationalities of Central Asia and Kazakhstan, 1959 and 1970

	Percent of Population Over 10 Years of Age Having Higher and Secondary Education (including incomplete secondary)		Percentage Change
	1959	1970	
Russians	37.8	50.8	13.0
Kazakhs	26.8	39.0	12.2
Kirgiz	29.9	40.0	10.1
Tadzhiks	29.9	39.0	9.1
Turkmens	36.3	43.0	6.7
Uzbeks	31.1	41.2	10.1

Sources: 1959 and 1970 Soviet censuses (see note 6).

TABLE 14

Students in Higher Education Per 1,000 Population Aged 16-24
by Russians and Major Nationalities of Central Asia
and Kazakhstan, 1959 and 1970

	1959	1970	Change
Russians	100.2	146.1	45.9
Kazakhs	95.8	143.1	47.3
Kirgiz	89.6	158.0	68.4
Tadzhiks	63.6	111.1	47.5
Turkmens	88.0	122.4	34.4
Uzbeks	81.0	134.4	53.4

Sources: Tsentral'noye Statisticheskoye Upravleniye pri Sovete Ministrov SSSR, Narodnoye Khozyaystvo SSSR v 1964 G. (Moscow: Statistika, 1965), p. 691; Tsentral'noye Statisticheskoye Upravleniye pri Sovete Ministrov SSSR, Narodnoye Obrazovaniye, Nauka i Kultura v SSSR (Moscow: Izdatel'stvo "Statistika," 1971), p. 196. Data on student enrollments for 1959 are not available. Accordingly, we have utilized figures for the 1962-63 school year, the earliest available, and have standardized these on the 1959 population. In reality, therefore, the 1959 data presented here are slightly inflated, but the overall relationships remain valid.

TABLE 15

Specialists with Higher and Secondary Education Per 1,000 Population
Aged 16-59 by Russians and Major Nationalities of
Central Asia and Kazakhstan, 1959 and 1970

	1959	1970	Change
Russians	72.8	134.9	62.1
Kazakhs	41.5	94.0	52.5
Kirgiz	38.5	84.0	45.5
Tadzhiks	32.7	67.5	34.8
Turkmens	39.8	79.9	40.1
Uzbeks	30.3	75.7	45.4

Sources: 1959 specialist data from Tsentral'noye Statisticheskoye Upravleniye pri Sovete Ministrov SSSR, Narodnoye Khozyaystvo SSSR v 1959 G. (Moscow: Gosstatizdat, 1960), p. 617; 1970 specialist data from Tsentral'noye Statisticheskoye Upravleniye pri Sovete Ministrov SSSR, Narodnoye Obrazovaniye, Nauka i Kultura v SSSR (Moscow: Izdatel'stvo "Statistika," 1971), p. 240.

modernized work force (specialists) also indicate that in this important sector the Russians enjoy a considerable lead over the Central Asians and Kazakhs and increased this margin between 1959 and 1970 (see Table 15).

Another implication of the lack of integration of the indigenous population of Central Asia and Kazakhstan into the modernized sectors of the society is the continued high rate of natural increase of the indigenous population, which is largely rural, has relatively low educational levels, numbers about 20 million people, and has increased almost 4 percent per year over the past decade. This, of course, means that if this rate persists the indigenous population will double in less than 20 years. Because Russians and other outsiders have been migrating in large numbers to the urban areas of Central Asia and Kazakhstan, the rural-urban migration of the indigenous population has been impeded, and the indigenous population has had a low rate of mobility. Even if this in-migration from outside the region did not occur, it is extremely doubtful that the Central Asia and Kazakh cities could absorb the rapidly growing indigenous work force. Currently, there are labor surpluses in the rural areas of Central Asia and Kazakhstan, and labor deficits throughout the Soviet economy, particularly in unskilled jobs, which traditionally have been taken by migrants. During the decade of the 1980s, most "European" areas of the USSR will have a nearly stationary work force, excluding migration, and some of the more industrialized areas will experience an absolute decline in work force. Over half the entire increase in the Soviet work force during this decade will come from Central Asia and Kazakhstan. Similar conditions elsewhere have resulted in considerable out-migration, as migration has equalized the supply of and demand for labor on a regional basis. (Note the situation in the United States in this century and recent foreign immigration in Western Europe.)

To date Russians have been moving into the cities of non-Russian areas in large numbers, and Russian areas have remained largely homogeneous. It can be expected that with continued economic development (which has occurred primarily in the Russian areas) and continued population growth in the less-developed, non-Russian areas, particularly Turkic-Muslim areas, there will be a significant migratory flow of non-Russians into Russian areas. The simple truth is that economic development of a country, being uneven, normally results in a massive redistribution of population, and in a multinational state much ethnic mixing, which for a variety of reasons results in ethnic tensions.[22]

CONCLUSIONS

In conclusion, the system of ethnic stratification that developed in Kazakhstan and Central Asia after the imposition of tsarist and Soviet rule provided the Russians with an inherent advantage in competition for both preindustrial (agricultural) and modernized roles. Thus, the indigenous Central Asians and Kazakhs have been excluded to a significant degree from the advanced society in their own nationality homelands.

This is not to suggest that the nationalities of Central Asia and Kazakhstan have not benefited at all from Russian rule. We hasten to mention that the material achievements of the Soviet government, and even of the tsarist regime, in Central Asia and Kazakhstan have been dramatic and in large measure deserving of praise. It is widely recognized that the Russians have effected improvements in the fields of public health and medicine, education and literacy, transportation, the emancipation of women, and in the establishment of general order and security.

Yet two inescapable considerations remain. First, the Central Asians and Kazakhs continue to be characterized by lower levels of modernization than outsiders within their own traditional territories. Despite the well-publicized comparisons with neighboring Muslim countries urged upon the nationalities of Central Asia and Kazakhstan, is it not more likely that the Central Asians and Kazakhs will contrast their position with that of the Russians, who occupy such a large share of modern society within their regions? One is reminded here of the invidious suggestion that blacks in the United States need only contrast their socioeconomic gains with blacks in Africa to "appreciate" their position in American society. Further, since the Soviet Union is a federation of ethnic territories and inasmuch as official propaganda has legitimized these nationality republics over the years, Central Asians and Kazakhs may expect certain advantages to accrue to them in their own titular units.

Finally, one must consider the subjective question of the continuing domination of nationalities and their homelands by an outside group. How does one balance the fact that there are many more hospital beds per capita in the Tadzhik SSR than in Afghanistan against the plain fact that the Afghans are independent and the Tadzhiks are not? Referring to situations such as Central Asia and Kazakhstan, where the indigenous population may have benefited in material terms from foreign domination, Tamotsu Shibutani and Kian M. Kwan have noted: "In many cases subjugated peoples have enjoyed material advantages as a result of the contact, but they have invariably dwelled upon the indignities."[23]

Modernization, in the global context, seems to have disjunctive potential for multinational states, according to Walker Connor.[24] The modernization and subsequent population change in Central Asia and Kazakhstan may lead to social and political tensions unless the nationalities of the area are integrated into modernized society in larger numbers.

NOTES

1. The concept of ethnic stratification is developed in Tamotsu Shibutani and Kian M. Kwan, Ethnic Stratification: A Comparative Approach (New York: Macmillan, 1965).
2. Ibid., chapters 6-9.
3. See Cyril E. Black, The Dynamics of Modernization (New York: Harper and Row, 1966), chapter 1.
4. Shibutani and Kwan, Ethnic Stratification, chapter 1, pp. 63-66.
5. The background of and procedures utilized in this project are in J. William Leasure and Robert A. Lewis, Population Changes in Russia and the USSR: A Set of Comparable Territorial Units (San Diego: San Diego State College Press, 1966).
6. Russian Empire, Tsentral'nyy Statisticheskiy Komitet Ministerstva Vnutrennikh Del, Pervaya Vseobshchaya Perepis' Naseleniya Rossiyskoy Imperii, 1897 G., 89 vols.; USSR, Tsentral'noye Statisticheskoye Upravleniye SSSR, Vsesoyuznaya Perepis' Naseleniya 1926 Goda, 66 vols.; USSR, Tsentral'noye Statisticheskoye Upravleniye pri Sovete Ministrov SSSR, Itogi Vsesoyuznoy Perepisi Naseleniya 1959 Goda, 16 vols.; and USSR, Tsentral'noye Statisticheskoye Upravleniye pri Sovete Ministrov SSSR, Itogi Vsesoyuznoy Perepisi Naseleniya 1970 Goda, 7 vols. For a list of the censuses and other sources for surrounding countries, see note 3 of Robert A. Lewis and Richard H. Rowland, "Urbanization in Russia and the USSR: 1897-1966," Annals of the Association of American Geographers 59, no. 4 (1969): 777.
7. Edward Allworth, "Encounter," in Central Asia: A Century of Russian Rule, ed. Edward Allworth (New York: Columbia University Press, 1967), pp. 7-19.
8. Helene Carrere d'Encausse, "Systematic Conquest, 1865 to 1884," in ibid., pp. 131-50.
9. Allworth, "Encounter," pp. 19-35, 53-59; Richard A. Pierce, Russian Central Asia, 1867-1917 (Berkeley: University of California Press, 1960), chapter 2.
10. George J. Demko, The Russian Colonization of Kazakhstan, 1896-1916 (The Hague: Mouton, 1969), chapters 2, 3.

11. J. William Leasure and Robert A. Lewis, "Internal Migration in Russia in the Late Nineteenth Century," Slavic Review 27, no. 3 (1968): 375-94; "Internal Migration in the USSR: 1897-1926," Demography 4, no. 2 (1967): 479-96.

12. Pierce, Russian Central Asia, 1867-1917, pp. 107-38.

13. Theodore Shabad, Basic Industrial Resources of the U.S.S.R. (New York: Columbia University Press, 1969), pp. 284-308.

14. Lewis and Rowland, "Urbanization in Russia and the USSR: 1897-1966," pp. 776-96. The urban definition employed by Lewis and Rowland is based on all centers with a population of 15,000 or more. This will be the urban definition generally utilized in this study. When the census definition is used, it will be so indicated.

15. Ibid., p. 782, Table 3.

16. Karl W. Deutsch, Nationalism and Social Communication, 2d ed. (Cambridge, Mass.: MIT Press, 1966), pp. 96-104.

17. V. I. Perevedentsev, "O Vliyanii Etnicheskikh Faktorov na Territorial'noye Pereraspredeleniye Naseleniya," Izvestiya Akademii Nauk SSSR, Seriya Geograficheskaya, no. 4 (1965): 34-36.

18. Non-Soviet data from United Nations, Department of Economic and Social Affairs, Demographic Yearbook, 1971 (New York: United Nations, 1972), pp. 139-58.

19. Ralph S. Clem, "The Impact of Demographic and Socioeconomic Forces Upon the Nationality Question in Central Asia," in The Nationality Question in Soviet Central Asia, ed. Edward Allworth (New York: Praeger Publishers, 1973), pp. 35-44.

20. Leslie Dienes, "Investment Priorities in Sovict Regions," Annals of the Association of American Geographers 62, no. 3 (1972): 437-54. The figures in Table 1, p. 438, reveal that as of the mid-1960s Kazakhstan and Central Asia lagged behind the Union-wide average in all key indicators of development.

21. Gertrude Schroeder, "Regional Differences in Incomes and Levels of Living in the USSR," in The Soviet Economy in Regional Perspective, ed. J. N. Bandera and Z. L. Melnyk (New York: Praeger Publishers, 1973).

22. For a detailed discussion of this problem, see Robert A. Lewis, Richard H. Rowland, and Ralph S. Clem, Nationality and Population Change in Russia and the USSR: 1897-1970 (forthcoming).

23. Shibutani and Kwan, Ethnic Stratification, p. 5.

24. Walker Connor, "Nation-Building or Nation-Destroying," World Politics 24, no. 3 (1972): 319-55.

NAME INDEX

Allende, Salvatore, 116, 123, 124, 125

Brezhnev, Leonid I., 33, 34, 137

Dubcek, Alexander, 78, 81, 82, 85, 86, 87, 88, 90
Dzhagarov, Georgi, 182, 187

Ehrenburg, Ilya, 165
Engels, Friedrich, 115, 126, 127

Fadeev, Aleksandr A., 168

Gierek, Edward, 59, 67, 69, 71
Gomulka, Wladyslaw, 55, 59
Grossman, Vasilii, 165, 166, 168, 169, 170, 172

Kautsky, Karl, 128
Khrushchev, Nikita S., 137, 143, 154
Kolakowski, Leszek, 179

Lenin, Vladimir I., 144, 148, 181, 204; on democratic centralism, 188; on dictatorship of the proletariat, 128-29; on nationalities, 203, 204; on political communications, 133-35, 144, 154; on public opinion, 139-40

Malenkov, Georgii M., 163, 171
Marx, Karl, 10, 11, 12, 113, 115, 119, 122, 129; on dictatorship of the proletariat, 111, 115-16, 120, 125-29; on nationalities, 202
Mlynar, Zdenek, 79, 80, 85

Novotny, Antonin, 77, 78

Ovechkin, Valentin, 171, 172

Polrovskii, Mikhail N., 204, 205, 206, 208

Slavik, Vaclav, 80, 81
Smrkovsky, Josef, 81, 85
Solzhenitsyn, Aleksandr I., 152, 171
Stalin, Josif V., 10, 12, 121, 133, 142, 150, 152, 206; last year of rule, 161, 168, 169, 172; on nationalities, 204-05, 211
Svitak, Ivan, 79

Tvardovskii, Alexander, 168, 169, 171, 173

Virta, Nikolai, 162, 163, 172

Zhdanov, Andrei A., 121, 170
Zhivkov, Todor, 182, 184, 190, 193

SUBJECT INDEX

Action Program, Czechoslovakia, 81, 84, 88-91
army: in Bulgaria, 192; in Chile, 123, 126; in Czechoslovakia, 126

Chile, political developments 1970-73, 122-26
Communist Party, 10-11, 12-14; of Bulgaria, 180-82, 183-84, 185-87, 188-92, 193-95; of Czechoslovakia, 77, 78, 79-91, 114, 115, 121, 122; of Hungary, 105; of Poland, 51, 53, 55, 71-73; 6th Congress of the Polish United Workers (Communist) Party, 59, 63, 65; of USSR, 19-37, 137; Conferences and Congresses of the CPSU, 171-72, 173
constitution, of Czechoslovakia, 80, 90; of USSR, 150

dictatorship of the proletariat: in Chile, 122-25, 129-30; in Czechoslovakia, 79, 110-22, 126-29; in Kautsky's view, 128-29; in Leninist ideology, 128-29; in Marxist ideology, 111-12, 115-16, 120, 126-28; in Russia, 112, 128
dissidents: in the USSR, 135, 140, 142, 144, 147-53, 154
Doctors' Plot, 162, 163

intelligentsia (intellectuals): Bulgarian, 180-81; in Marxist ideology, 179-80; Polish, 47, 179; Soviet, 137, 140-43, 166

Kiev Rus', 205-06, 208

modernization process, 12, 14; in Hungary, 95-96, 98, 99-100, 101, 102, 104, 106-07; in Poland, 41-43, 48-49, 50; in USSR, 218-19, 222-23, 224-25, 227, 229

National Front: in Czechoslovakia, 80, 83-84, 85-90, 113, 114, 120
"New Soviet Man," 10, 12-13
no-conflict theory of literature (USSR), 162-64, 170, 172

Paris Commune, 113, 124, 127
people's councils (Poland), 58-74
public opinion reporting, 7, 8; in Bulgaria, 189-90, 193-94; Harvard Project on the Soviet Social System, 143; in Hungary, 98-99; in Poland, 48; in the USSR, 138, 141-42

radio broadcasting to the USSR, 135-36, 138-39, 144, 150-51

samizdat (self-publishing), 144-47
stratification, ethnic, in USSR, 217-18, 224-29
stratification, social: in Hungary, 100-04, 106, 107; in Poland,

[stratification, social] 43, 45, 47-48, 50; in USSR, 141

workers' councils: in Czechoslovakia, 90-91; in Poland, 41, 50-56

ABOUT THE EDITORS AND CONTRIBUTORS

PETER J. POTICHNYJ is Professor of Political Science at McMaster University in Hamilton, Ontario. He is Chairman of the Interdepartmental Committee on Communist and East European Affairs at McMaster and Secretary-Treasurer of the Canadian Association of Slavists. He is author of Soviet Agricultural Trade Unions, 1917-1970 (University of Toronto Press, 1972), The Ukraine and Czechoslovak Crisis (Canberra, 1972), Ukraine in the Seventies (Mosaic Press, 1975), and editor-in-chief of Current Soviet Leaders.

JANE P. SHAPIRO is Associate Professor of Political Science and Department Chairman at Manhattanville College, Purchase, N.Y. She is coeditor of Communist Systems on Comparative Perspective (Doubleday, 1974).

RALPH S. CLEM is Assistant Professor in the Department of International Relations, Florida International University, and editor of The Soviet West: Interplay between Nationality and Social Organization (Praeger Publishers, 1975).

EDITH ROGOVIN FRANKEL teaches in the Political Science Department, Hebrew University of Jerusalem. Her particular interest is in culture and politics in the Soviet Union.

GALIA GOLAN is Director of the Soviet-East European Research Center of the Hebrew University of Jerusalem and author of The Czechoslovak Reform Movement (Cambridge University Press, 1971) and Reform Rule in Czechoslovakia (Cambridge University Press, 1973).

LUBOS G. HEJL is Associate Professor of Economics and Political Science, Graduate School of Management, University of Rochester, on leave at the University of Chicago Graduate School of Business. His main interest is in the application of Marxist theory to socialist societies.

GAYLE DURHAM HANNAH is a Fellow of the Radcliffe Institute, Cambridge, Mass., and author of Soviet Political Indoctrination (Praeger Publishers, 1972).

JOSEPH HELD is Associate Professor of History and Hungarian Studies at Rutgers University, New Brunswick, New Jersey, and coeditor of Social and Intellectual History in the Hapsburg Monarchy from Maria Theresa to the First World War: Essays in Honor of Robert Adolph Kann (East European Quarterly, 1975).

STEPHAN M. HORAK is Professor of History at Eastern Illinois University, Charleston. He is author of Poland and Her National

Minorities 1919-1939 (Vantage Press, 1961) and Poland's International Affairs, 1919-1960 (Indiana University Press, 1964), and Chairman of the Association for the Study of the Nationalities (USSR and East Europe) Inc.

ROBERT A. LEWIS is Professor of Geography, Columbia University, and coauthor of The Population Changes in Russia and the USSR: A Set of Comparable Territorial Units (San Diego University Press, 1966).

ALEXANDER MATEJKO is Professor of Sociology, University of Alberta, Edmonton, Canada, and author of Social Change and Stratification—Eastern Europe: An Interpretive Analysis of Poland and Her Neighbors (New York, Praeger Publishers, 1974).

DAVID W. PAUL is Assistant Professor of Political Science and a member of the Institute for Comparative and Foreign Area Studies, University of Washington, Seattle. He has written several articles on East European affairs.

PETER RAINA is Research Fellow at the Ost-Europa Institute, Free University of Berlin. Among his books are Gomulka-Politische Biographie (Cologne, 1970) and Internationale Politik in den 70-er Jahren (Frankfurt, 1973).

RICHARD H. ROWLAND is Assistant Professor of Geography, California State College, San Bernardino. His main interests are demographic change and modernization in the Soviet Union.

PHILIP D. STEWART is Professor of Political Science at Ohio State University, Columbus, and author of Political Power in the Soviet Union (Bobbs-Merrill, 1968).

RAY TARAS is Lecturer in Politics, Lanchester Polytechnic, Coventry, England, and Researcher in the Department of Sociology, University of Essex. His main interest is local government and political culture in Poland.

PUBLICATIONS FROM THE FIRST INTERNATIONAL SLAVIC CONFERENCE, BANFF 1974

I. Volumes in the Social Sciences, published by Praeger Publishers, Praeger Special Studies, New York:

Economic Development in the Soviet Union and Eastern Europe: Reforms, Technology, and Income Distribution, edited by Zbigniew M. Fallenbuchl, University of Windsor.

Economic Development in the Soviet Union and Eastern Europe: Sectoral Analysis, edited by Zbigniew M. Fallenbuchl, University of Windsor.

Education and the Mass Media in the Soviet Union and Eastern Europe, edited by Bohdan Harasymiw, University of Calgary.

Soviet Economic and Political Relations with the Developing World, edited by Roger E. Kanet and Donna Bahry, University of Illinois, Urbana-Champaign.

Demographic Developments in Eastern Europe, edited by Leszek Kosinski, University of Alberta.

Environmental Misuse in the Soviet Union, edited by Fred Singleton, University of Bradford.

Change and Adaptation in Soviet and East European Politics, edited by Jane P. Shapiro, Manhattanville College, and Peter J. Potichnyj, McMaster University.

From the Cold War to Detente, edited by Peter J. Potichnyj, McMaster University, and Jane P. Shapiro, Manhattanville College.

II. Volumes in the Humanities, published by Slavica Publishers, Cambridge, Mass.:

Russian and Slavic Literature to 1917, edited by Richard Freeborn, University of London, and Charles A. Ward, University of Wisconsin, Milwaukee.

Russian and Slavic Literature, 1917-1974, edited by Robin Milner-Gulland, University of Sussex, and Charles A. Ward, University of Wisconsin, Milwaukee.

Slavic Linguistics at Banff, edited by Thomas F. Magner, Pennsylvania State University.

Early Russian History, edited by G. Edward Orchard, University of Lethbridge.

Nineteenth and Twentieth Century Slavic History, edited by Don Karl Rowney, Bowling Green State University.

Reconsiderations on the Russian Revolution, edited by Carter Elwood, Carleton University.

III. Additional Volumes:

"Nomads and the Slavic World," a special issue of AEMAe Archivum Eurasiae Medii Aevi, 2 (1975), edited by Tibor Halasi-Kun, Columbia University.

Russian Literature in the Age of Catherine the Great: A Collection of Essays. Oxford: Willem A. Meeuws, 1976, edited by Anthony Cross, University of East Anglia.

Commercial and Legal Problems in East-West Trade. Ottawa: Carleton University, Russian and East European Center, 1976, edited by John P. Hardt, U.S. Library of Congress.

Marxism and Religion in Eastern Europe. Dordrecht and Boston: D. Reidel, 1976, edited by Richard T. DeGeorge, University of Kansas, and James P. Scanlan, The Ohio State University.

Detente and the Conference on Security and Cooperation in Europe. Leiden: Sythoff, 1976, edited by Louis J. Mensonides, Virginia Polytechnic Institute and State University.

Augsburg College
George Sverdrup Library
Minneapolis, Minnesota 55454